MAJOR-GENERAL SIR LOUIS JEAN BOLS, K.C.B., D.S.O.

THE RANGERS' HISTORICAL RECORDS

From 1859 to the Conclusion of the Great War

Edited by

CAPTAIN A. V. WHEELER-HOLOHAN

and

CAPTAIN G. M. G. WYATT

CHENIES STREET
TOTTENHAM COURT ROAD
LONDON

THE RANGERS'
HISTORICAL
RECORDS.

CONTENTS.

FOREWORD.
(By Major-General Sir L. J. Bols.)

PART THREE.

THE SECOND BATTALION.

vii

PAGE

PART FOUR.
THE AMALGAMATED BATTALION.

PART FIVE.
THE DEPOT AND THE RESERVE BATTALION.

APPENDIX.

EDITORIAL FOREWORD.

THE Editors feel that the subscribers to this book are entitled to some explanation of the time that has elapsed between the Armistice and its publication. It is the support (and subscriptions) of these early subscribers which alone have made its production possible and it is due to them that they should be made acquainted with some of the difficulties that have been encountered by the Editors.

These difficulties have mainly been threefold, connected respectively with the Editorship, with contributions in writing, and with finance. As to the first, everyday business affairs has hindered work on what, to do it justice, required whole-time attention. One of the Editors, Lieutenant the Hon. Bryan Buckley, was forced, by the calls upon his time, to relinquish his share in the editing of the work. For some considerable time Captain Wheeler-Holohan carried on alone, and it was not until Captain Wyatt came to the rescue that any real progress with the actual publication could be made.

As to the second, while in the first flush of enthusiasm promises were plentiful and responsibilities for portions of the task were lightly undertaken, when a call for results was made in many cases the former went unredeemed and the latter were ignored. As to the third, the most sincere thanks of all concerned in the production of the book must be given to those, who, by the prompt and early proffering of their subscriptions on the promise of performance, enabled the foundation stones to be laid. Mention, however, must be made of the fact that the vast majority of those who have borne the name of " Rangers " have felt

x

too little interest or too great scepticism in the success of the undertaking to adventure hard cash before they could see something accomplished in return.

Perhaps this explanation, tardy as it is, will satisfy some of those people whose delight it has been to worry the Editors with enquiries both polite and impolite.

This is not the moment, perhaps, to dwell upon the nearness of failure, and the anxiety of the task of those responsible ; rather is it to be hoped that the early subscribers will welcome the production as the justification of their faith, and that the book, born after such protracted and anxious labour, may attract the belated interest of other members, past and present, of the Regiment.

A. V. W.-H.
G. M. G. W.

Chenies Street, W.C.
    May, 1921.

FOREWORD.

THE Historical Records of the Rangers, covering a period of one hundred and forty years, disclose many acts of gallantry and devotion, and, unquestionably, other deeds as gallant as those described in these Records have been performed without witnesses, by men of this distinguished Regiment. But none can excel in self-sacrifice and devotion to duty the action witnessed by me one day early in 1915, when the Rangers, to save another battalion, counter-attacked under well-nigh hopeless conditions, and by so doing saved Ypres.

The 84th Infantry Brigade had been fighting incessantly for three weeks, fighting desperately against new and horrible weapons as well as against greatly superior numbers.

The day came when, driven back to the main line of defence, a Unit on the right flank of the Brigade ceased to exist, and fresh German troops pressed for the opening, flinging back the right Battalion of the 84th Brigade. Eight hundred yards behind lay our last reserve, some two hundred men, all that was left of the Rangers after those bloody weeks.

" *You will counter-attack and re-capture the Trenches of our right Battalion.*"

This was the order that the Rangers received while lying in shallow trenches, subjected to heavy artillery and machine-gun fire.

Fifteen minutes later, two lines of Rangers sprang up in perfect order and alignment and moved, without hesitation, forward over that stricken ground ; half an hour later, less than one hundred Rangers held the rise of ground where the trenches had been, and, with their rifles and machine guns, almost destroyed the dense mass of Germans which had been destined to roll up our lines and clear the road to Ypres.

This was the finest local counter-attack which I had the honour of seeing during the Great War.

Let us salute those who have shown us how to attain the great honour of giving ourselves for our Empire and our comrades, and may the discipline, comradeship and devotion which made such deeds possible always influence the Rangers.

L. J. BOLS,
Major-General, Chief of the General Staff, Egyptian Expeditionary Force, Hon. Colonel of the Rangers, formerly commanding the 84th Infantry Brigade.

PART ONE.

From 1859 to August the Fourth, 1914.

CHAPTER I.

THE foundation of the Rangers as a valuable unit of the Volunteer Force was laid in 1859, although the regiment claims with every justification that its history dates in a connected line from 1780, when the "Gentlemen Members of Grays Inn" were organised. True, this force had a meteoric career, the man power which could be called upon being limited, but when "line" organisation was established in 1859 (nearly eighty years later) in order to take in members of all the other Inns of Court the old force merged its identity into "The Central London Rifle Rangers," and all ranks readily accepted the new formation.

The Battalion has always had its Headquarters in Grays Inn, and the object of its formation in 1859 was for the accommodation of those military minded members of the various Inns of Court who had not associated themselves with the Battalion familiarly known as the "Devil's Own." To quote in full the rules and orders which governed the "Gentlemen Members" is impossible. A copy of them is preserved at Grays Inn, and is a document of considerable interest, especially the clause referring to uniforms, which runs as follows :—"That each member shall provide himself with a scarlet coatee, faced with cloth of the same colour, silver buttons, white cloth waistcoat, breeches, and white stockings, a blue cockade, and silver shoe buckles." Discipline was maintained by the primitive, but doubtless effective, means of fines. Thus a member, if well and in town, for not answering Roll Call at 6 a.m. was fined 6d.; for disobedience of orders after the word "By the Right, Dress," 6d. But perhaps the strongest testimony to the spirit of the time was the

regulation that " if any member, being well, and in
town, absent himself for three consecutive days, he
shall be put into the Awkward Squad."

When the " Rangers," as such, came into existence,
the Regiment began in a modest way, and from
that day its records show nothing but sound, solid
progress. Two Companies were formed in the first
year and they were placed under the command of
Captain John B. Waters and Lieut. H. Isaac, the
official title being " The Central London Rifle
Rangers" [numbered the 40th Middlesex]. The
Benchers of Grays Inn readily conceded to the Corps
the privilege of drilling within the precincts of the
Inn, and here Headquarters were established in Field
Court and South Square.

The 40th Middlesex Rifle Volunteers (" The
Central London Rifle Rangers ") always wore the
uniform of the King's Royal Rifles, namely, dark
green with scarlet facings, the men's tunics were of
the K.R.R. pattern without the scarlet piping down
the front edge. The shako was black with a black
ball tuft, while a leather waist belt, a pouch and
bayonet frog completed the men's kit. The Officers'
uniform was of K.R.R. pattern with scarlet facings,
light green cord in the sleeve knots according to
regulations, while the shako plate and chin chain were
silver plated. The design of the former and the
central ornament on the pouch belt was an 8-pointed
star with a bugle and " XL," with the regimental
motto " Excel " thereon ; the Crown above the
ornaments on the men's shako was bronzed. Up
till 1875 dismounted Officers as well as mounted
Officers wore knee boots of rather soft leather with
the trousers tucked into them. The Pioneers wore
busbies of the Guards pattern. The Battalion in
1862 was authorised to raise eight Companies, Lieut.-
General Sir J. Yorke Scarlett, K.C.B. (who had
commanded a heavy brigade at Balaclava) became
Honorary Colonel, and at the same time Lieut.-Colonel

A. Plantagenet F. E. Somerset of the 13th Light Infantry took active command.

Lieut.-Colonel Somerset did not remain long in command of the Regiment. This Officer, who left to command the 2nd Tower Hamlets Militia in 1866, was succeeded by Lieut.-Colonel the Hon. Halliburton-Campbell (who afterwards became Lord Stratheden and Campbell), and his brother, the then holder of the title, became Honorary Colonel upon the death of Sir J. Yorke Scarlett in 1872. The Adjutant was Captain F. B. Cooper, who was a good drill instructor, but was possessed of a very fiery temper, and fond of shaking his umbrella (when in mufti), and using very strong language to the defaulting man or company. At this time the corps had Sergt.-Major Humphries as chief of the N.C.O. instructors, and a finer drill instructor it would be hard to find in the army, for he had the way of making his drill instruction interesting and could always rely on a good attendance on parade. The regimental range was at " Park," Tottenham, with the old target with the steel bull's-eye, and was available up to 600 yards. As the rifle in the early days was muzzle loading until the first breech loading rifle was issued (the " Snider ") the distance was all that was required. The Battalion was, however, unhappily fated now to a quick succession of Commanding Officers. After Colonel Campbell came Colonel Adrian Hope in 1872, who held command for about twelve months before going to the London Rifle Brigade R.V. ; he was always mounted upon beautiful Arab horses. Then for some period the Regiment was under the command of Major Weir, who was asked to take over the command of the Regiment, but declined on account of health, greatly to the regret of the officers and men. Then Major Miller for a time commanded the Regiment, which had gradually been falling off in numbers till it barely numbered four hundred members. Then followed

Colonel Henry Hozier, C.B., a Staff College graduate, who had been assistant Military Secretary to Field Marshal Lord Napier of Magdala in the Abyssinian campaign and afterwards military correspondent of *The Times* during the Franco-Prussian War. Captain Cowper (the Adjutant) having retired, Captain H. Higgins, King's Own Scottish Borderers, was appointed to succeed him, and it was to his untiring efforts and efficient management of the internal economy of the Regiment that the Corps began to show again its value as a Volunteer force. At this period a marked change came over the 40th Middlesex R.V., they being renumbered the 22nd Middlesex R.V., and attached to the Royal Fusiliers, and not being transferred to the K.R.R. until 1883-4; they retained their old title as the Central London Rifle Rangers and the old motto Excel (XL). Then Sir Howard Vincent (late 23rd Foot), whose general interest in the Volunteer movement is so well known, took command of the Regiment in 1875. Up to this date the internal economy of the Regiment was vested in a regimental committee, which dealt with all finances and regimental clothing, the Officer Commanding and his army staff being responsible to the War Office for the training and discipline. Colonel Vincent, with the aid of his able adjutant, Captain Higgins, resolved that the system should be altered; there was some opposition at first from the finance members of the committee and others, but Colonel Vincent applied to the War Office for support, and fresh arrangements were made for the ensuring of numbers, proper discipline and proper control of the finances of the Regiment. It was solely due to Colonel Vincent that matters were investigated by a small committee of commanding officers of the Volunteer Force, and he himself drafted a scheme which was adopted throughout the Volunteer Force with War Office sanction. Colonel Vincent did more for volunteer movement than any other officer ; he was keenly interested in his work and spared himself no labour to improve the conditions of the service and its efficiency, and was thanked by the War Office for his good work in improving the efficiency of the Volunteer Force. When he was married a detachment of officers and N.C.O.'s attended the ceremony. Colonel Vincent resigned the command, much to the regret of the officers, N.C.O.'s and men, to take the appointment as Chief of the Criminal Investigation Department of Scotland Yard. During this period—1878-9— the helmet was issued to the Regiment, a heavy, clumsy head gear which was disliked by all ranks, especially the younger men of the Regiment, as it simply extinguished them. The Field Officers at the same time adopted a short neckline looped up on the right breast. Until the alteration in the financial arrangements of the Regiment at this period members upon enlisting for 4 years had to pay for their uniforms and 4s. towards the band fund. The issue of uniforms was on the same scale as previously described, helmet, tunic, trousers, waist-belt, pouch and frog—there were pockets in the back of the tunic, and these were the only ones (and many men carried their rations for a day and a half in them !). The Regiment attended all the Brighton reviews, parading at something like 1 or 2 a.m., and getting back the next night about the same time. Each man provided his own overcoat, and rolled it or wore it in his own way ; there were no such things as haversacks or water bottles, so that men would be seen with all kinds of bags worn on their waist-belts or strapped on their backs, with bottles of all descriptions both in the bags and hanging from their belts. One can readily imagine on a wet day what the men looked like—some in mackintoshes and in all manner of overcoats and colours. Up till this period the funds of the Regiment were helped in several ways, Major Miller organising theatricals, and through his efforts a great deal of money was raised by displays given chiefly at St. George's Hall.

Lieut.-Colonel Sir Henry Malet, late Grenadier Guards, was then gazetted to the vacancy caused by the retirement of Colonel Vincent, and immediately had the Regiment trained upon the lines of the Brigade of Guards with their high idea of discipline ; he was, however, not long with the regiment and his junior Major, W. J. Alt, took over the command in 1881, which he retained for twenty years—very much to the benefit of the Regiment ; upon his retirement he received the Companionship of the Order of the Bath. Besides holding active command for by far the longest period in the history of the Corps, Colonel Alt did invaluable work for the Regiment and brought it up to its full strength of 800 men. During his command the Regiment adopted machine guns, after some opposition from the War Office : recognition did not come till later, but Colonel Alt purchased two Nordenfeldt five-barrel rifle calibre guns and himself designed a carriage suitable for their use, and, the War Office still holding aloof, Colonel Alt demonstrated the use of this new arm for Infantry Regiments by establishing a private gun club from the men of the Rangers under their Officers, Captain Armitt in command : the members took part in the combined display at the First Military Tournament held at the Agricultural Hall, and for many years after. In 1893, the War Office relented so far as to allow Colonel Alt to take the guns to Aldershot for experimental practice and finally sanctioned the adoption of the guns. *The " Rangers " can claim that they were the first Infantry Battalion in the British Army to use machine guns.* At the outbreak of the Egyptian campaign the Regimental Gun Detachment volunteered to take the guns out, but Lord Wolseley, while acknowledging their public spirit, could not see his way to accept the offer. In 1882 Colonel Alt had presented to the Regiment a shield with money prizes for a Company Drill competition, the condition for a Company desirous to compete being a parade in Review Order with not less than 18 files, no Sergeant in the ranks, each Company to have its complement of one Colour Sergeant and three Sergeants. This competition became very popular and was competed for up till 1914 with varying success, all Companies sharing in the honour of having successfully competed for the Prize. During Colonel Alt's command the Gas, Light & Coke Company allowed the Regiment to recruit two Companies from their gas works at Beckton and contributed very handsomely to the Prize Funds ; also the highly-trained Regimental Brass Band was formed, which was said to be the finest Volunteer Band in the Service. In 1885 the men wore a tunic of the K.R.R. pattern except that they had an Austrian knot in light green braid above the scarlet piping on the cuff ; the shoulder straps were black edged with scarlet, and with 22nd MX on them in light green. The buttons were of black composition, not of bronzed metal. The black cloth helmet with bronzed mounting was now worn by everyone in the Regiment, including Medical Officer, Pioneers and Band. The helmet and pouch plates were changed to a Maltese Cross, at first with a small lion in the four angles, but these were soon afterwards cut away to resemble as much as possible the K.R.R. Cross ; the men's trousers were plain black ; leggings and Glengarries were possessed by nearly all the men, but other equipment was only issued specially for Camp, Reviews, &c., consisting of haversack, water-bottle and (for marching columns only) great coats. The Officers' uniform was according to K.R.R. pattern, and the light green Austrian knot, which did not harmonise with the scarlet cuff, began to disappear. The whistle chain was worn of treble thickness so as to be shorter and not to swing about ; and no cap lines at all were worn. Mess jackets and vests (of K.R.R. pattern) were in use, but not quite universal until about 1890. Officers had rifle pattern great coats with black buttons. A signalling section was first formed in the year 1886. During 1887 and 1888 a few changes were made in the direction of bringing the Officers' uniform more up to date and more in accordance with the K.R.R. Lambskins were worn on the mounted Officers' horses in review order only. The Austrian fatigue cap came into use, whistle chains were again worn long, and the pouch belt was discontinued in drill order, except for the Captain and Subaltern of the Day.

In 1890, thanks to the efforts of Sir William Whitehead, the then Lord Mayor, the Metropolitan Volunteers received a more adequate outfit than it had hitherto been possible to procure for them. A form of the " Slade Wallace " equipment was issued to the Battalion in March, and this and the Regimental great coat were worn for the first time on Easter Monday. The great coats had no capes or shoulder straps—they were black with 22 MX worked in scarlet on the turn-down collar. The term " Rifleman " was officially substituted for " Private " during this year. The new Rifle busby was taken into wear in 1892—this was the K.R.R. pattern for all ranks, the small bronze plate in front of the Officers' busby being of the Battalion pattern, and the end of the cap lines was now attached to the back of the busby by all Officers.

The Battalion was particularly fortunate in the Adjutants appointed. On the retirement of Captain Higgins in 1882, Major C. W. Adderly, of the Royal Fusiliers, was posted to the Regiment : in 1886 he assumed the surname of Cradock in lieu of that of Adderly and, retiring in 1887, was gazetted to the Honorary Colonelcy in 1901. In October, 1887,

Captain and Brevet-Major E. W. Herbert, King's
Royal Rifles, took over the post of Adjutant and
the King's Royal Rifles for many years supplied
his successors. Captain—afterwards Colonel—Sir
Thomas Pilkington, Bart., in 1893 ; Major—now
Colonel—C. J. Markham in 1897 ; Major Lord
Robert Manners, D.S.O., in 1903 ; and Captain
H. F. W. Bircham, D.S.O., in 1908 (both these
gallant soldiers were destined to fall in the Great
War). Captain W. K. Venning, Duke of Cornwall's
Light Infantry, became Adjutant in 1913, and was
with the Regiment during its mobilisation and
training for its active part in the European War.
In March, 1901, Colonel W. F. Leese, V.D., who had
commenced his military career in the Corps, succeeded
to the command, being deservedly popular with all
ranks, and he maintained the high opinion of the
Headquarters Staff for the state of efficiency to
which he brought the Battalion. During Colonel
Leese's command the house in South Square, the
Headquarters of the Regiment for so many years,
was required by the Benchers of the Inn, and the
Battalion had to seek new quarters at 3, Henry
Street, Gray's Inn Road. While not of a palatial
or imposing character the new offices were a great
improvement on anything which the Corps had
ever possessed. They comprised Stores, Armoury,
Orderly Room, Officers and Sergeants' rooms, Morris
tube range, and a fair size lecture-room, as well as
accommodation for the machine guns. In February,
1905, His Majesty the King was graciously pleased
to approve of the Battalion, in recognition of services
rendered during the South African War, 1899-1902,
bearing on all its appointments the words " South
Africa, 1900-1902." During Colonel Leese's service
with the Battalion he formed the Regimental
Orchestra of over thirty performers, and with
great patience and musical ability brought it to
such perfection that it gave performances in various

parts of London. Colonel Leese's hard work as Commanding Officer left the Battalion in the forefront of the London Regiments. He was followed in 1907 by Colonel H. S. Coldicott, V.D , who had previously served in the Rangers for twenty years, had received his first Commission as ensign in a Worcestershire Corps on March 31st, 1872, and was one of the first to receive the Volunteer Officers' Decoration. In the same year (1907) Colonel Cradock, to the regret of all, relinquished his appointment as Hon. Colonel, which was offered to and accepted by Colonel W. J. Alt, C.B.

On March 31st, 1907, the old Volunteer Force ceased to exist, by virtue of the Territorial and Reserve Force Act of 1907, and on the following day the Corps went over as a unit to the new Territorial Army, and was henceforth known as " The Rangers," the 12th (County of London Battalion), The London Regiment, forming the 4th Battalion of the 3rd Brigade of the 1st London Division, which was commanded by Colonel F. T. Maxse, C.V.O., C.B., D.S.O. (Coldstream Guards), and the Division by the former Brigadier, Major-General A. E. Codrington, C.V.O., C.B. The Rangers on June 20th, 1908, marched in and took over their present Headquarters in Chenies Street, Tottenham Court Road. The Rangers still remained a rifle regiment, and the Brigade was made up of the four London Regiments, the 9th (Queen Victoria's Rifles), the 10th (the Paddington Rifles), the 11th (the Finsbury Rifles), and the 12th (the Rangers). The Battalion was honoured at one of its Prize distributions, in January, 1908, by the presence of Mr. R. B. (afterwards Lord) Haldane, then Secretary of State for War, to whose scheme the Territorial Army was due, and in a speech he explained the organisation which had been adopted and which proved to be so valuable when the war broke out. Upon the death of the Honorary Colonel,

W. J. Alt, C.B., in January, 1909, Colonel Sir Corbett
Woodall was appointed in his stead ; he had been a
very great friend to the Regiment as Governor of
the Gas, Light & Coke Company and had encouraged
the employees at the several Depôts to join the
Rangers by giving them holidays in order to enable
them to attend Camp ; the Company, too, was a
liberal subscriber to the Prize Funds.

Upon the retirement of Colonel Coldicott, the
command of the Regiment was taken over by the
late Lieut.-Colonel T. Wilton, an officer who joined
the Beckton Company as a subaltern and for many
years commanded one of the companies formed
from the gas workers. He was a most popular
officer and under his command many improvements
were made to the Headquarters and to the Regiment.
During his command the Rangers were mobilised for
the Great War in August, 1914, and he, with the
assistance of Captain Venning, trained the Corps for
the great part they so gallantly fulfilled until Peace
again came to Europe.

Walking-out Dress.

Review Order.

Marching Order.

Drill Order.

The "Rangers" Uniform in 1914.

CHAPTER II.

THE SOUTH AFRICAN WAR.

IN December, 1899, owing to the black outlook in South Africa it was eventually decided to call for volunteers for active service. Offers had been thrust on the War Office but, until what was known as the "black week," these had been offered in vain. The Lord Mayor of London (Sir Alfred Newton) had offered to raise a battalion of infantry with mounted infantry attached, and to clothe, equip, and transport them to Cape Town where they were to be taken over by the War Office. This offer was finally accepted by the War Office, and Colonel W. H. Mackinnon (Grenadier Guards) was appointed to command. It was understood that this force was to be raised from the existing Volunteer Regiments in London, and was to be known as the City of London Imperial Volunteers, or the famous C.I.V. The Rangers, then the 22nd Middlesex Rifle Volunteers, were called upon to furnish a contingent of one officer and twenty-six other ranks. There was great competition to be selected, and Lieut.-Colonel H. S. Coldicott (commanding in the temporary absence of Colonel Leese) had the difficult task of choosing the men. Every man had to be thoroughly fit, a first-class shot, and unmarried. On January 4th, the Rangers detachment paraded at Gray's Inn and marched to the Guildhall, where they were sworn in by the Lord Mayor ; on January 12th, 1900, each man was presented with the Freedom of the City of London. Rifles were drawn from the Tower at the identical spot where, fourteen years later, the 2nd Battalion were to draw them (one member of the contingent taking part on both occasions—then as an N.C.O., and later as a Senior Captain). On January 19th, the Regiment attended a farewell Church Parade at St. Paul's, followed by a supper, provided by the members of Lincoln's and Gray's Inns, and the following morning proceeded to Nine Elms Station to entrain for Southampton. H.R.H. the Duke of Connaught was present to see the Battalion start, and the roads to the station were lined with London crowds. On February 16th, the Regiment disembarked at Cape Town and a few days later reached Orange River Camp. The Rangers' detachment were posted to H Company, and comprised the whole of No. 4 section of that Company, Lieutenant Brian Alt (a Ranger officer) commanding the left half company (Nos. 3 and 4 sections) of H Company and Lieutenant B. C. Green (now Lieut.-Colonel B. C. Green), of the London Scottish, commanding the right half company, while Captain C. A. Mortimere was Company Commander. For some weeks the Battalion was employed on outpost duties on the Lines of Communication, the Rangers being stationed at Wigton and being responsible for a section of railway line on the route to Kimberley, but at the end of March the Battalion moved up to Bloemfontein to take its part in the main advance of Lord Roberts upon Pretoria, and on April 16th (Easter Monday), the long trek was commenced. The C.I.V., with the 1st Sussex, Derbys, and Cameron Highlanders, comprised the 21st Brigade under General Bruce Hamilton, which formed part of a mixed force, which, commanded by General Ian Hamilton, was the right flank of Lord Roberts' advance. On May 4th, the Rangers, being a part of the advance guard, fired their first shots at the retiring Boers after a 16 mile march. Their advance was through Winburg, across the Zard River, where a slight stand was made by the enemy, and through Kronstadt, where, on May 14th Lord Roberts inspected the Battalion. After Kronstadt the advance was continued through Lindley and Heilbron, and then General Hamilton's force was moved to the left of Lord Roberts' main army. On May 29th, the Battalion was advance guard to the division, H Company being the leading company of the Battalion. The force moved off at 6.30 a.m. and at 11.45 orders were received to form up for attack on Doornkop (the hill where the great Jamieson surrendered). The Boers put up a stiff resistance and for the first time a Battalion of English Volunteers took a prominent part in a big engagement, the Rangers' contingent having the good fortune to be the first troops engaged. Nine thousand five hundred rounds were fired during the fight, and General Ian Hamilton sent a message of congratulation to the Regiment. General Smith-Dorrien, who commanded the Infantry, was also highly complimentary in his despatch. On June 5th, 1900, the Battalion had the distinction of taking part in the march past Lord Roberts in the square of Pretoria. Up to that time the advance had lasted fifty-one days, forty of which had been marching days, the distance covered being 523 miles. The Boers were now holding strong positions south-east of Pretoria, and General Ian Hamilton's force was sent to dislodge them, and on June 11th and 12th, took part in the Battle of Diamond Hill. The Boer position was very strong and was stubbornly held, the whole of the infantry being hotly engaged until nightfall on the 12th, when the Boers evacuated their position. Colonel Mackinnon, in his diary, makes special mention of H Company's part in this engagement. On June 12th, the Rangers' contingent were unfortunate in losing Lieut. Alt, who was shot through the head. He was an officer of exceptional ability and loved by his men, and his death was a great loss to the Battalion. After the dispersal of the Boers at Diamond Hill the Battalion took part in various operations for rounding up the Boer commandoes still in the field, and for some time served under General Archibald Hunter, and later under General Smith-Dorrien (during the manœuvres after De Wet), eventually reaching Pretoria again on August 24th, having completed a trek of 1,000 miles. On October 2nd, Lord Roberts inspected the Regiment, and the following day the Battalion entrained for Cape Town *en route* for England. On October 29th, London was reached where, after a service at St. Paul's, the Regiment was entertained at Finsbury Barracks by the Corporation of London. After a month's furlough the detachments were re-transferred to their original Units.

NAMES OF RANGERS' CONTINGENT.

Lieut. W. B. Alt.
Lance-Sergeant H. K. Cheshire.
Lance-Corporal H. Littlejohn.
Lance-Corporal S. Chart.
Lance-Corporal E. Cuningham.
Rifleman P. Abbis.
Rifleman W. Nichols.
Rifleman W. R. Gazzard.
Rifleman C. F. Whitworth.
Rifleman C. Paine.
Rifleman F. Shaw.
Rifleman A. J. Gray.
Rifleman J. Orton.
Rifleman O. J. Triplette.
Rifleman F. Fennell.
Rifleman H. W. Rawlings.
Rifleman C. Hall.
Rifleman H. Barnett.
Rifleman C. Smith.
Rifleman E. Moore.
Rifleman G. Burton.
Rifleman J. W. Hammond.
Rifleman C. A. Pollett.
Rifleman L. R. Evans.
Rifleman A. Young.
Rifleman C. W. Messenger.
Rifleman H. Lloyd.

To face page 17.]

COLONEL A. D. BAYLIFFE, C.M.G., T.D.

PART TWO.

The First Battalion.

CHAPTER I.

THE FIRST BATTALION IN ENGLAND.

ON the morning of Sunday, August 2nd, 1914, the Battalion paraded in Gray's Inn Square, prior to the annual training, which was this year to have taken place in Camp at Wool, Dorsetshire. From Gray's Inn Square the Battalion marched to Waterloo, and there, after the customary delays incidental to such an operation, entrained in two trains for Wool. The first train was stopped at Southampton West, the second at Winchester, and in each case was returned to Waterloo. From Waterloo the Battalion marched back to Alfred Place, and there awaited the orders of higher authority. After some time the parade was dismissed, everyone having first been warned that mobilization was imminent, and to return home and prepare himself and his kit against the moment of its actual occurrence. Thus, there reached their homes again, unexpectedly, sometime after seven at night, all those who had set forth some twelve hours previously, expectant of spending, many a fortnight, others a week, of training for the defence of their Country in time of war, the likelihood of the necessity for such defence being now appreciably nearer and correspondingly brought home to them.

In the evening of Tuesday, August 4th, 1914, mobilization was put into operation, the summons being sent by telegram to Officers and Senior N.C.O.'s and by card to the remainder. Many Officers and Senior N.C.O.'s slept that night at Chenies Street, or at the Central Y.M.C.A. in Tottenham Court Road, where the passing from peace to war status was to take place.

At 8 o'clock on the morning of Wednesday, August 5th, 1914, began the stream of men to be medically examined and fitted out: during the next few days the then serving members of the Battalion reported, many old members re-enlisted, and many recruits joined, and all were medically examined and fitted out, stores and transport were collected, and out of seeming chaos emerged a Battalion fully equipped and ready for the next move.

During this period, recruit drill took place in Gray's Inn Square, and training in Regent's Park, interspersed with route marches to Hampstead Heath. One night, shortly after 9 o'clock, the alarm was blown, and everyone within hearing fell in outside the Y.M.C.A., surrounded by a large crowd of civilians, of whom many were anxious relatives or friends; after standing-to for a short while, during which various and disquieting rumours were rife, the parade was dismissed, and no one in the Battalion to this day knows the reason for the alarm. During this period also, the Officers were all sounded on the question of volunteering for foreign service, whether unconditionally or for service with the Battalion as a unit; the enquiry was conducted confidentially by the C.O., and no statistics showing the result are therefore obtainable for publication.

On Friday, August 14th, 1914, the Battalion, with the remainder of the 1st London Division, set out to march to a training camp; on this day we marched to Richmond, where the Battalion was billeted for the night, the Officers in private houses whose owners generously took them in and treated them with great kindness, the remainder of the Battalion in empty schools and other buildings. There were left behind to form the Depot, Lieut. C. Hardy, and Col.-Sergeant Scott.

The next day we marched to Staines, and on the road passed General Sir Ian Hamilton, who sat in a motor-car watching us go by. Here again,

B 2

accommodation was provided in billets as at Richmond; here, owing to the want of condition of some of the troops in the Division, we spent two nights, with a welcome and restful Sunday in which the weaker brethren recovered themselves of their sore feet and other ailments.

On Monday, August 17th, 1914, we left Staines, and marched to Bullswater Common, where we found our Camp pitched amongst very pleasant surroundings.

Here we settled down industriously to a period of hard training, and here was asked of every officer and man the great question, whether he was willing to extend the obligation he had undertaken on becoming a member of the Territorial Force, to defend his home in this Country, to include its defence by volunteering to go abroad and meet the enemy in a foreign country; the C.O. addressed the Battalion, and Company Officers their Companies, but the first response was not as good as those who had their Country's defence at heart could wish. The Brigadier and the Divisional General added their speeches to those already made by the C.O. and other Officers, and the Bishop of London addressed a meeting of all ranks on the subject. Finally, a good percentage volunteered and undertook on A.F.E. 624 the liability for Service abroad, and those who did not see their way to do so left us, and were sent back to the Depot, where they became the *nucleus* of the 2nd Line Battalion which was formed shortly after; of these many, after having the opportunity of thinking the matter over at greater leisure and especially of going home, seeing and consulting with their relatives, and making arrangements for and settling up their domestic and business affairs, subsequently undertook liability for service abroad and rejoined the Battalion later.

While here, Lieut.-Colonel J. Wilton handed over the command to Major A. D. Bayliffe, being found medically unfit to serve overseas, and left us. Captain K. R. Wilson also returned to take charge of the Depot with Lieut. C. Hardy, who had been left behind, to assist him.

On Tuesday, September 1st, 1914, the Battalion, with the remainder of the 1st London Division, left Bullswater Common and set out to march to another training Camp. The first day we marched to Bramley, where billets were provided in empty buildings for the men, and again the Officers enjoyed the hospitality of private residents.

The next day we marched to Horsham, engaging in tactical exercises on the way ; the Battalion was in the front of the Column, and, while the main body deployed with its usual skill, the advance guard, who had not been warned of the existence of an enemy, peacefully proceeded on its way in blissful ignorance of the presence of the enemy between it and the main body. Owing to this unfortunate *contretemps* the advance guard, having no orders to halt there, proceeded right through Horsham and had reached a point a mile beyond before orders arrived to return to Horsham and to billets. The next day, the march was resumed to Haywards Heath, where two nights were spent in billets, in this case mostly, if not entirely, consisting for the men of accommodation in small houses and cottages with subsistence, a change from empty buildings. On the day after our arrival, in the afternoon, the Battalion was inspected on parade by General Capper. On Saturday, September 5th, 1914, we again took the road, and on this day had the honour of passing on the road and saluting H.M. the King, who had come from London expressly to see the 1st London Division pass by. In the evening we reached our new Camp, at Crowborough, in a deluge of rain which had started an hour or so previously.

During the period the Battalion spent in Camp at Crowborough, the inoculation and vaccination and re-vaccination of the whole Battalion took place, while the remainder of the time was spent in route marching, company, battalion and brigade training. While here, Major A. G. E. Syms left us to take command of the 2nd Battalion which had just been formed, and Captain R. C. Freeman and 2nd Lieut. Balfour transferred to the R.E. Signal Service. The following new Officers joined the battalion : 2nd Lieuts. Lang and S. W. Green.

Suddenly, at very short notice, orders were received overnight for the Battalion to entrain early on Sunday morning, 11th October, 1914, for the purpose of relieving units in guarding the railway ; each platoon was detrained at its appropriate centre on the section of railway from Waterloo along the London and South Western main line to North Camp. The detrainment took place between 12 midday and 1 o'clock p.m., and the train taking away the troops relieved in most cases followed within half an hour of our detrainment, a sufficiently short time in which to familiarise oneself with plans, sectors, relief groups, sentries, and detached posts and generally to take over. However, despite a shortage of Officers in most, if not all of the Companies, and the discovery that our strength was considerably less than that of the units relieved, the relief was carried through, and there ensued an anxious time of strenuous work for all. Gradually, new Officers were posted to the Battalion, and drafts of men, including many old members of the Battalion who had reconsidered their prior choice of service at home only, came from the 2nd Battalion and the position became easier, though never free from considerable hardship for all. While on this work, ration allowance in lieu of rations was drawn, and each detachment catered for itself, with the kindly and generous assistancé of local tradesmen and others : this part of the experience seemed to be a matter of thorough enjoyment for all, all detachments vieing with each other to produce a varied assortment of dishes that should be the envy of such other detachments as heard of them, the chief object of each such dish being undoubtedly that it should little resemble that inevitable accompaniment of Camp life, "shackles." This period spent on the railway passed without incident, except a few cases of shooting in the dark at supposed spies (mostly bushes and occasionally an explorer of empty carriages in a siding with felonious intent), the arrest of a few absentees, and one grave tragedy : this was the death of Lance-Corporal Trant, a member of " F " Company, the only casualty throughout the seven or eight weeks spent in railway guarding, which occurred a few days only before the last detachment quitted its post. He was knocked down by a train in a cutting, the approach of which was masked by the noise and smoke of a train which had just passed, and killed instantly. He was the first member of the Battalion to make the supreme sacrifice, and gave his life for his country no less truly than those who subsequently gave theirs on the battlefields of Flanders and France.

While on the railway, the following new Officers joined the Battalion :—2nd Lieuts. Moss Vernon, Newton, Dunlop, Beausire, Wildsmith, and Troutbeck.

The Battalion was relieved by Companies and by detachments from its vigil on the railway, the work of guarding which was then taken over by the Volunteers : the final relief was effected on December 16th, 1914. On relief, the Battalion reassembled in Roehampton House and Dover House, Roehampton, and training, in which the time spent on the railway had induced something of rustiness, was resumed in Richmond Park. While here, orders were received for the Battalion to proceed to France to take its share in events overseas. Leave was given to everybody (36 hours only was possible) in two shifts, new arms were issued, transport equipment, clothing and necessaries renewed where requisite, and completed for service abroad, the final selection by medical examination made, and those rejected sent away to the 2nd Battalion. At last all was in readiness and orders to move were received ; entrainment took place in two trains from Barnes Station early in the morning of Wednesday, December 23rd, 1914, for Southampton in the expectation of crossing that day to France. However, on arrival there, it was found that no boat was available that day, and billets in empty schools and other buildings were found for the men and the Officers distributed among hotels.

The next morning there was a boat available, the Battalion was embarked, and the journey to France commenced that evening, escorted by a destroyer, which sent us seasonable greetings through a megaphone : the voyage was without mishap and the boat was berthed very early on Christmas Day, 1914, at Havre. The crossing had been calm, cold, and made for the most part in bright moonlight.

CHAPTER II.

DECEMBER 25TH, 1914, TO MAY 10TH, 1915.

DISEMBARKATION was shortly commenced and soon completed, and the Battalion marched off through the town to a rest camp, passing on the way a large hospital with soldiers in the grounds in front and, later, the Belgian Government Headquarters. The rest camp was perched high on the outskirts of the town, with a cemetery on one hand and a hospital on the other—cheery surroundings for those newly from home! Moreover the only accommodation was in tents. However, the Battalion soon settled in and started on the task of writing the first letters home, the censorship of which provided plenty of employment for the Officers during the next few days. A local estaminet was found where the Officers indulged in a Christmas dinner, the chief component of which was omelette, and the meal concluded with various toasts and subsequently subaltern courts-martial on Officers " for wearing pyjamas on Active Service " took place : subsequent soldiering with pyjamas in rest billets, a *sine quâ non* for comfort, must have provided those present with a strange commentary on the proceedings of their first night in France. This Estaminet served as a mess for the Officers most nights of our stay in Havre.

Boxing Day started very cold with a severe frost, but later it turned to rain, which lasted off and on for the period of our stay at Havre, turning the whole camping ground into a veritable quagmire, and culminating in a tremendous storm on the night of December 28th, which wrought havoc among the tents. On this night orders were received for entrainment the next morning.

In pouring rain and a howling wind, the Battalion

turned out to parade for entrainment ; in the storm of the night many horses broke loose, dragging the pickets out of the soft and prevalent mud, and one horse was missing in the morning. The limbers and waggons, too, had sunk in the mud, and great difficulty was experienced in literally digging them out, which caused considerable delay in getting off, while those not engaged on fatigue work had to stand on parade, waiting to move off, in a series of blinding hail storms for close on two and a half hours. Here occurred our first casualty overseas, Rifleman Allison, one of the transport men and one of the youngest men in the Battalion, meeting with a fatal accident. All mourned the sad circumstances of his death. Eventually, entrainment was completed by 11.35 a.m. in cattle trucks, and we commenced our journey up country, reaching St. Omer, our detrainment station, at 8 a.m. the following morning. Detrainment took place at midday and the Battalion marched about three miles to a village called Blendecques, where billets were found in school rooms, in barns and in large houses, and on the whole, not uncomfortable ones. Here we stayed about a month, training with route marches, attack practices, digging, both individual and a defence system, and firing on the rifle range at St. Omer. During this period, letters from home commenced to arrive, belated Christmas puddings were sent out, and goatskin coats were issued to the Battalion. After various inspections of training the Battalion received orders to move forward. On the morning of January 29th, 1915, the Battalion left Blendecques about 9.30 a.m. for Hazebrouck, where the whole Battalion was billeted for the night in a large, partially furnished building intended for a hospital, which had, apparently, long and recently been used for the stabling of horses ; this was probably the dirtiest billet ever allotted to the Battalion, or so it seems, even after a lapse of four years and upwards and after considerable experience of billets in France and Belgium, though perhaps the effect on a mind comparatively fresh to the rigours of service abroad still lingers. It was a cold night accompanied by heavy frost which rendered the next day's march, to Outersteene, on slippery, uphill roads, an extremely slow process, with the inevitable necessity for much work for many fatigue parties to get the transport along. Here billets were allotted in farm buildings, not uncomfortable for the short time of the Battalion's stay.

On February 2nd, 1915, the Battalion again moved forward as Divisional troops of the 28th Division, marching in rear of the Divisional train, a position in which all the many slight checks incidental to the movement of the Divisional train reacted with multiplied effect, causing the maximum discomfort. After an all-day's march the Battalion reached Ouderdom, to find that the billeting arrangements had gone awry, and it was not till after dark that accommodation was eventually found in barns and farm houses for the much-wearied troops. Here the Battalion remained till February 8th, 1915, doing such training as the frequent signals of enemy aircraft permitted, watching the shelling of these, and, on one occasion, having a test " Alarm " which necessitated turning out in full marching order and reaching a rendezvous, after packing blankets, cook's waggons, &c., in less than half an hour, a feat successfully accomplished by three out of the four Companies.

On February 8th, 1915, the Battalion marched forward to Ypres, reaching this desolate city about 6.30 p.m., and was billeted in the Cavalry Barracks. In these days there were few inhabited houses, though many were still standing, but a few shops still doing business, and abundant evidences on all sides of hostile shell-fire, and an absence of windows that gave an effect of ruin greater than the reality. At this time the enemy were content to bombard the city twice a week at night for about an hour with medium weight of shell. Within two hours of the arrival of the Battalion in Ypres, parties to carry rations and stores up to the front line trenches had to be found. In these early days there was no attempt at communication trenches, and the only method of approach to the front line was across open country, right up to the actual front line trench, exposed to whatever bullets or shells passed over this, either aimed thereat or searching for troops coming up from the rear. Fatigue parties and reliefs had of necessity to proceed by night, dependent on guides sent down from the trench to bring them safely there, a task not always performed with conspicuous success. Despite this nervous work, which not infrequently entailed being out from between 7 and 8 p.m. till about 5 and 6 a.m., and was indeed trying to troops for the first time under fire, the Battalion gained (and this in a regular division, in which they were the only troops of the T.F.) an enviable and thoroughly deserved reputation for the greater certitude of the delivery of their burden to those for whom it was destined. The finding of fatigue parties continued till February 12th, 1915, on the night of which A and C Companies went into the front line trenches " S " and " T " for a tour of duty for the first time, to strengthen the depleted units then in the line.

On the following night they were relieved by B and D Companies, who were intended to stay in for 24 hours only : however, a successful German attack on troops of the Middlesex regiment developed, and the relieving troops had to be employed in the counter-attack, and it was impossible also to spare troops to carry out the full relief or to carry up rations ; C Company relieved D Company, but B Company had to undertake another 24 hours without further rations. During this tour of duty there was a constant and, at times, fierce artillery battle and infantry action quite close at hand, coupled with a terrific thunderstorm and torrential rain. Two platoons of A Company were detailed for special duty in establishing and keeping touch between 27th and 28th Divisions. Late on the following night, when the idea of relief had again been practically given up, the Companies in the trenches were relieved and returned to the Cavalry Barracks. During this short period in the trenches, heavy casualties occurred, Major V. R. Hoare, Captain L. F. K. Studd and 2nd Lieut. C. K. Beausire making the supreme sacrifice, the two first-mentioned being officers long associated with the Regiment, and very gallant gentlemen, the last named, one whose service with the Regiment had been short but sufficient to gain him the trust of all ranks. Second-Lieut. H. Infeld was wounded. After this period, too, many men went to hospital, suffering from frost bite or trench feet, due to the wet, unpleasant condition of the trenches. The same day, within four hours of the last relieved troops returning to the Cavalry Barracks, the Battalion paraded to march back to Ouderdom for a rest, the march to which, though only in actual distance a short one, was, nevertheless, after the incidents and sodden mud of the trenches, a truly wearisome event. Billets of the usual type, barns and farmhouses, were found, where the Battalion rested and was re-equipped during the next three days, while here the first draft from home under Lieut. T. D. Wakefield, and comprising 60 N.C.Os. and men joined the Battalion. On February 19th, 1915, a move a little further back was made to fresh billets of the same type in a little village on the outskirts of Poperinghe, where the distance from the line, some eleven to twelve miles, seemed to promise a rest. The next day, however, orders were received to return to Ypres : arriving there about 9 p.m. A and D Companies proceeded further forward, partly in trenches " R," " S " and " T," and the remainder in support on the Canal Bank, while B and C Companies were housed in reserve in a disused factory. Here the next day was spent, but a move back to our last billets near to Poperinghe started at 12.30 a.m. on February 22nd, 1915, and these were reached soon after dawn. Here the Battalion rested till February 28th, when once again it took the road to Ypres, during the journey to which a D.R. brought the news that billets were again at the Cavalry Barracks and that nobody would be required to go forward from there that night. On the next night, B and C Companies were sent into the trenches to strengthen the troops then in the front line, where they spent a tour of 24 hours. During this tour 2nd Lieut. Wildsmith was killed, and Lieut. H. W. Wightwick was wounded. Second Lieut. Wildsmith's platoon was later taken over by the second reinforcing officer to come out, 2nd Lieut. V. Wheeler-Holohan. The following night, A and D Companies were sent into the front line, C Company was relieved and B Company withdrawn to the Canal Bank in support, where they had to dig temporary shelters in the pouring rain just behind the front line system. C Company were again in the trenches the following night for another 24 hours, the other three Companies being relieved and returning to billets in Ypres. The following night the Battalion returned to the billets near Poperinghe, C Company, which was relieved later, returning the next morning. Here the Battalion rested till March 16th, only supplying fatigue parties for night work in or behind the trenches near Ypres, two companies at a time, on the nights of March 10th-11th to 13th-14th, proceeding to Ypres and back in motor buses. On March 16th, the Battalion proceeded at short notice to Vlamertinghe, where the night was spent in huts. The following day a further move was made, by companies independently into Ypres, to billets again in the Cavalry Barracks. While here, the second draft from home, 184 N.C.Os. and men, joined the Battalion. Here the Battalion remained till March 22nd, in reserve, but without being required for active duty. On our last day, the G.O.C. Division, Major-General E. S. Bulfin, inspected the Battalion and addressed a few words of unstinted and much-appreciated praise for the work done while in this singularly unpleasant and cheerless area. On March 22nd, the Battalion moved to fresh billets in Bailleul. While here the Battalion ceased to be Divisional troops and were definitely attached to the 84th Brigade. On March 24th, the Battalion moved to fresh billets at Dranoutre from which night working parties were supplied for the trenches in front of the Lindenhoek cross-roads until March 28th. On March 28th, A and B Companies proceeded to the front line and support trenches, to join the 2nd Northumberland Fusiliers and 2nd Cheshire Regiment, where they remained until the early morning of April 2nd, Good Friday, a quiet and pleasant tour after the experience of the trenches at Ypres. During this period, C and D Companies provided working parties each night and again on the night of Good Friday.

On April 3rd, the Battalion moved to fresh billets at Ravelsburg : almost immediately after arrival, the Battalion again paraded to march to Locre, past the recent billets at Dranoutre, to a service by the Bishop of London, for which his Lordship was close upon an hour late. The coldness of the weather, the long wait in full marching order, the long march of eight miles each way immediately after a change of billets, all these factors conspired against a proper appreciation of the honour and true motives of the Bishop's visit, and pointed in a sense not intended by him some of his remarks, and prompted the inevitable sequel to his opening

remark . . . " As you could not come to the
Church I have brought the Church to you " . . .
a subdued chorus of . . . " Pity you did not
bring it a little nearer " . . . On Easter Sunday,
a quiet, but greatly appreciated, Battalion Service
was held, the last opportunity for some weeks. On
April 6th were held Battalion Sports, thoroughly
successful and much enjoyed, with a really clever
comic element, including a band of varied instruments, composed largely of signallers. The Battalion
remained in reserve at Ravelsburg until April
7th. On April 7th, the Battalion marched to an
inspection, with the remainder of the Brigade, by
the G.O.C., 2nd Army, General Sir Horace Smith-
Dorrien, who afterwards spoke to the assembled
Officers and representative W.Os. and N.C.Os., in
the course of his remarks mentioning, with commendation, the work done by the attached T.F.
Battalions, 12th London and Monmouth Regiments,
and also hinting at a hard time to come in the near
future. After the inspection the battalion marched,
in pouring rain, to Bailleul, where billets were again
obtained. Here the Battalion trained for the succeeding five days. On April 10th, Captain W. K.
Venning, the Adjutant, attached from the D.C.L.I.,
who had been with the Battalion over two years
and who had done so much to make the Battalion
fit so early and so successfully to take its share in
the fighting overseas alongside the regiments of
the Regular Army, left the Battalion for Staff
training at G.H.Q. : he went, greatly regretted by
all ranks and with the most heartfelt wishes for the
success which it was felt certain would be his, and
which he afterwards so well and truly attained.
His place as Adjutant was taken by Captain W. G.
Worthington. On April 11th, the Battalion, with
the Cheshire Regiment, underwent an inspection
by the G.O.C., V Corps, Lieut.-General Sir Herbert
Plumer. On April 12th, the Battalion moved to

billets at Vlamertinghe, in which it remained until April 16th. While here we had our first experience of a Zeppelin raid, a German airship passing overhead in the direction of Bailleul on the night of our arrival and dropping bombs close to hutments just alongside the village in the direction of Ouderdom, the only casualty, one horse : the station guard (Vlamertinghe being now advanced railhead and therefore probably the object of the attack) turned out and fired volleys from their rifles at the Zeppelin ; it was too early days to realise the futility of this manœuvre : finding ourselves in close proximity to the 9th London Regiment, with whom the Battalion had been brigaded in peace time and in the early days of the war while yet in England, a football match was arranged and played on April 13th under Association rules on a ground in their hutments : a close and fast game was won by us by two goals to nil. While still at Vlamertinghe there passed through the Canadian Division, for whom hospitality was prepared by the Battalion : a fine body of men, soon to know the ultimate horrors of war in the German gas attack. In the evening of April 16th, after an alarm to be ready to move on the 15th, the Battalion left Vlamertinghe for St. Jean, where A and B Companies were billeted for the night, C and D Companies going forward to dug-outs on the railway between Ypres and Zonnebeke. On April 17th, the Battalion moved forward to Zonnebeke where D Company occupied trenches 17 and 18, and C Company trench 19, A and B Companies being in support : in these trenches, with inter-company reliefs, the Battalion remained until relieved on the night April 23rd–24th, a period of little activity and few casualties, though, on the front of the Welsh Regiment on our left, there was greater activity and a certain liveliness with Minenwerfer. The Battalion, on relief, proceeded to bivouac in open fields near Verloerenhoek with a few flimsy

straw-covered shelters, arriving about 2 a.m. : about
4 a.m. orders were received to be in readiness to
move at a moment's notice in conjunction with the
Suffolks. All the morning the Battalion waited in
bivouac, while Lieut. Hunter and a signaller en-
deavoured to get in touch with the troops to the
North, only to find no formed bodies of troops in
that direction, and watched a stream of Canadians,
wounded, gassed, exhausted, passing slowly back
from the direction of St. Julien : many stragglers
were collected by the R.S.M. About 2 p.m. orders
were received to advance in support of the Suffolks
in the direction of St. Julien, attacking any enemy
that was met. During the advance, the C.O.,
Lieut.-Colonel A. D. Bayliffe, was wounded in the
leg, the command of the Battalion devolving on
Major H. G. Challen : about 6 p.m. the Battalion
dug in facing St. Julien, with the Suffolks on the
left. After passing the Field Artillery, no formed
body of our own troops was encountered, only
stragglers from the gas-shattered Canadian units :
the advance was under considerable shell fire, with
occasional cross machine-gun fire, the casualties
being 18 o.r. killed, 3 officers (Captain G. S. Tucker
and Lieut. R. L. Hoare, in addition to the C.O.) and
38 o.r. wounded. In this line the Battalion remained
until relieved on the night of April 26th–27th, by
the Yorkshire L.I., momentarily expecting an attack
by gas or otherwise which never came, and struggling
against the drowsy effects of the gas which still hung
about. The casualties from shell fire were not light.
After relief the Battalion returned to bivouac again
at Verloerenhoek, where the intelligence summary
and the daily papers for the first time informed
us of the terrible German gas attack on April 22nd
and the narrow escape from being cut off in the
salient at Zonnebeke the Battalion had had. From
here fatigue parties for work at Zonnebeke were
supplied nightly, while by day the Battalion remained

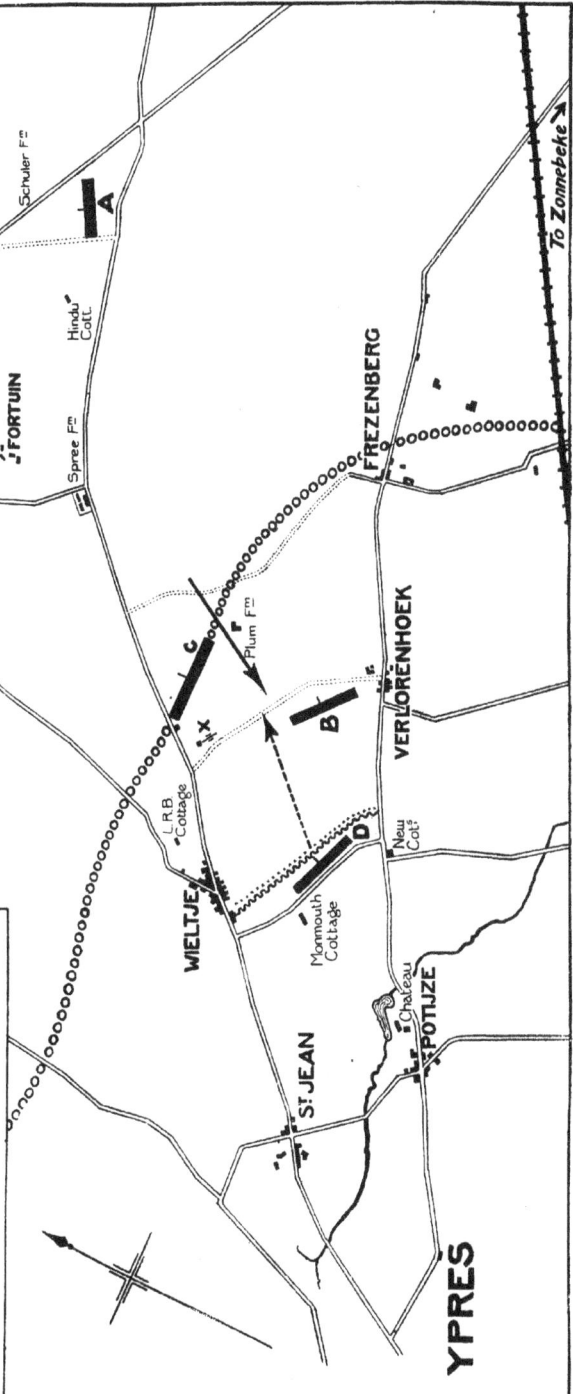

SECOND BATTLE OF YPRES

━━ Rangers.

∧∧∧∧∧∧ GHQ Line.

ooooo Firing Line.

A 24ᵀᴴ to 26ᵀᴴ April.

B 24ᵀᴴ April. 26ᵀᴴ April to 2ᴺᴰ May.

C 3ᴿᴰ to 8ᵀᴴ May.

D 8ᵀᴴ May (4 to 11 A.M.)

──▶ German Advance.

- - ▶ { Rangers' Counter Attack.

X Machine Gun.

Schuler Fᵐ

A

Hindu Cott.

ST JULIEN

FORTUIN

Spree Fᵐ

FREZENBERG

Plum Fᵐ

C

X

B

VERLORENHOEK

L.R.B. Cottage

WIELTJE

D

Neu Cotᵗ

Monmouth Cottage

ST JEAN

Château

POTIJZE

To Zonnebeke →

YPRES

in bivouac, enduring intermittent shell fire, hearing the heavy shells passing overhead to the destruction of Ypres, and watching the hazardous passage of artillery ammunition limbers up the shell-swept road. On one day a German aeroplane was brought down in close proximity to the bivouac, which many were tempted to visit until German shrapnel directed on the spot induced wiser counsels. On the night of May 2nd–3rd, the Battalion was sent to dig a trench line, fire and support trenches, on the Frezenburg ridge, and to man this, which was to become the front line in the event of a retirement from the salient at Zonnebeke taking place. This retirement took place the following night (May 3rd–4th) on which night the new line was improved. The German artillery soon found the new line on the Frezenburg ridge, and shelled it repeatedly, causing numerous casualties. Relief by the Monmouths, eagerly looked for by the troops now wearied with the strain of many days under continual shell fire, took place on the night May 7th–8th, and the Battalion retired to dug-outs behind the G.H.Q. line, arriving about 4 a.m. Heavy shelling of these dug-outs from about 6 a.m. onwards caused numerous casualties and forbade rest. At 11.15 a.m. came the order to advance in support of the Monmouths, the right of the Brigade line having been broken by the German advance. The Battalion, now about 200 strong, advanced with A, B and C Companies in the front line, led by Major Challen and Major Foucar, and D Company, under Captain Jones, in support, the Machine Gun Section with one gun only left, moving independently on the left flank. The Battalion had to pass through a gap in the barbed wire in front of the G.H.Q. line on which German machine-guns were trained, and suffered heavily in its passage. The whole of the ground over which the further advance took place was heavily shelled, and in places exposed to heavy rifle and machine-gun fire, so that the Battalion rapidly dwindled. A small remnant pushed forward to the rise where the trench line had been and there dug in, and stayed the German advance. The Machine Gun Section under Lieut. J. K. Dunlop, operating independently, did extremely useful work and was able to bring enfilade fire to bear on the advancing Germans, until the gun was struck and disabled by shell fire. Of survivors there were ultimately collected by Sergeant W. J. Hornall (every Officer having been either killed, wounded, or taken prisoner), 53, mainly pioneers and signallers. All the remainder were either taken prisoner, killed, missing or wounded. The determination of the attack, it is said, was such that the Germans thought it could only have been made by troops sure of speedy and strong support, not, as in fact was the case, by practically the last remaining troops between them and Ypres, and so the enemy dug in without further advance, and thus was achieved the object for which so many gallant souls gave up their lives.

The few survivors, after assisting to dig trenches in the vicinity for the next two or three days were ultimately withdrawn to the rest they so richly deserved.

[*To face page* 36.

Machine Gun Section, 1st Battalion, The Rangers.

CHAPTER III.

A PERIOD OF TREKS.

THERE were many sad and many glorious days to come, but for sheer tragedy the Second Battle of Ypres stands out most prominently from the many vicissitudes through which the Rangers went during the War. The brave effort on the Frezenburg ridge had brought about the end of the original Battalion. Of the Officers and men who had so whole-heartedly and unselfishly prepared themselves for war during the days of peace, only fifty-three men, headed by Sergeant Hornall, struggled out of the shell-fire and the mud and slush in front of Ypres.

Meanwhile Lieut. Withers Green, the Battalion Transport Officer, had brought up to Ypres every man of Battalion Headquarters, every detail on whom he could lay his hands, and some reinforcements that had lately arrived under Lieut. Benns and 2nd Lieut. Bentley. By May 10th, however, the German advance had been stemmed and the eighty odd men that composed Lieut. Green's party were not needed. Accordingly they proceeded to a camp near Ypres and slept the night in some huts. It was here that Sergeant Hornall and the band of fifty-three survivors, begrimed with mud, dazed and utterly weary, reported to Lieut. Green in the early hours of May 11th. They had little enough time that day to sleep and recover from their experiences, for at 5 o'clock in the afternoon the Battalion, now numbering five officers (counting Lieut. Lindop, the Quartermaster and Lieut. Uloth, the Medical Officer) and two hundred N.C.O.'s and men, took its place in the brigade column and marched down the shell-broken cobbled road to Poperinghe.

Days spent in trekking and nights spent " A la belle etoile " followed, but they were pleasant enough to men worn with battle. After leaving the outskirts of Poperinghe, the Battalion slept one night in a field off the Poperinghe-Steenvoorde road, where they were joined by Lieut. Perkins, who, as senior officer, assumed command, and a draft of ten men. The next night was spent in a farm south of Wippenoek, a few hundred yards off the French frontier. On the 14th, motor-buses conveyed the Battalion across the frontier to the hamlet of Herzeele, where, on the 19th, Lieut. Monsell assumed command. After a farewell speech from the General Commanding the 84th Brigade (Brig.-General L. J. Bols), in which he complimented the Battalion on its splendid work, a final bus ride on the 20th brought the two hundred odd men into the Pas de Calais and deposited them in the small town of Tatingham, a few miles west of St. Omer. Bathing parades, route marches and company training whiled away the next ten days.

On the last day of May the wanderings of this nomadic party, now 250 strong, came to an end, when a composite battalion was formed for work on Lines of Communication to which the remnants of the Rangers and the remnants of the 1st Battalion of the Kensingtons each supplied two companies. No. 1 Company, which consisted of all details and C Company, went to Etaples, where Headquarters was established, and No. 2 Company, composed of A, B and D Companies to Calais. So the remnants of the Battalion had done with fighting for many months to come, and, like the Greeks after the disastrous end of the expedition of Cyrus, had once more reached the sea.

CHAPTER IV.

LINES OF COMMUNICATION.

THE history of a battalion on Lines of Communication does not make very interesting reading. We will review the work and experiences as briefly as possible.

On the last day of May, Lieut. Monsell and No. 1 Company detrained at Etaples. They marched away about a mile north of the small town and pitched camp on the sand-dunes that lie between the railway line and the broad shallow mouth of the river Canche, where Napoleon concealed his fleet of flat-bottomed ships in readiness for an attempt to invade England.

The duties of this Headquarters detachment during the summer were not very arduous. It supplied both clerical and manual labour in connection with the siting and building of what was to become one of the largest reinforcement camps in France, of the vast hospital of wooden huts (bombed frequently in the latter part of the war by Boche airmen), and the training ground on the side of a high sand peak a little to the north of the hospital, which came to be known afterwards as the " Bull Ring." In leisure hours, officers and men went for bathes in the estuary or long walks or rides over the lonely sand-dunes to Camiers, or else they took the train from Etaples to Paris Plage, where the Hôtel des Bains and the Au Chat Bleu Restaurant were favourite haunts of officers in the afternoon.

By the end of September, Lieut.-Colonel Bayliffe, who had been decorated a month before with the C.M.G., Major Jones, Captain Worthington, now returned to the duties of Adjutant, Captains Wightwick and Dunlop, the latter decorated with the Order of St. Anne of the 1st Class for skilful handling of machine-guns in the Second Battle of Ypres, had recovered from their wounds and returned to the Battalion. Officers and men had also been drafted out from the second and third lines in England and the strength of the Battalion had risen to close on six hundred.

A vigorous programme of training was carried out, runs up the beach before breakfast, officers' tactical schemes under Major Syms and Major Jones (a certain trench scheme produced by subaltern officers under the guidance of Major Jones, which involved many miles of foot slogging over the inland hills, will not be forgotten, even now, by those subaltern officers, nor moreover, by the mess waiters who had to serve an extra lunch to them at about three in the afternoon for many days running), route-marches and attendance at the icy-cold " Bull Ring," where instruction was given in bombing, bayonet work and trench duties.

Sergt.-Major Rayner of A Company gives a good account of this period :—" Great efforts were made both to counteract the ill-effects on discipline and physical fitness of ' cushy ' railhead jobs, and to provide entertainment and relief from monotony for the men in the sandy camp. Concerts were organised, in which I remember Lieuts. Benns and Monsell were particularly active—the latter's ' Bo-Hunkus ' and Irish songs being immensely popular. Cross-country ' Pack ' team races were arranged— they were run over the sand-hills and marshy fore-shore of the river Canche in which, I think, the Battalion Headquarters team were successful as a rule (with C.Q.M.S. Sewell as a comical but effective member of their team). Lieut. Liveing, Rifleman (afterwards Sergeant) Worthington and myself were, I believe, the most frequently scoring individuals . . . .

" We certainly had an excellent football team— managed, I think, by Staff-Sergeant Mellor of the

A.O.C., who had been attached to us from the beginning. It did very well, indeed, in hot competition in the Etaples League—some of the hospitals having fine teams. Of the team, I can remember Ted Batten (now R.Q.M.S.), Cerrutto, Jack Batten, Church, Edwards, Northam, Popple, Tommy Bowers, C.S.M. Stevens (afterwards R.Q.M.S.) and those two fine backs, Lieut. Higgins and Jack Davies (R.A.M.C. attached to us from the beginning)."

CHAPTER V.

PREPARATION FOR THE ATTACK ON GOMMECOURT.

WHEN the 167th Brigade took over the Hebuterne sector in May, the opposing lines were, on an average, 750 yards apart. Our front line ran roughly 100 yards east of the trees and orchards surrounding Hebuterne. No Man's Land was an open, grassy terrain sloping slightly towards the German lines guarding Gommecourt, and, to the south thereof, Nameless Farm. An attack over such a wide stretch of ground without any cover would have little chance of success. It was decided, therefore, to dig out a new system of trenches in No Man's Land, connecting up with the old front line. On a night in May, the 167th Brigade went out audaciously into No Man's Land and commenced to dig this new system. The whole plan was accomplished so cleverly that hardly any casualties were incurred, and the trenches, deepened and improved on subsequent nights, brought us to within 300 yards of the German lines.

From June 3rd to the 8th, six nights running, the Battalion, with the exception of A Company, who reported for special work to the R.E's. in Hebuterne on the morning of June 3rd and were billeted in the " Keep," marched from Sailly into the trenches and worked solidly from 9 p.m. to 1.20 a.m. on the new system. By this time the Boches were quite aware of the presence of these trenches (in fact, they had already raided them once), and they had the range of them to a nicety. The trenches were still very shallow, so that the work was really done " on top " and frequent " strafes " by minenwerfers and machine guns, during which men would have to take cover in shell-holes, caused a few casualties each night, in all one officer and seven other ranks wounded. A Company were also engaged, under R.E. supervision, on the construction of dug-out and other work in the trench system in front of Hebuterne.

At 3 p.m. on the 8th, the Battalion commenced moving into Hebuterne by companies along the duck-board walk (which ran through the battery positions and was the only route which could not be observed by the enemy from Gommecourt Wood), to relieve the London Scottish. By midnight the relief was complete, and the Battalion was occupying the W Sector, as it was called, in front of Hebuterne, with A and B Companies in the new front and support lines, C Company in the old support line, Cross Street, which ran just behind a belt of trees bordering the Hebuterne Orchards, D Company and Battalion Headquarters in the village itself.

On the night of the 10th there was a re-distribution of companies, chiefly with the object of bringing C Company up into the " R " line (the original front line), and D into Cross Street to take the place of C. The enemy maintained a casual minenwerfer bombardment during the night, killing Lieut. Meo and a rifleman of D Company, and wounding two other riflemen. The flight of these " minnies " was soundless, though, by constant watching, the red trail which they made could be detected, and at the final moment the projectile dodged. It was whilst keeping well out of the trench to watch these unpleasant projectiles and to point his men into safe positions that Lieut. Meo was killed by one of them prematurely bursting in the air.

On the next day, a Sunday, the enemy maintained a continuous bombardment of the new trench system with shells of all calibre. Many fire-bays in the front line were blown in, and any attempt to cross and repair these positions was at once detected, and "strafed" with "whizz-bangs" and machine-gun fire. A and B Companies had some difficulty in evacuating their wounded, about ten in number, along the still extremely narrow communication trenches, down which stretchers could not be taken. A remarkable case was that of Lance-Corporal Hopkins of B Company, wounded severely in the head with shrapnel. It took five hours for stretcher-bearers to carry him down, by means of sand-bags under his arms and knees, into Hebuterne. A speedy operation, however, saved his life.

On the night of the 11th, A and B Companies were relieved by C and D. It was a very wet night. By the next morning the trenches, especially the new system, were in an extremely muddy state. All Companies went to work "over the open" on their new positions on the night of the 12th, and succeeded in deepening them considerably despite the pulpy state of the ground. We were relieved by the Kensingtons on the evening of the 13th, after sustaining eleven more casualties, all wounded, and marched by platoons to Souastre, covered with mud, and exhausted, but singing cheerily.

The Battalion was billeted in Souastre for a week. Every morning companies marched out at 7.30 with picks and shovels to dig the divisional cable line, which had reached Sailly-au-Bois, and which had to be extended thence to Hebuterne, returning at 4.30 in the afternoon. After tea one could visit the "Bow Bells." There was one song in the show, as it was played then, that had more encores than any others, and that was "My Old Kentucky Home," rendered and clog-danced to by Mark Leslie. Even now when a barrel-organ comes round and plays that song beneath the windows of any 1916 member of the 56th Division, his memory will travel quickly back to the old barn at Souastre, the smoke from pipes rising on the warm air, and the laughing faces of his "pals" around him; he will smile at the recollection of that pleasant interlude in a life of toil and danger, but he will sigh when he realises how many of those laughing companions have since " gone west." " And then to bed," as Pepys would say, or rather, blankets on the floor of a barn, and sleep to the hammering of a machine gun two miles away.

It has been said that we stayed in Souastre for a week. As a matter of fact, the last two days and nights (June 20th–21st) were virtually spent in the trenches. A and B Companies took over the support line in the " W " Sector, and worked throughout the night on the new system of trenches, as also did C and D Companies, which were billeted in the daytime in Hebuterne, and those two nights were weird enough. In the dim moonlight parties of all battalions of the division moved about in the open to their tasks of wiring or digging in the slushy ground of the one-time No Man's Land. The Boches had begun to " get the wind up " at our preparations. Their usual method of tackling night working-parties was to give intense machine-gun fire over a small sector, and, when they thought their enemy had gone to earth, to send over their " minnies," for which he would not be prepared. The process was used *vice versa*, a heavy burst of machine-gun fire being given as soon as he considered that we were " on top " and keeping a look-out for his " Minnies." The " Gaby Glide " and " Lone Tree " were the nastiest spots of the new line. The " Crow's Nest," a region of scrub through which ran the support line, was also a medium for the expression of Boche hatred. Some jester had pinned up an ironical notice on the wall of the support line trench, just before it crossed the sunken road to Puisieux : " If you don't want to become a landowner in France, keep well down whilst crossing the sunken road." There was method in his madness.

During these two days in the trenches, one officer, 2nd Lieut. A. B. Phillips, was killed while out with a party in front wiring, and Captain Withers Green, of transport fame in 2nd Ypres, very seriously wounded on the same job. Of other ranks, three were killed, one died of wounds, and three were wounded.

A and B Companies left the trenches by platoons at mid-day on the 21st. Though weary, they marched back strenuously over the duck-boards to Sailly, along the " screened " road to Bayencourt, then to Souastre, with the ripening corn and red poppies on either side of them making them forget, for the time being, the dark days left behind.

In a green field beyond Souastre the companies collected and rested, and then marched as a body through Henu, down the long tree-bordered hill into Pas (5th Corps Headquarters) and up again to Halloy, which they reached at 6 p.m., four hours later than the other companies. That peaceful little village seemed miles away from warfare. An Army canteen had been installed, and there were several " estaminets " where " Veuve Clicquot " could be bought at 9 francs the bottle and " vin ordinaire " and beer were wonderfully cheap, so that altogether Halloy was an ideal spot after Hebuterne. The only drawback to our comfort was the rain, which poured through the canvas huts in which the two brigades were billeted.

After battalion, brigade and divisional practice-attacks over the replica trenches, the final one being a " full-dress rehearsal " with smoke, aeroplanes and the Brigade, Divisional and Corps Staffs looking on, the two Brigades, 168th and 169th, moved up to billets and bivouacs behind the line on the 27th. The Rangers reached Bayencourt at five o'clock on the evening of that day. Meanwhile, the Germans at Gommecourt had been enduring a gruelling time.

To face page 47.]

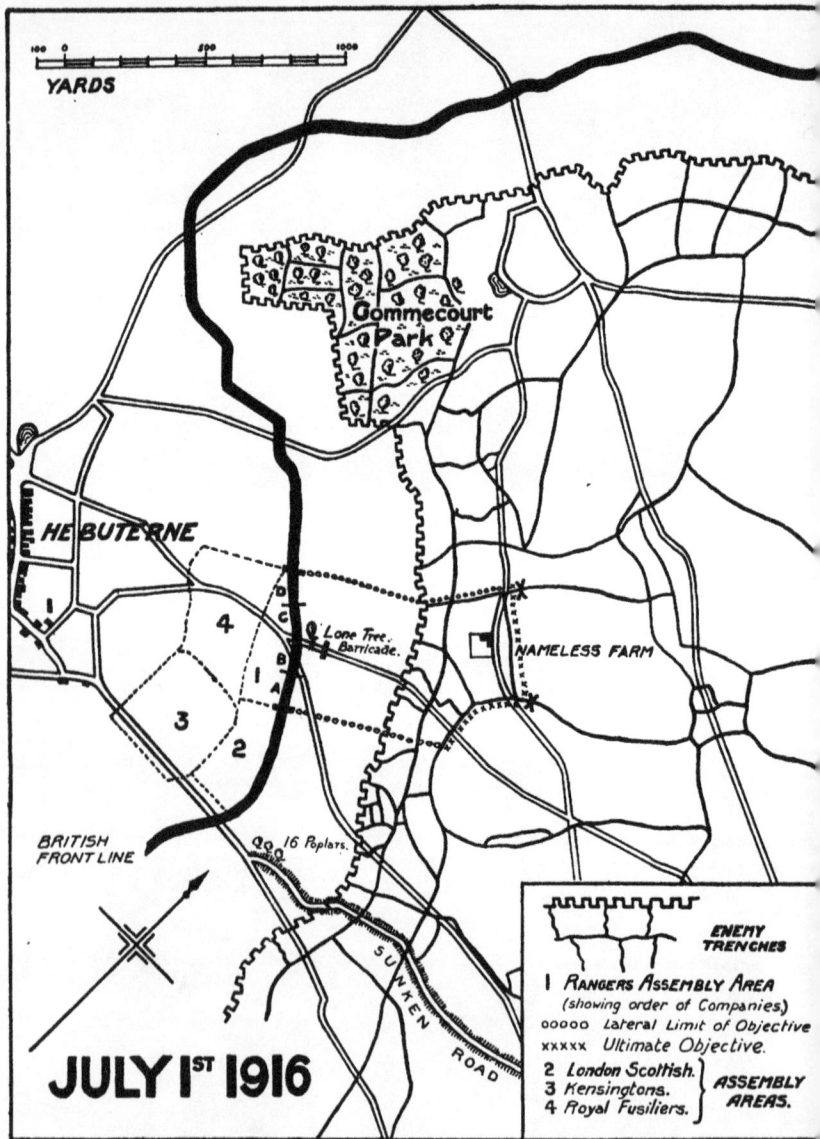

YARDS

Gommecourt
Park

HEBUTERNE

4

1
B
A

3

2

Lone Tree.
Barricade.

NAMELESS FARM

BRITISH
FRONT LINE

16 Poplars.

SUNKEN ROAD

JULY 1ST 1916

ENEMY
TRENCHES

1 RANGERS ASSEMBLY AREA
(showing order of Companies)
ooooo Lateral Limit of Objective
xxxxx Ultimate Objective.

2 London Scottish.
3 Kensingtons.
4 Royal Fusiliers.

ASSEMBLY
AREAS.

CHAPTER VI

THE BATTLE OF JULY 1st, 1916.

THE combined Anglo-French offensive, to be handed down to history as the Battle of the Somme, was originally intended to start on June 29th, but the offensive was at the last minute postponed for two days, taking place ultimately on July 1st. During the period of waiting an untoward incident happened to the Battalion. Throughout the night of the 27th–28th a battery of 9·2 long-range guns stationed at Bayencourt maintained a strong bombardment of the enemy lines. About six o'clock the next morning the Boche artillery retaliated, searching for our gun position with several "crumps" and shrapnel shells. This gun position happened to be just behind B Company's billets. The gunners "went to ground," but they need not have done so, for the shells fell short and did havoc in B Company, killing a very excellent N.C.O., Corporal Goldsmith, and wounding seven riflemen.

We must now turn for a short time from the doings of the Battalion and consider in some aspects the first day of the Somme Battle. And be it said, before we go any further, that the average soldier knew nothing, beyond his own division's attack, of the size and type of the offensive in which he was to play his small part. He only knew that a very hard and bloody struggle awaited him and his comrades, and he knew, too, that he would be lucky if he was wounded and not killed. There were, of course, the usual wild rumours. One was that wedges were to be driven into the enemy's lines from the coast to a distance far south, and these wedges were to be afterwards linked up, the German garrisons between being isolated. A very wild rumour reached us on June 30th that the Royal

Scots had advanced ten miles to the east of Albert and that the Germans were evacuating long portions of their line. To these tales the average soldier gave their due significance ; he gauged the task in front of him at its true difficulty, and looked ahead with all the fortitude and cheeriness that he could muster. It would be uselessly argumentative to say when the fighting spirit of the British infantry reached its prime during the war, but certainly the new " civilian army " of this time, rebuilt as it was from the regulars and pre-war territorial veterans and the early volunteers, tempered as it was with the rigours of trench warfare and the long period of training that occupied the period of comparative quiet on the British front between the Battle of Loos in September, 1915, and July 1st, 1916, and imbued as it was with an " esprit de corps " which could hardly be regained later owing to the difficulties of reinforcing battalions with their own men, was a foe which the Germans regarded with considerable dismay.

The main plan of the offensive on July 1st was a combined Anglo-French attack on a twenty-mile front astride of the Somme assisted by several containing attacks to the north of the Ancre. It was recognised that these latter attacks would not be likely to succeed in themselves, but, if fortune attended them, they could be pushed forward and linked up in co-operation with the main offensive further south.

It was the task of the 48th and 56th Divisions to make the most northerly of these assaults, namely, on the fortress position of Gommecourt Wood. The 48th Division was to drive down behind the wood from the north, the 56th Division was to attack south of the wood in an easterly direction, the idea being that the two assaults should finally link up in the village and cemetery, thus " pinching off " the wood itself, which was too powerfully fortified, both naturally and artificially, to be stormed frontally.

The famous writer, Mr. John Masefield, who visited the Somme battlefield in 1917, has admirably described the Gommecourt position in his introduction to Lieut. Liveing's book, " Attack " :—

" Though the Gommecourt position is not impressive to look at, most of our soldiers are agreed that it was one of the very strongest points in the enemy's fortified lines on the Western Front. French and Russian officers who have seen it since the enemy left it have described it as ' terrible ' and as ' the very devil.' There can be no doubt that it was all that they say . . .

" A traveller coming towards Gommecourt from the west sees nothing of the Gommecourt position till he reaches Hebuterne. It is hidden from him by the tilt of the high-lying chalk plateau, and by the woodland and orchards round Hebuterne village. Passing through this village . . . one comes to a fringe of orchard, deep in grass, and of exquisite beauty. From the hedge of this fringe of orchard one sees the Gommecourt position straight in front, with the Gommecourt salient curving round on slightly rising ground so as to enclose the left flank.

" At first sight the position is not remarkable. One sees, to the left, a slight rise or swelling in the chalk, covered thickly with the remains and stumps of noble trees, now mostly killed by shell-fire. This swelling, which is covered with the remains of Gommecourt Park, is the salient of the enemy position. The enemy trenches here jut out into a narrow pointing finger to enclose and defend this slight rise.

" Further to the right this rise becomes a low gentle heave in the chalk, which stretches away to the south for some miles. The battered woodland which covers its higher end contains the few stumps

D

and heaps of brick that were once Gommecourt
Village.   The lower end is without trees or buildings.
.   .   .   From a mile or two to the south of Gomme-
court the valley appearance becomes more marked.
.   .   .   The salient shuts in the end of the valley
and enfilades it.   .   .   .

"The position is immensely strong in itself,
with a perfect glacis and field of fire.   Every in-
vention of modern defensive war helped to make it
stronger.   In front of it was the usual system of
barbed wire, stretched on iron supports over a
width of fifty yards.   Behind the wire was the
system of the First Enemy Main Line, from which
many communication trenches ran to the central
fortress of the salient known as the Kern Redoubt,
and to the Support or Guard Line.   This First Line
.   .   .   is a great and deep trench of immense
strength   .   .   .   at intervals it is strengthened
with small forts or sentry-boxes of concrete, built
into the parapet.   Great and deep dug-outs lie below
it.   .   .   .   At the mouth of some of these one
may still see giant-legged periscopes by which men
sheltered in the dug-out shafts could watch for the
coming of an attack.   When the attack began and
the barrage lifted, these watchers called up the
bombers and machine-gunners from their underground barracks and had them in action within
a few seconds.

"Though the wire was formidable and the
trench immense, the real defences of the position
were artillery and machine-guns   .   .   The enemy
had not less than a dozen machine-guns in and in
front of the Kern Redoubt.   Some of these were
cunningly hidden in pits, tunnels and shelters in (or
even outside) the obstacle of the wire at the salient,
so that they could enfilade the No Man's Land, or
shoot an attacking party in the back after it had
passed.   .   .   .   Besides the machine guns outside
and in the front line, there were others, mounted in

the trees and in the higher ground above the front line, in such position that they, too, could play upon the No Man's Land and the English front line. The artillery concentrated behind Gommecourt was of all calibres. It was a greater concentration than the enemy could then usually afford to defend any one sector. . . . On July 1st it developed a more intense artillery fire upon Hebuterne, and the English line outside it, than upon any part of the English attack throughout the battlefield."

On the evening of June 30th the Battalion marched to Hebuterne by platoons at 100 paces interval along what was called the " Blue Track." This track on leaving Bayencourt kept somewhat to the right of the Bayencourt-Sailly Road, dipped into the valley behind Sailly-au-Bois, climbed the further side through an artillery and anti-aircraft encampment and, turning east, rounded the southern outskirts of the village into the plain between Sailly and Hebuterne, where many battery positions lay concealed.

At Hebuterne, the track ended and platoons were taken along various routes through the village by their guides. Up to the time of entering the village the Battalion had suffered no casualties, though shrapnel bursts above the battery positions just behind the cemetery had proved rather unpleasant. Several platoons which were to be used as " consolidators " on the next day had to pick up their wire-netting and other materials at a dump near the church—-or rather its ruins. The remainder went straight ahead. Considerable darkness, a disproportion between troops and the number of communication trenches, which had not been sufficiently widely cut, and a somewhat damaging minenwerfer bombardment delayed movements, but all companies were in position by 3.40 a.m. on July 1st, and the commanders of the front platoons had patrolled the enemy's wire, finding a considerable portion of it cut.

We were now occupying a frontage about 400 yards wide in the new system, our right being on the communication trench, Woman Street, where we adjoined the London Scottish, and our left flank extending about fifty paces to the left of Wood Street, where we adjoined the Queen Victoria's Rifles. The companies from right to left were A, B, C, D. The platoons were so arranged as to go over in four successive waves at 70 yards interval, the first platoon of each company occupying the front line, the second the Boyeau de Service, and the third and fourth the Support Line. Rum was served out, and pea soup in petrol tins The latter most of us drank in turn from the " spout," a somewhat difficult operation considering the crowded condition of the trenches.

The hours before the attack were far from pleasant, and heavy shelling gave us many casualties.

Our intense bombardment, the largest of the kind that had been effected up to that date in the war, started at 6.25 a.m.

The Boche artillery retaliated considerably, though the explosions of their shells, unless very near, were drowned by the noise of our own bombardment. This lasted up to 7.30 a.m. when the artillery lifted on to the final objectives, and the infantry, covered by a smoke screen, moved forward to the attack.

The Battalion had a particularly difficult task in front of it. With the exception of the Q.V.R. it had to cross a wider stretch of No Man's Land than any other battalion in the two divisions attacking Gommecourt Wood. Its orders were to fan out slightly as it crossed No Man's Land (roughly 400 yards wide), cross the German first and second line trenches, leaving " nettoyeurs " to mop up any resistance in these lines and proceed to and consolidate the support line from a position on the right in what was termed by us Fame Trench, along a portion of Elbe Communication Trench and along the whole length of Felon Trench from its junction with Elbe to its junction with Epte. Its final frontage, after all objectives had been seized, would be about 559 yards, and its furthest objective, namely, the junction of Elbe Communication Trench and the fire-trench, Felon, would be 700 yards from our front line. The trench system which it had to capture included the ruins of " Nameless Farm," which had been fortified into a strong point.

Of the right company (A), a considerable number, including three out of the five officers, became casualties while crossing No Man's Land, and only a few reached the German line untouched. Between the first and second German lines this remnant was enfiladed from the left by a withering machine-gun fire, and took cover in a communication trench leading to the second line. Captain Wyatt, under cover of fire from the Lewis Gun Detachment, which pluckily operated from some slight cover afforded by a turn in the trench, seeing that the second line could not be taken by advancing across the open, organised a bombing party, which attempted to bomb up the trench into the second line. They were held up by a party of Germans, who had erected a block in this trench and were bombing from behind it. After some counter-bombing Captain Wyatt, on getting up on the side of the trench to reconnoitre and observe the effect, was immediately wounded. A gallant and successful attempt was made to rush the block, and 2nd Lieut. Parker, who had taken over the command, at the head of a handful of men, forced his way into Fall about 9.30 a.m., and, reinforced by the remnants lying outside the trench, his party, 15 to 20 in number, with some London Scottish added, consolidated and held for six hours a portion of the second line astride the head of the communication trench.

We must leave A Company for a time and turn to B, the right centre company. The Company had suffered more casualties before going over than any other ; its leading waves had considerable difficulty in getting through their own wire, and reached the German lines only to find themselves confronted with a broad belt of wire, through which possibly 2nd Lieut. Taplin—certainly Sergeant King and some men of the leading wave—found a gap and reached temporarily the German line, but from which the remainder were beaten back by a withering fire of bombs, machine guns and rifles.

They were reinforced by the remnants of the third and fourth waves, which had been severely handled by enfilade and frontal machine-gun fire whilst crossing No Man's Land. Very gallant attempts were made to file through a gap in the wire which was " taped " by a machine gun until a pile of dead and wounded lay before it. Undoubtedly, a few odd men reached the further side, including Sergeant Shimmel and Corporal and Rifleman Mason (two brothers and the sole survivors of No. 5 Platoon) while later Corporal Tombleson and three men (the survivors of a party of twelve) got through, but had to take cover in a shell hole in front of the first line. The crew of the one surviving Lewis gun did good work for some period from a shell hole in front of the German wire, and the remnants of the Company also maintained strong rifle fire on the German lines from shell holes in No Man's Land. All officers except 2nd Lieut. Taplin, of whose experiences nothing, or next to nothing, is known and who has ever since been " missing," were seriously wounded before reaching the German trenches.

The left centre company (C), crossed the enemy line, though a large portion of it under Captain Hoare was held up by uncut wire, and with its gallant leader was annihilated with rifle and bomb fire.

By the time the rest of the Company had crossed
the enemy line, it had been badly diminished by
machine-gun fire, and all waves were merged. These
remnants advanced towards Nameless Farm under
withering machine-gun fire from that strong point.
Second-Lieut. Josephs was killed whilst bravely
charging a machine gun. The line began to retire,
covered by the Company Lewis gunners, under Lance-
Corporal Saville, who opened fire with the remaining
Lewis gun and fired off all available ammunition.
With both flanks in the blue, no officers left, and
the Lewis gun out of action, the remnants of the
Company were forced back to our original line,
though Lance-Corporal Saville and Rifleman Bartleman, with ammunition replenished, again took their
gun forward across the German line, beyond which
they brought it into action, though engaged from
several directions by enemy machine guns. They
were compelled to retire once more, with all ammunition used up, and in company with other members
of C Company went forward again with a reinforcing
company of the 4th London Regiment. By this time,
however, there was a terrific German artillery barrage on No Man's Land, together with an increase
of machine-gun fire, and it is doubtful if any of this
reinforcing party reached the German lines.

The left company (D), was held up by uncut wire
in front of the German line, and came under enfilade
fire from a machine gun on their left. Attempts
were made to get through the wire, during which
2nd Lieut. Davey was killed. The Company now
opened rifle fire on the Germans, who were standing
with their heads and shoulders above their parapets,
throwing box-shaped hand-grenades. This gallant
fight in the open lasted ten minutes, after which
hardly a man of the first three waves remained unwounded. Major Jones, leading the remains of the
fourth wave, about eight in number, attempted to
rush a twenty-yard gap in the wire, whilst the Lewis

gun teams, also just arrived, opened fire on the German bombers from two shell holes. Major Jones fell wounded about two yards in front of the enemy's parapet, and the only surviving member of the party, Rifleman Perkins, on jumping the trench, was seized by two Germans, whom he struck in the face with a bomb which he held in his hand, afterwards leaping on to the German parapet and throwing bombs into the trench. The survivors, consisting only of three N.C.Os. and nine men (including Rifleman Perkins), saw nothing for it but to return to our own lines. Undoubtedly, another detachment of D Company got through the wire at some other spot and reached a point further into the German lines, which they were seen to be consolidating about 10 a.m., and where they had got into touch with the 169th Brigade on their left much earlier in the day.

From noon onwards it is impossible to review the experiences of individual companies. In fact, companies no longer existed, and the remnants of the Battalion were mingled with remnants of other units. By noon the German artillery had developed such a tremendous barrage on No Man's Land and our front line trench that carrying parties taking over much-needed bombs were all killed or wounded before reaching the enemy lines, whilst the two machine-gun teams despatched to reinforce the party of D Company, just mentioned, also failed to reach their objective. The party of D Company and some Q.V.R. very bravely held out, repelling several bombing attacks, until about noon. It was shortly after noon that the Germans counter-attacked in force all along the line. A very heavy counter-attack was launched on our party, so that, left without bombs and ammunition, they had to fall back gradually, joined on the way by some Queen's Westminster Rifles, and men of C and B Companies, until finally, about 3.30 p.m., after having been driven southwards by the advancing enemy, they joined the party under Lieut. Parker. Here the combined parties collected all available bombs and made a determined stand, but their supply again gave out and a further southward movement had to be made till a junction was effected with the remnants of the London Scottish, from whom they collected some bombs and again checked the Germans till all these were expended. The enemy then bombed our party back until they had perforce to retire back through the German lines and cross No Man's Land into our " W.R." line between 4 and 5 p.m. Other survivors of B and C Companies had been driven back, and crossed into our lines about 3.10 p.m.

Second-Lieut. Parker, who had got detached from the London Scottish, remained with some men in the German lines, and was with them eventually captured. After many attempts to escape, with some temporary success, he was finally caught, late at night, in a sap by a German, whom he suddenly found standing over him with a bayonet.

Night came at last. By 12 o'clock the remnants of the Battalion had been relieved by the 8th Middlesex, and, filing through the heavily-shelled streets of Hebuterne, reached the Corps line east of Sailly, which they occupied at 1.30 a.m. Of the sixteen officers who had gone over, one remained ; of the 745 other ranks, something like 200.

Many wounded of both sides lay out in No Man's Land. A local truce was called the next morning, and our own men and the Boche stretcher bearers carried on rescue work side by side in that valley of death between the opposing lines, until the artillery of both sides unfortunately fired. There were wounded men who lay out in shell holes for several nights, unable or not strong enough to find their way back. One of our wounded men, Rifleman Hegarty, of C Company, though wounded, remained of his own accord to look after some wounded comrades in a shell hole, and for three nights running he crawled out and fetched them food and water from the haversacks and water-bottles of dead men. On the fourth night he crawled into our lines in a terribly weak state, but before being sent down, insisted on guiding a rescue party out into No Man's Land to bring in his wounded friends.

The attack on Gommecourt Wood had been a terrible battle against terrible odds. Every effort had been made beforehand to draw the enemy's forces to our sector, and so keep them from moving to the Somme. It had never been expected that this attack would be successful in seizing ground. The 46th Division north of the wood had only been able to penetrate the German lines for a few hours. It was remarkable that the 56th had not only seized most of its objectives, but had also held them against overwhelming forces and with hardly any ammunition and bombs, until late in the afternoon.

When General Allenby, then in command of the 3rd Army, inspected the Division some days later, he said : " I can find no words to express my opinion of the splendid way you have fought. The great accumulation of German forces on your particular front—the accumulation of nearly 100 German batteries—and the Reserve of the Prussian Guard, made your task a desperate one ; but you seized all points designated as your objectives, and your achievement will stand out and compare favourably with any fight in history. It has been the foundation of the success further south, and of the triumphant battle the sound of which is now dinning in our ears."

So far as the Battalion itself was concerned, July 1st, 1916, marked the end of its days as a regiment composed exclusively of actual " Rangers." So far as the individual members of the Battalion were concerned, it came as the end and abrupt finish of a comradeship which they will never forget during their lifetime.

CHAPTER VII

SOMME, 1916.

First Phase.—September 1st–14th.

AFTER the battle of Gommecourt the Hebuterne
Sector became a haven of peace and quiet
in which the 56th Division remained for the best
part of the ensuing two months. The early days of
July were occupied in clearing the *débris* from the
shattered trenches and salving the remnants of the
large quantities of stores which had been distributed
in the trench system for that battle.

Afterwards we spent uneventful weeks in carrying out ordinary trench duties and working hard at
reclaiming and rebuilding the forward portions of
the trench system. The experience and training in
constructing and maintaining field works which the
Battalion acquired during this period was invaluable.

On August 18th, the 56th Division left the
Hebuterne Sector and the VIIth Corps and moved
to the St. Riquier training area north of Abbeville,
spending three days at Doullens on the way. The
G.O.C. VIIth Corps in a farewell order said : " The
gallant manner in which the Division fought at
Gommecourt will be appreciated in history, but the
Corps Commander wishes the Division to know that
the less spectacular but more irksome work which
the Division has put into the line which they have
been holding, has not escaped notice. It is invidious
to make distinction when all have worked so well,
but he particularly congratulates those units who
have so well repaired that part of the line knocked
about in the fighting on July 1st."

The Rangers appropriated some of the latter
praise to themselves as a set off against the chaff
they had to endure for a fine piece of model trench

construction which our old friend and genial neigh-
bour, the C.O. of the 4th Londons, christened " Eye-
wash Alley."

Our billets in the St. Riquier area were in the
village of Neuilly L'Hopital (commonly called
" Nearly-in-Hospital ") and the actual training
ground was about two miles from the village. We
were kept pretty busy training during the few weeks
spent there, but managed to lighten our labours
with Battalion sports and concerts, a certain amount
of football and an occasional visit to Abbeville.
Whilst here the first demonstration of tanks was
carried out in the neighbourhood and the writer
was privileged to be amongst the first of the B.E.F.
to witness these new engines which ultimately played
so large a part in winning the war.

As an example of how well the secret was kept
it may be mentioned that we were merely ordered
to attend a demonstration by the Heavy Machine
Gun Corps at a certain map reference. (As we were
holding our Battalion Sports that afternoon we were
not a bit keen on going.) On approaching the rendezvous we found the surrounding hills picketed by
Mounted Police, and after getting through the
cordon we could see in the far distance some strange
looking objects, emitting clouds of smoke, which we
took to be a new brand of cooker.

When we finally got up to the new monsters
the scene was not unlike Derby Day. Every " brass-
hat " and staff car seemed to be there, and the
spectators included H.R.H. the Prince of Wales,
and the Commander-in-Chief, and General Foch
(General Joffre witnessed a demonstration the
following day). The demonstration was extremely
interesting, but the universal criticism was that the
tanks would need speeding up in order to keep pace
with advancing infantry.

At 6 p.m. on the afternoon of September 3rd
the Battalion entrained at St. Riquier for Corbie,

which was reached at 11.45 p.m., whence an hour and a half march brought us to our billets at Vaux-sur-Somme. Next day, in the middle of dinner, we got orders to move in half an hour, a feat which we managed to accomplish and which was our record for rapid move.

An incident involving the Padre, the M.O. and the lady at Headquarters Mess will always be associated in the writer's mind with this move.

The M.O., as Mess President, was engaged in settling up with our hostess for " extras " when she discovered the loss of one of her antimacassars and, with a lamentable absence of tact, roundly declared that one of the officers must have stolen it. In vain the M.O., in his best bedside manner, tried to pacify her. Not a bit of it, one of us had stolen it and it would have to be paid for ; moreover, it was a singularly valuable antimacassar, and had been worked by her grandmother, &c., &c. (here followed a long extract from her family history), and she would not take less than 10 francs compensation. Time was getting short, so the M.O. paid up, mounted his steed and rode off to join the Battalion. About 100 yards up the road he overtook the Padre serenely striding along to the starting point with the missing antimacassar dangling on the hook of his jacket.

Madame's property was restored to her, but her joy at finding that which was lost was in no way commensurate with her bitter grief over the losing of it, tempered, as it was, with the repayment of the 10 francs.

Our route lay across country over a " dry-weather " track, but, unfortunately, the weather had been far from dry, and the new hand-carts for Lewis guns were being used for the first time. To enable a civilian reader to realise the result, let him try pushing his infant son in a perambulator over his allotment. If ever Rangers swore terribly in

Flanders our Lewis gunners surpassed themselves in Picardy on that day.

We reached Bray Citadel (deceptive name) at 8 p.m. that night to find that, instead of the old-world fortress conjured up by that name, we were to spend the night in tents on a bare hill side.

Next afternoon, the Brigade started off in the rain for the line, but shortly after we had cleared the camp a message came that only the Scottish and Kensingtons would proceed and the Rangers and Fusiliers would return to camp.

That night orders came, just as we were settling down to sleep, to move at once to Casement Trench, near the Briquetrie, 500 yards south of Bernafay Wood on the Maricourt-Longueval Road, and at 12 a.m., in pitch dark, we started off to march there via Fricourt and Maricourt over a route which we had had no chance of reconnoitring by daylight.

The start was marred by an unfortunate incident. The two battalions were formed up in column of route ready to move off when someone in the leading platoon of the Fusiliers trod on an old Mills grenade buried in the mud causing it to explode, with the result that several of their men were injured, and also a horse, which added to the confusion by trying to stampede.

The march was very trying owing to the darkness and bad state of the roads, and for part of the way we were constantly passing bodies of French troops and transport coming back from a relief.

Eventually we reached our destination at 7 a.m. having taken 6½ hours to do about 10 miles.

At 6.30 p.m. on the afternoon of the 6th we moved up into Maltz Horn Trenches in Chimpanzee Valley. Headquarters Company were leading and their arrival occurred at an unlucky moment when the enemy put over two 5.9 shells, causing casualties amongst the signallers.

Here we remained until we moved up to relieve

the 7th Inniskilling Fusiliers in Sunken Road Trench, near Guillemont, at midnight on the 7th–8th.

On the night of the 8th-9th, the Battalion moved up into assembly trenches at the head of Angle Wood Valley just below the crest along which runs the road from Leuze Wood to Guillemont, preparatory to an attack on the enemy's position at Ginchy Telegraph next morning.

The attack started at 4.45 a.m. on the 9th. Immediately on crossing the ridge in front of the assembly trenches all companies came under very heavy machine-gun and rifle fire. This fire was coming from a German position half left from the line of advance. (This position was afterwards known as The Quadrilateral.) The right leading company (C) encountered no enemy during their advance to the first objective except a small party of about twenty in a listening post, the survivors of whom were captured.

The left leading company (D) advanced under heavy machine-gun and rifle fire and by the time the Company reached the crest of the slope their strength had been reduced considerably. The men were ordered to lie down and open fire on the German trenches which were sited in a basin on the left front of the Company. The 7th Inniskillings did like-wise. D Company then advanced to the trench "C—D" which was unoccupied and which they proceeded to consolidate, at the same time keeping up rifle fire on the enemy trenches.

At nightfall, the 7th Inniskillings found their left flank exposed rendering their position untenable and forcing them to withdraw, which circumstance they reported to O.C., D Company, who thereupon decided that his only course was to fall back on our front assembly trench and hold it.

The right support company (A) followed in support of C Company. One of their platoons succeeded in reaching the line of the final objective and came under the orders of O.C. C Company.

The remaining three platoons only succeeded in reaching their first objective and came under the orders of O.C. D Company.

The left supporting company (B) followed in support of D Company and on reaching the first objective came under the orders of O.C. D Company.

To return to the action of C Company. This Company reached the road from Leuze Wood to Ginchy at 6 a.m. The advance to the final objective was carried out thence by a series of rushes, the advance being exposed all the time to rifle and machine-gun fire from their left rear. On arrival, at about 6.45 a.m., they found the 4th Londons (Fusiliers) and some Kensingtons in the position with the Q.V.Rs. (169th Brigade) on their right. After a consultation between the senior officers present with the various units the distribution was arranged and a " block " established on the left flank by a mixed party of Ranger and Fusilier bombers.

At about 11 a.m. the London Scottish came up on to the position, some of them moving up on the extreme left where, in conjunction with some Rangers, they succeeded in holding back the enemy bombers. On the morning of September 10th, the distribution was finally settled as follows :—

Rangers and London Scottish bombers.	London Scottish.	Rangers.	Fusiliers.	Q.V.Rs.

the line running approximately from the northern-most corner of Leuze Wood in a north-westerly direction as far as the light railway.

At midnight on September 10th–11th, the Rangers were relieved by the 8th Middlesex and moved back to Billon Farm Camp, south-west of Carnoy, where they remained until the 14th, resting and refitting.

The expression " contemptible British Army " has become history, but the troops on the vast camping area at Billon Farm were assuredly entitled to the epithet " contemptuous."

Concealment was thrown to the winds. The countryside crawled with troops, horses, and transport and was simply " blistered " with dumps. Tents and tarpaulins sprang up like fungi, and at night the " twinkling watch-fires," so dear to the war poet, illuminated the landscape. Everybody who could find anything to burn had a fire.

What the enemy's intelligence department thought about it we do not know.

What the German prisoners thought about it was apparent from their faces one sunny afternoon when the dull monotony of being stared at by their captors was relieved by the appearance of the 56th Divisional Band who discoursed sweet music to the troops within 100 yards of the prisoners' cage, and were followed by the " Bow-Bells " (56th Divisional Concert Party) who gave selections from their repertoire, using a G.S. wagon as a concert platform.

Unfortunately, the troupe was in uniform—had the leading " lady " been in one of her " chic " confections the caged Huns, undoubtedly, would have endorsed the continental opinion as to the insanity of the English.

CHAPTER VIII.

SOMME—1916.

Second Phase—September 15th to October 30th.

ON the evening of September 14th, the Battalion moved from Billon Farm Camp to Falfemont Farm about half a mile south-west of Leuze Wood. Of the farm itself no traces remained except a few scattered bricks, and the name merely represented a portion of the old German trench system.

We arrived at our destination at about 1.30 a.m. on the 15th, preparatory to certain projected operations which had been planned for that day and which were conditional upon the success of other operations on our left. The proposed operations were subsequently cancelled.

The French were on the high ground across the valley to our right in Savernake Wood and from our position we could see the eastern portion of Combles. The weather was brilliantly fine and with the assistance of field-glasses we had a very interesting view of various minor operations carried out by our gallant Allies by way of "feeling" in the direction of Combles. We remained here until the evening of the 16th, when we moved back about 500 yards to the reserve trenches in Angle Wood Valley.

Here the command of the Battalion passed to Lieut.-Colonel F. W. D. Bendall, who remained in command until the end of October during the temporary absence of Lieut.-Colonel A. D. Bayliffe, employed on other duties. The Battalion remained at Angle Wood in divisional reserve until the night of the 18th, when they moved into trenches at Hardecourt to be moved back again the following night to Angle Wood, moving again on the night of the 20th into the trench system at the north-west corner of Leuze Wood in relief of the 12th Gloucesters.

Here they remained until the night of the 22nd when they moved back to Chimpanzee Valley.

The night of the 24th found them back again in the Leuze Wood area in Bully Trench preparatory to the operations on the 25th, which resulted in the capture of Combles.

During the above period, from the 16th to the 24th, the Battalion, with the rest of the Brigade, was employed in making and perfecting the trench system which was constructed as a " jumping off " place for the operations on the 25th, and was a very interesting example of " peaceful penetration." It is hardly relevant to a regimental history to go deeply into the operations of the Brigade as a whole, except in so far as the Rangers co-operated, but it may be of interest to record that a trench system constructed at a right angle to our front line, and facing the western edge of Bouleaux Wood was pushed out to a distance of 1,200 yards in the direction of the enemy, and included four strong points and a length of trench, dug by the 5th Cheshires (the Divisional Pioneer Battalion) in the dark under fire, which for symmetry and accuracy of direction and dimension could not have been bettered in daylight in a back area. So good was it that the air photograph was circulated throughout the 3rd Army to show what could be done in the way of trench digging in the face of the enemy.

A length of trench at the extreme north of the system was dug by our Battalion, and named Ranger Trench to record the fact. Also the northernmost strong point (which was dug first and linked up afterwards) was occupied daily by two or three Ranger observers, who, in spite of their isolated position, succeeded in remaining concealed and obtaining valuable information until the " linking up " was complete.

E 2

In the operations of the 25th, the rôle of the Rangers was to support the Fusiliers and the London Scottish, but so well did these two battalions carry out their task that the Rangers were not called upon to take any active part in the battle, during the course of which they remained in Bully Trench, and, fortunately, suffered very little there, in spite of very heavy shelling which, however, caused several casualties amongst carrying parties coming up from Angle Wood.

On the morning of the 26th, Combles was in the hands of the 56th Division and the French. The 6th and Guards Divisions on our left had secured the Flers line, but a length of trench known as Mutton Trench was still in the hands of the Germans, and at 3.30 p.m. the Rangers were ordered to clear it with the assistance of two tanks.

B and A Companies moved to an assembly area in a fold of the ground within striking distance of the enemy, with two platoons of D in support in the first instance, but subsequently, the remainder of that Company were moved up also in support. The reserve company (C) moved up into Ranger Trench.

At 4 p.m., the tanks passed Battalion Head-quarters (which was established in two deep German pits north of the railway embankment, east of Bouleaux Wood) making a somewhat heavy passage owing to the very unfavourable state of the ground, which was deep in mud and pitted with shell-holes every yard. Simultaneously with the forward move of the tanks the two forward companies of the Rangers deployed into assaulting formation under the crest of the rising ground in front of the objective.

About this time, the Battalion Scout Officer (2nd Lieut. A. O. Colvin) returned with a patrol which had been up to the portion of Mutton Trench held by the 6th Division on our left. He reported that the portion of that trench immediately on the right of the 6th Division was held by the Germans in some strength, and that, although the trench was damaged by shell fire, it was wired. This information had been imparted by him to the O.C. the two forward companies (Captain Copeland).

At 6 p.m. the O.C. forward companies asked that a company from the brigade on his flank should be moved up in line with the support company (which was accordingly done).

At 7.45 p.m. the O.C. Tanks reported that his machines were in difficulties and had not arrived at their destination. Upon receipt of this news it was decided not to attempt the assault in the dark without the tanks, and accordingly, the two forward companies were ordered to dig in on their position and two machine guns were sent up to reinforce them.

At 4.45 a.m. the forward companies were ordered to prepare to assault at 10 a.m. supported by tanks, three of which passed Battalion Headquarters and, after proceeding another 500 yards, halted, apparently in difficulties.

After a conference between the O.C. Tanks and Battalion Headquarters, the position was reported to Brigade Headquarters and arrangements were made for two more tanks to be sent up, with a view to the assault being delivered in the afternoon. These experienced the same difficulties owing to the appalling condition of the ground and eventually, at about 4 p.m., orders came through that the assault would not take place, and that the Division would be relieved that night by the French who were " side-slipping " northwards as far as the Guillemont-Morval road. The 2nd Battalion of the 33rd Regiment d'Infanterie arrived at 11 p.m., and by 3.30 a.m. on the 28th the relief was complete, and the Battalion returned to Chimpanzee Valley, arriving there about 7 a.m.

It is due to the companies detailed for the

assault on Mutton Trench to say that they were genuinely disappointed in not being allowed to carry on without the tanks, and their commander delivered himself in picturesque language of the opinion that " they would have been capable of putting it across every qualified Hun in the con-demned trench without the aid of any mechanically-propelled sardine-boxes." However, neither he nor his command were to know why the higher command considered it inadvisable to carry on without the tanks. The Battalion left Chimpanzee Valley at 3 p.m. on the 28th to march to Morlancourt in anticipation of a fortnight's rest, but in this they were disappointed, for the 30th saw the Division back again in Bray Citadel en route for the line once more.

Whilst here we received a strong draft of officers to the number of 13 and about 80 other ranks, mostly " Derby " recruits. A very fine type of man these latter were, but, alas, most of them became casualties, as also did many of the newly-arrived officers, before many days were over. Some of them could almost have reckoned their experience of fighting in minutes.

The two first days of October were spent at Bray Citadel. On the afternoon of the 3rd the Battalion moved at about 3 p.m. and arrived at about 10 p.m. in the reserve trenches east of the site of what had once been the village of Guillemont. No traces of the village were remaining except a few bricks here and there and an occasional barn.

The next move took place on the 5th, on which day the Battalion left at 5 p.m. to relieve the Fusiliers (4th Londons) in the front line east of Les Bœufs, thus entering up their final and worst experience of the inferno which is to go down to history as the Battle of the Somme.

The trench system in front of Les Bœufs was very irregular and sketchy, having been dug under fire during the course of the advance and not having been properly connected up and organised. Consequently, this relief was a long and tedious affair and was not finally completed until 4 a.m. on the 6th.

That afternoon the Battalion received orders to attack the German position next day in conjunction with the 167th Brigade on our left and another battalion of the 168th Brigade on our right, the objective allotted to the Rangers being known as Dewdrop Trench.

The task of the 168th Brigade was to attack and capture the German position between Les Bœufs and Le Transloy. There were two objectives. First, a line just west of the crest about 800 yards to our front. Secondly, a line of detached German positions further east.

The Rangers were to assault on a three-platoon front in four waves. The " leap-frog " method of attack was employed, the two leading waves being detailed to move at 50 yards interval, secure the first objective and dig in, the third and fourth waves to move 20 minutes later, overrun the first objective and capture and consolidate the second objective.

The order of battle was as follows :—

First wave : 2 platoons, D Co. ; 1 platoon, A Co.
Second wave : 2 platoons, D Co. ; 1 platoon, A Co.
Third wave : 2 platoons, A Co. ; 1 platoon, C Co.
Fourth wave : 3 platoons, C Co.
Reserve, B Co. (less 1 platoon).

The remaining platoon of B Company with two Lewis guns was ordered to move 50 yards in rear of the left flank on the fourth wave along the road which formed the Rangers' left boundary. The rôle of this platoon was to establish a strong point on the left flank of our final objective so as to be able to command the road in the direction of the enemy and bring fire to bear itself right along the front of the position when captured.

The two leading waves moved forward at Zero (1.45 p.m.), and immediately on leaving Rainy Trench came under very heavy and accurate machine-gun fire from Dewdrop Trench on their left front.

After going some 50 yards only about 15 men of the leading wave were left and the advance was checked.

The second wave suffered a similar fate, and as neither of the succeeding waves were able to get up in sufficient strength to carry the attack forward, the remnant of the first and second waves hung on in shell holes until dusk, when they re-occupied Rainy Trench.

The third and fourth waves, whose positions of assembly were in Burnaby Trench and a line of shell holes 50 yards in rear, advanced to the attack at 2.5 p.m. They had been shelled steadily since Zero and began to suffer further heavy casualties directly they advanced. A wounded officer reported that by the time they had gone 40 or 50 yards he could see no man of the third wave left standing and a like fate subsequently overtook the fourth wave.

The fate of B Company's Platoon detailed for the strong point is unknown.

The officer in command (he had only just joined us from England—an actor by profession and a right merry fellow from all accounts) was never seen again, and most of his men were missing also at the end of the day. Brigade Headquarters received a very definite report from an aeroplane scout that he had seen British troops consolidating a strong point on the objective allotted to this Platoon, and the inference is that this gallant little party died in a manner worthy of the best traditions of British infantry.

October 7th, 1916, was a disastrous day for the Rangers and for many others. The attack of the brigade on our left failed as also did that of the troops on our right. The weather was appalling, the ground was greasy and slippery with recent rain and there was more than one subsequent abortive attack after we were relieved before the position was finally won.

At 2 a.m. on the morning of the 8th the Battalion was withdrawn to the old German third line, our places in the front line being taken by the Q.V.R. who with the L.R.B. had been placed under the command of the 168th Brigade for the purpose of further operations fixed for that afternoon.

Parties from the reserve company were employed all night in collecting wounded. At 11.30 p.m. we moved up to Shamrock Trench and the night was again spent in collecting wounded.

At 6.30 p.m. on the 9th we moved back to Trones Wood and morn next day found us at Mansel Camp.

During the day the Corps Commander saw the Commanding Officers and Brigade Commanders at Divisional Headquarters and thanked them for their services in the Battle of the Somme.

We spent the following day at Mansel Camp resting and cleaning up and were lucky in having glorious autumn weather to enable us to forget the dangers and hardships of the preceding month.

The early hours of the 12th saw the Battalion on the move towards a well-earned spell of peace and quietude. Marching as far as Treux, we were picked up there by a column of French motor buses and lorries. The embussing arrangements were excellent. On arriving at Treux we found the bus conductors all paraded under the French officer responsible for the arrangements. Most of the conductors were natives of the French Colonial Troops. As the Battalion filed by, each bus load was told off and led to its vehicle by the conductor. Those parties of Rangers who drew native guides were delighted and instantly fitted them with appropriate names, usually " Rastus," " Whistling Rufus " or " Uncle Tom," and the guides strode along in a state of happy importance to find themselves actually leading some of the redoubtable British infantry, even though the objective was but a humble bus. Everybody thoroughly enjoyed the ride and it was a truly delightful sight to see the Headquarters char-a-banc with Major Worthington and a " coloured monsieur " seated side by side, both faces covered in dust and wreathed with happy smiles.

We reached Belloy-sur-Somme that afternoon and spent a very pleasant week there " resting and refitting " and doing a certain amount of training.

By an interesting turn in Fortune's wheel our next destination was Merelessart and it was hard to realise that only nine months previously had the Battalion left there with the then newly-formed 56th Division. Truly had the Division made history and a name for itself during that period.

Arriving at Merelessart on the 19th the Battalion remained there until the 23rd when they entrained at Lonfre at 8 p.m. for an all-night journey to Merville which was reached at 6 a.m. the following morning. Here the Battalion took to the road once again and marched to Estaires, remaining until the 29th when a further move was made to Laventie, the Battalion coming into Brigade reserve on arrival.

CHAPTER IX.

NOVEMBER, 1916, to MARCH, 1917.

THE arrival of the 168th Infantry Brigade in the Laventie Sector (or, as it was officially called, the Fauquissart Sector) was marked by most unneighbourly conduct on the part of the Hun. Whether he got wind of the relief or whether it chanced to synchronise with a premeditated outburst of hate is not known, but the fact remains that the night our " sister " battalion, the London Scottish, took over from the outgoing brigade, the enemy raided the Red Lamp Salient and gave the Scottish a very uncomfortable time.

The line in that sector consisted of breastworks, and the Red Lamp Salient was so called because every night a red lamp was kept burning in such a position that it could be seen from the front line south of the salient, thus minimising the risk of our own Lewis guns and riflemen shooting into the salient in the dark.

The presumed object of the enemy's raid was to damage the shafts of the mines which an Australian Tunnelling Company was running under No Man's Land towards the German trenches. If such was the object, it failed, largely owing to the fact that the preliminary bombardment reduced the salient to a " pudding " of shattered sandbags and liquid mud, making it impossible for anybody unacquainted with the trench system to find any mine shaft under the circumstances.

The more probable explanation of the raid is that the enemy had got wind of the relief and wanted to discover who had taken over. Many of the inhabitants were still living in Laventie and even nearer to the line, and, as the Germans had formerly occupied the town, it was more than probable that they had established an efficient spy system there.

As the result of the smashing of the Red Lamp Salient we were all let in for many weeks of hard work to repair it as well as to improve other parts of the line.

So far as the Rangers were concerned the occasion produced the man, for amongst a draft of nine officers who joined the Battalion in the first week of November was one, no longer in the bloom of his first youth, who, in response to a call for a " Trench Pioneer Officer," modestly stated his willingness to try what he could do, and right well did he perform the job. He had been drafted to the Battalion from another regiment and his real name has probably been forgotten by many, but those Rangers who served with the Battalion during the winter of 1916–1917 will remember the good work of our energetic and popular little " Duckboards."

The Battalion went into line here for the first time on November 1st, and for several weeks thereafter we lived a quiet and uneventful life, except for occasional "alarums and excursions," such as are represented by the following entries in the War Diary :—" November 3rd, 1919, 7.30 p.m. —A Patrol Action took place at N.13.d.7.9$\frac{3}{4}$ —one German was shot dead and brought in." " November 4th, 1919, 2.38 a.m.—S.O.S. call received from Brigade Headquarters emanating from 95th Brigade. Everybody ' stood to '—one other rank arrived." " 3.30 a.m.—S.O.S. cancelled."

Reliefs between the Rangers and Scottish took place every four days. They were effected at the gentlemanly hour of 10 a.m. and, as a rule, were completed in time for lunch.

When out of the line the time was spent in carrying out platoon and company training, having baths and attending Working Parties, which does not mean knitting comforters for the troops, but shovelling liquid mud or putting up wire in No Man's Land.

Two stories in this connection are perhaps worth retailing.

On one occasion two men on a wiring party had a dispute (the cause was variously ascribed by some to a lady, and by others to a question of the ownership of a coil of wire) which ended in blows, and called for the interference of other workers to separate the disputants. The other incident was when "reinforcements one" fresh from England proceeded to light his pipe in the middle of No Man's Land apparently unaware that there were such things as Germans about, and in happy ignorance of the distance at which a lighted match can be seen. As the wiring party lay flat on their faces in the mud waiting for the burst of machine-gun fire, which fortunately never came, their muttered curses swept like a blight along the front of the line.

After his raid on the Red Lamp the enemy had remained very quiet, and on the night of November 12th the O.C. our right company became consumed with curiosity as to what the Hun was up to.

Starting at midnight from the Red Lamp with his runner, the pair made their way across to the Wick Salient in the German front line, and, crawling over the parapet, made the discovery that his front trench system was under water, and was apparently not occupied, except by occasional posts.

On the night of December 1st we collected our first real live Hun officer. The word "collected" is used advisedly, as we can hardly claim to have "captured" an individual who came wandering down a deserted length of trench and accosted, in German, an astonished Ranger sentry who was on duty at the entrance to a fire-bay.

The sentry was a bit of a linguist and, on realising what he had found, gently insinuated the point of his bayonet against the visitor's windpipe, whilst he briefly outlined the situation to him in German.

The prisoner proved to be an officer in a Bavarian Regiment. His story was that he had been out with a patrol of three men to examine our wire. The patrol had been fired on and had to make a bolt for it. In doing this, he had fallen head first into a shell hole full of water, and (so we gathered) his men had not thought it necessary to stop and fish him out. When he had succeeded in extricating himself he found he had lost all sense of direction, and made for our line under the impression that it was his own. It must be remembered that the Rangers were holding a very long stretch of front with only two weak companies in the line, which was very complicated and winding, and it was only possible to hold every fifth fire-bay or so, and rely on patrols to do the rest. Consequently, it was possible (as happened in this case) for a single Hun to get in on a dark winter's night if he were lucky enough to strike a point between two sentry posts, but once in he could not get far without meeting someone.

The prisoner in due course arrived at Battalion Headquarters, and it is due to him to say that he did his best to keep his end up under difficult circumstances. His manner was haughty, distinctly haughty. Twice did he " tell off " the Adjutant for asking questions which he declared " No English officer had a right to ask a captured German officer."

Unfortunately his personal appearance made his attitude a difficult one to sustain.

He was a youngish fellow of rather a mild caste of countenance with thin fair hair and " pince-nez." He was wet to the skin from top to toe and his uniform was covered with mud and slime. Poor devil ! It must have been a bitter moment for him, for (if his story is to be believed) he had been recommended for the Iron Cross, had just got his commission and this was the first time he had been out on patrol as an officer.

Nothing of importance happened after this until the 23rd, when we thought it was about time to have another look at the German front line and see what was going on there. Accordingly, a party visited the Wick Salient and reported that the trenches were flooded, and showed no signs of regular occupation, from which we gathered that the wily Hun had decided to winter on Aubers Ridge, knowing full well that if we did occupy his trench system we should be no better off than we were in our own, and that he could amuse himself shelling the breastwork communication trenches we should have to build if we moved across to the opposite side of the way. The brigade which relieved us in this sector later on used to establish posts by night in the enemy front line until one very cold winter's night the enemy successfully raided these posts, the cold being so intense that the garrisons were too cramped to use their rifles and Lewis guns with full effect.

A description of the famous Red House which was Battalion Headquarters in the line may be of interest.

The block of buildings comprising this farm formed a complete square and were in excellent condition, having been rebuilt just before the war. They consisted, on the side facing the road, of the dwelling-house and on the other three sides, of barns and outhouses, one of the barns being so large that a shed had been erected inside it for use as a canteen. The building had not been touched by shell fire, and there were no shell holes very near. Rumour had it that the Kaiser had once stayed there when it was a Bosch Headquarters in the earlier days of the war, and had promised the owner that it should not be shelled. Be that as it may, the fact remains that nothing fell near it whilst we were there, although its location must have been known to the enemy. The same was the case with both Brigade Headquarters in Laventie one of which,

Cockshy House, was a landmark for friend and foe for miles around. The more probable explanation is that the enemy knew perfectly well that so long as we were left there in peace he could always smash up the Headquarters of two brigades and a battalion whenever it became desirable to do so, but that, if he drove us out prematurely by his unwelcome attentions, it would take him some time to find where we had gone.

A wrecked estaminet stood near Red House. When we arrived, the main walls and the framework of the roof were still standing, but the place soon began to melt away in a mysterious fashion, the rate of demolition being marked by the disappearance, one by one, of the letters of the word " Estaminet " painted along the entire length of the building.

Then the authorities woke up, put the place out of bounds as dangerous and demanded the blood of the " scroungers." But who would be likely to steal a few bricks? The Rangers had all *they* wanted, for the Transport Section had just completed the building of some fine brick-floored horse standings in their lines near Laventie.

During our stay in this sector we were all genuinely pleased to receive a visit from the second in command and adjutant of the 2nd Battalion, who came out from England to study the conditions of trench warfare.

We were not able to show them much warfare in such a quiet sector, but we did our best to show them what trench life was like under the conditions of " peace warfare."

In the early hours of December 8th another party made its way across to the Bosch front line, and found matters much as they were on the previous occasion. They visited a machine-gun post which had been previously located, but on this occasion the garrison was not at home, so there was nothing doing. They apparently disturbed a sentry who was heard floundering and splashing back to safety, but they were not molested.

The Brigade had a stroke of luck at Christmas as that festival coincided with their turn for Divisional Reserve. Consequently, the Rangers spent the period from December 21st to January 2nd, 1916, at Robermetz, near Melville (now a heap of ruins, but then untouched), and Christmas Day was celebrated by companies in the traditional manner.

On our return to the line we relieved the 2nd London Regiment in the Moated Grange Sector (south of our former sector), the line there being held by a series of posts known as Winchester, Grants, Dreadnought, Erith, Lonely, Min, and North Tilleloy.

Here we and the Scottish relieved one another every six days, and the periods out of the line were spent in providing working parties, bathing, and Lewis gun training. The 27th saw us back again at Robermetz, where we remained until February 2nd, on which day we relieved the 13th Royal Fusiliers (37th Division) in the Neuve Chapelle Sector, this entailing a further move southward in the line.

We remained in this sector until the 27th when we relieved the 1st Norfolks in the Ferme du Bois Sector (yet another move further south).

The final relief of the Battalion from the front line in this part of the front was effected by the Scottish on March 5th, and the Battalion moved into support in billets at Seneschal Farm, where we reorganised on the new system within companies (i.e., Bombing Section, one Lewis Gun Section and two rifle sections, with Company Headquarters as a separate unit).

On the 9th we were relieved by the 4th West Ridings and moved to Lestrem.

Next day we marched to Merville and entrained for Doullens, arriving at 4.30 p.m. the same day at that place, whence we marched to Le Souich.

F

The transport moved by road and rejoined on the 11th.

The 12th saw us in billets at Ivernay, where we remained until the 22nd employing our time partly in company training and partly in forestry work in the Bois de Robermont.

Whilst here, No. 10 Platoon worked up a demonstration of a platoon attack under the new organisation with " live " bombs, rifle grenades and Lewis gun and rifle fire, which would have been quite a " star turn " at the Military Tournament. (Incidentally, we were credited with having kept another battalion, which was training on another area behind the line of fire, lying flat on their faces for a quarter of an hour.)

The demonstration was originally given for the benefit of the Brigade, but was considered good enough to justify a " command performance," to which the nobility and gentry of the various divisions round about were invited. Of course, as usually happens when one is expected to " show off," the repeat performance was not quite as good as the original, although somewhat more impressive, as, owing to a slight mis-calculation, the rifle sections charged perilously close up to the rifle grenade barrage.

On the 23rd the Battalion marched to Guoy-en-Artois, where we spent our time training for the forthcoming Battle of Arras until the end of the month, moving up into Beaurains to relieve the Queen's Westminsters in the line on April 1st.

An historic event occurred whilst we were at Guoy in the first meeting between the 1st and 2nd Battalions of the Rangers, the latter being quartered near by in the villages of Bavincourt and Laherliere.

CHAPTER X.

LAVENTIE.

(Winter, 1916.)

AFTER the trials and troubles of the Somme, we came to Laventie, as unto a haven of rest. No longer did the roar of the barrage disturb our nights or deafen our days. We had left behind us the desolation of Les Bœufs, and entered into a land where civilians abounded, and where houses had roofs, and, in some cases, even glass in the windows.

True, Laventie had its own particular worries. Who, among us, will forget those everlasting fatigues and working parties ? Our routine became six days working *in* the line, and six days working *on* it. When we were " relieved " it was often a bit of a rush to get back to billets in time for the first working party to start back for " Red Lamp Corner "—and it often became necessary for officers commanding companies to employ expert mathematicians to solve the problem of " How to find a Working Party of 100, out of a Company of 60."

But, I think our chief source of worry was really the ubiquitous rat. The whole of the London Scottish could not provide a " Pied Piper " capable of exorcising the " big rats, little rats, grey rats, brown rats " from those old trenches. The Quartermaster used to look more than a " little blue " when we turned up with monotonous regularity after each tour in the line and demanded a complete new issue of webbing equipment, packs, &c., to replace those consumed, and many an unfortunate man soon learned that to advance " Eaten by the rats " as an excuse for missing equipment, was almost as dangerous as to try the old " Lost it on the Somme " wheeze.

Very few lively incidents came to break the peaceful monotony of our existence ; but just one or two events still colour one's memories of those days. There was the " Episode of the Kidnapping Huns," when two (or more) bold bad Huns got on to an Island Traverse and nearly kidnapped a D Company officer and his runner, though the actual explanation of how either, or both, or all, escaped, has not been officially vouchsafed even unto this day, though many affirm that the runner could tell us a tale, an he so wished.

Then there were the raids when we used to blacken our faces, and dash over into Hun-land with great expectations and with " Nil Returns."

And I don't think C Company will ever forget " Standing-to " till about 4 a.m.—or should it be 0400 ?—on one of those nights, ready to lend a hand should the raiders get into trouble—only to find in the end that the raiding party had been back since midnight and had all been asleep for hours.

And occasionally we got back to Estaires and heard the jolly old " Bow Bells " (" Old Roger Rum " still rings in my ears)—and ever and anon the Padré got up a regimental concert in that little hall by the shell-torn church, and L—— would give us some of his " Classical Dances." Poor old L——, you don't dance now, I'm afraid ! Are you still in hospital, I wonder ? You were last time I heard from you.

Yes ! I think, in after days, we all used to look back upon those quiet Laventie times and wish that they would come again.

* * * * *

Poor little Laventie ! The war has passed over you since we were there, and there have been dreadful days when you were neither peaceful nor quiet, nor safe, nor civilised. For the hand of the Hun fell heavily upon you during those fateful days of April,

1918, after the thin khaki line of British " Tommies "
had withheld it from you, by a hair's-breadth, as it
were, for over three years.

I hope you have not disappeared altogether like
so many other places of greater renown.

I hope the little kiddie who used to sing :—

" Après la guerre finit "

to us round at the estaminet by the Quartermaster's
stores and C Company Headquarters, is back there
again. I hope the two girls at the estaminet down
by D Company's billet have escaped a repetition of
the appalling horrors which had fallen upon them
earlier in the war. I hope all the poor old folk
whom we knew in those days are back once more
in their peaceful old homes, and I trust that among
all the dreadful memories which must crowd upon
them, they may have just one bright spot—just
one recollection to brighten so much that must
be black and horrible—the recollection of those
strange " les Anglais "—those London boys who
dwelt among them during the winter of 1916.

CHAPTER XI.

MERVILLE.

(Christmas, 1916.)

MANY of us, I think, must have felt a pang of regret and almost dismay when the news reached us in April, 1918, that Merville had fallen into the hands of the Hun—a feeling almost akin to that which we should have felt had our own native town been desecrated by the invader.

For we knew Merville well : we had friends there —not the ordinary "Mesdames" of the chance estaminets, but real friends with whom we had been on real terms of intimacy. And what jolly people they were ! I do not know whether the prevalent rumours as to the place having been rescued by British troops at the eleventh hour during the big Hun rush of 1914, were true or not, but it is undoubtedly true that of all the towns and villages where we made our temporary homes during all the years there was none where we received a warmer welcome than at this jolly little town.

Christmas, 1916, was a real good time for all of us —all things being considered, though I seem to remember some trifling misunderstanding between the Brigadier and ourselves on a matter of cleanliness of equipment that resulted in a day's "C.B." just when we all wanted to be out and about arranging for various festivities !

It was Christmas Eve, if I remember rightly, when we really began to let ourselves go. C Company officers had just settled down to a quiet evening in their little mess at Robermetz, when the sound of "harmony" was heard without, and the door was opened to reveal the stalwart forms of the Company sergeants, who had come carol-singing to celebrate the occasion. Naturally, they were invited in, and officers and sergeants had just settled down to drink each others' healths in Madame's somewhat fiery champagne, when another burst of melody outside betokened the arrival of the Company cooks and sundry other " etceteras " who had also hit upon the idea of serenading Company Headquarters.

They also were invited in—or as nearly " in " as the proportions of Madame's parlour would allow, and another cork had just " popped," when a further, louder and even more discordant " carol " was heard outside.   The writer, praying the while that Madame's cellar would prove equal to the occasion, opened the door—only to be hurled aside by a crowd of the most rowdy, untidy rapscallions he had ever beheld —in khaki or out.   He was about to raise his voice in indignant protest at this gross breach of discipline, when a chance light falling on the face of the leading " Tommy," revealed the features of his old friend C—— from B Company, and closer inspection showed that the whole party consisted of officers—in disguise !

What followed is a little vague—but I know that the night's programme included a promenade round the neighbouring streets singing carols, and visits to various company messes *en masse*. Indeed, it is rumoured that A Company officers are still wondering who stole their—er—shall we say " citron " ?—and that a certain officer, who shall be nameless, has yet to discover the identity of the " men " who invaded his private sanctum and " pied " his bed as surely no bed was ever " pied " before !   And I can still hear ringing in my ears the wonderful word of command by which C—— started the party on its tour : " By the left in England, by the right in France, therefore—By the Centre—Quick-March ! "

*   *   *   *   *

What other memories have I of that particular Christmas ?

There was the dinner at the Hôtel de Ville on Christmas night—surely one of the most wonderful dinners on record !

And there were those festive company " feasts " —when officers and men of the various companies met together on terms of the utmost camaraderie and laughed and sang and made merry as though the war existed not. And here's the best of luck to the Y.M.C.A. official who said that though beer must not be served within the precincts of his hut, well !—there *was* a side door ! !

And there were the " Bow-Bells " with their wonderful pantomime (" Aladdin " wasn't it ?), and there was football, and—best of all—there were real nights of rest—undisturbed by visits to Epinette Dump or " Red Lamp Corner."

Ah, yes ! they were good days. And Merville always seemed so safe—so essentially a Back Area. Occasionally, a rumble of guns in the distance would remind us that away out there the war was still " carrying on." And always of nights one could see the inevitable Very lights rising and falling in the distance reminding us of that line whence we had recently come—and whither, in due course, we should return. But all this was unreal and distant— the idea that the little town with its busy streets, and quaint little shops, and its kindly folk would ever again see the invader never entered our minds.

Well, well ! War is war, and the Hun is the Hun. And I fancy that Madame L——, if she managed to escape and has been spared to return to her old home-town, and has looked upon the abomination of desolation that now exists there— will have shrugged her shoulders with that marvellous stoicism of her race, and remarked : " C'est la guerre."

CHAPTER XII.

" APRIL FOOLS."

(APRIL 1ST, 1917.)

" Oh ! my ! I don't want to die !
—I want to go 'Ome ! "

I DON'T know that I ever felt that " Want to go 'Ome " feeling quite so keenly as on that most foolish of April Fool's Days—April 1st, 1917, when the Battalion left the peaceful fastnesses of Gouy-en-Artois, and made its way towards that sector of the line in front of Arras, which a week later was to be the scene of one of the best scraps in which we ever participated.

The weeks of training in Iverguy and Gouy had come to an end, and we were (the great majority of us for the first time) actually marching into a real live battle. It was quite a clear day, and when we emerged on the main Arras–Doullens high road there were not wanting those signs which to a practised eye betokened the imminent approach of various operations. Far up in the heavens the angry rattle of machine-gun fire, and an occasional puff of white smoke against the blue sky proclaimed that the struggle for aerial supremacy had already begun. Up and down the road unending streams of motor lorries rattled on their way, while far ahead—away towards Dainville—the road itself was being shelled by some enterprising " 4·2 " battery from Brother Hun's lines.

In the afternoon we halted—having approached as near to the line as was considered safe. A last meal from the cookers—all water-bottles filled (" God knows when you'll get 'em filled again " says the Doctor cheerily—nasty fellow !)—and as dusk falls we hump our packs on our backs and start off into the unknown—by platoons at 200 yards interval.

It gets darker and darker, and by the time we approach Achicourt we might as well be marching by platoons at 2 miles interval for all we can see of the rest of the Company. Now that night has fallen the stream of traffic has increased in volume, and as we make our way forward we have to thread our way in between and around motor lorries, and ambulances, and G.S. waggons and ammunition limbers, and guns and tractors, and all the rest of the paraphernalia that appertains unto modern warfare.

By the time we reach the square at Achicourt we are completely isolated from the rest of the Battalion, and runners sent forward and backward to keep touch with neighbouring platoons merely disappear into the pervading blackness and are lost.

Vaguely I try to recall to memory the route as marked on my map, and to recognise in the nightmare of confusion round about some landmark that will give me a clue as to my whereabouts. A chance turn to the right, and we are soon clear of the village, and at once the jostling crowd has disappeared and we find ourselves, as it were, completely isolated and alone. We wander on in the darkness, and by and by stumble across a dejected body of engineers who are mending a bridge that bears unpleasant signs of having been hit recently. Enquiries elicit the reply that "there ain't been no infantry past there for weeks," and that "Beaurains is over there where those shells are falling," neither of which statements are in the least soothing.

One man volunteers the statement that a few days ago "this 'ere place was in No Man's Land," and the party lapses into silence, and we make our way sadly forward towards those most unpleasant shells. (Later in the war I discovered that it was far better to have falling shells as a guide on a dark night than to have no guide at all, but at that time I thought it a very poor scheme !)

On a very dark night, with a very heavy pack on one's shoulders, one could choose a better track for one's journey than a No Man's Land that has very recently been the scene of a merry little fight—and we really were a very depressed little platoon when we eventually reached Beaurains. It seemed as though hours had passed since we left the sad engineers away back there by the bridge, when we eventually reached the pile of bricks that marked the outskirts of the village. And then the miracle happened ! A mumble of voices ahead, a cluster of shadowy figures moving in the darkness, and we actually found ourselves once more united to the remainder of the Battalion. By mutual consent everybody halted and laid down to rest, we young officers got together and compared notes, and congratulated ourselves upon our achievements, and generally thought what brilliant and able fellows we were. . . . It was not till late that we learned that the corner where we had all halted was the favourite objective for the Hun's half-hourly strafe with his very best 5·9's !

I suppose the word " guide " will always send a cold shiver down the average platoon commander's back. In later days I learned that that magic sentence " Guides will meet the Battalion at X.22.a.7.5½ " which always appeared in orders, was merely a pleasant little fiction on the part of the Adjutant—or of all adjutants—and that the words were not intended to be taken seriously.

Any officer who in these later days may set out to spend the years of peace in writing a dictionary, will, I am sure, define a Guide as " A man whom one places at the end of one's platoon and loses at the earliest possible moment." There was the man up by Glencorse Wood, who—but that is another story ! The real point is that we were supposed to meet guides at Beaurains. . . . And did not !

Half an hour's frantic confusion followed—with the whole Battalion huddled up in mass while nasty large shells crashed among the ruins around—but eventually we got directions, and set off along the Neuville-Vitasse Road towards our final destination. And what a destination! A horrible " slit " trench —used by the Boche as a " C.T." till a few days previously—about 8 feet deep with at least 2 feet of sticky, oozing mud at the bottom. No dug-outs, no shelters! A few hurried instructions from the Westminsters whom we were relieving, and we were left alone in our new home. A steady shower of rain as the first light of dawn began to appear over the Hun lines, and as I waded round the trench to see that all was well (well? I ask you !)—a voice behind me muttered " Blankety-blank-blank—April Fools ! "

*   *   *   *   *

I think he was right.

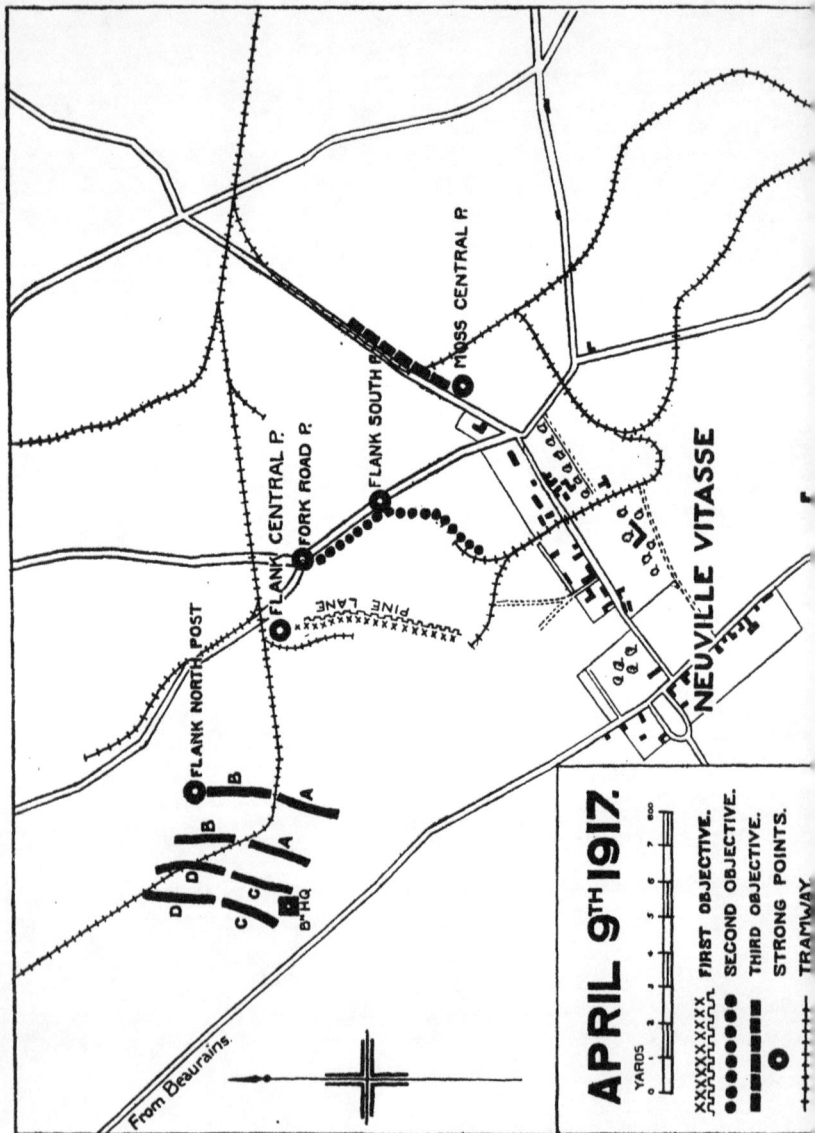

APRIL 9TH 1917.

YARDS 1 2 3 4 5 6 7 800

XXXXXXXX FIRST OBJECTIVE.
●●●●●●●● SECOND OBJECTIVE.
▬▬▬▬▬▬ THIRD OBJECTIVE.
⊙ STRONG POINTS.
┼┼┼┼┼┼ TRAMWAY

MOSS CENTRAL R

FLANK SOUTH P.

FLANK CENTRAL P.
FORK ROAD P.

FLANK NORTH POST

PINE LANE

NEUVILLE VITASSE

From Beaurains

BATTLE OF ARRAS.

APRIL 9TH, 1917.

THE Battle of Arras was originally intended to take place in March, the subsequent postponement being occasioned by the retirement of the enemy from his original position shortly before the date intended for the battle.

Had the original plans been carried out the task of the Rangers would have been the capture of the village of Beaurains, an unpleasant looking job when viewed from our original front line, and when we subsequently regarded it from the enemy's position we were thankful that he had saved us the trouble.

The enemy's retirement in March took him back to a position about 1½ miles in the rear of Beaurains on a ridge roughly parallel to his former position.

The front allotted to 168th Brigade as their first objective was the village of Neuville-Vitasse, and about 600 yards of the ridge northwards.

The capture of the village was entrusted to the Kensingtons, and the ridge northwards to the Rangers.

The ultimate objective of the Brigade was the capture of the Cojeul Switch and the establishment of the line about 2,700 yards further on.

The attack was planned on the " leap-frog " principle, the London Scottish being detailed to pass through the leading battalions on the first objective, capture the Cojeul Switch and push forward an outpost line on the final objective.

The 4th Fusiliers were in Brigade reserve except one company allotted to the Kensingtons for " mopping up " purposes.

The time allowed for the first objective to be secured before the London Scottish were to pass through was 4 hours 20 minutes. The objective was in our hands in 1 hour 45 minutes.

Our Brigade Orders stated that one section (4) tanks had been allotted to co-operate with the Division. These were to start close behind the leading wave. Two of them were to be directed round the north side of Neuville Vitasse with the special mission of attacking the strong point just inside the northern edge of the village, and would move diagonally across the Rangers line of advance.

It is with the task of the Rangers that this narrative is concerned.

To enable that task to be appreciated, a short description of the ground is necessary.

The country east of Arras is rolling land not unlike Salisbury Plain. Normally, there are few trees, except round the villages, and by the day of battle all these, as well as the villages themselves, had been blotted out by shell fire.

Beaurains stands on a 95-feet contour, Neuville Vitasse at about 82 feet, and the valley between at about 50 feet.

The Rangers "jumping off" place was at the bottom of the valley which rose immediately on their left flank to the high ground of Telegraph Hill, standing on the 100-feet contour.

The task of securing Telegraph Hill fell to the 43rd Brigade belonging to the division on our left, and as the "jumping off" place of that brigade was somewhat to our left rear, it was decided that they should be allowed 11 minutes start of us to ensure that the enemy on Telegraph Hill were well engaged before the Rangers started their attack.

This decision was not arrived at without careful consideration.

It was open to the objection that, inasmuch as the whole plan of battle started with the Canadian attack on Vimy Ridge up north and was to spread like a " feu de joie " southwards, by the time it came to our turn the enemy would probably have tumbled to what was happening and would seek to pin us to our assembly trenches with shell fire.

On the other hand, it was obviously unsound to launch our attack with our left flank exposed to the enemy on Telegraph Hill before the attack on his position there had developed.

The result justified the decision and although the enemy did put down a barrage on our assembly trenches he left it too late and when it arrived it was a comparatively small affair and fell on empty trenches, about a couple of minutes after the last wave had cleared them.

The Rangers attacked on a front of two companies, with two companies in support. Each company attacked on a front of two platoons, with two platoons in support. The objectives were :—

First.—Pine Lane Trench.
Second.—Fork Road Point to tramway.
Third.—Road, left of Moss Central Point.

The two leading Companies, A on the right, and B on the left, were to overrun the Pine Lane Trench and secure and hold the Second objective.

The support companies, C on the right, and D on the left, were to move through A and B Companies direct to the Third objective and capture it.

In addition to their allotted tasks, C Company was to be prepared to assist the advance of the Kensingtons on their right (if necessary), and to form a defensive flank on our right, in the event of the Kensingtons attack being held up. Neither of these contingencies arose, as the attack of the Kensingtons went without a hitch.

In the event of the attack by the 43rd Brigade on our left being held up, D Company was to assist A and B Companies to form a defensive flank.

This was done by D Company alone, for a short period during which the advance of the 43rd brigade was temporarily delayed, but on that Brigade continuing its advance D Company completed its original task.

So much for the plan of attack. Before proceeding to a description of the actual battle, it is desirable to refer to some of the events which preceded it.

During the latter part of March, the Rangers were billeted in Gouy-en-Artois, a small village about 8 miles south-west of Arras and 2 miles north of the Arras-Doullens road.

Here the Battalion carried out intensive training, and, in view of the coming battle, constant practice in the attack formations intended to be used on that occasion. In the course of training an opportunity arose for carrying out a preliminary rehearsal, which was of the utmost value to all concerned.

The ruined village of Ransart (about 5 miles south-east of Gouy-en-Artois) was allotted to the Battalion to enable practice in fighting amongst ruins to be carried out. On comparing the maps of this village and Neuville Vitasse, it was noticed that a striking similarity as regards the general lie of the land and the relative positions of roads and tracks appeared to exist between Ransart when approached from the south-west and Neuville Vitasse when approached from the direction of Beaurains.

A visit to Ransart showed that not only was this resemblance quite remarkable, but disclosed the additional fact that the old trench system and wire there corresponded with that in front of Beaurains.

Accordingly, a full rehearsal was arranged, only those who were to take part in the real attack actually participating, and a whole day was spent in practising the attack, over and over again, until all details had been thoroughly mastered. To this day's work is ascribed the excellent manner in which the platoons kept direction on the actual day of the battle.

On April 1st, the Battalion moved up to Beaurains and relieved the Queen's Westminsters in the front line.

The 2nd and 3rd were spent in improving the assembly trenches and stocking them with ammunition, stores, water, &c., required for the attack, also in familiarising all ranks with the appearance of their objectives and the approaches to them.

The first thing that struck us was the formidable obstacle presented by the enemy's wire in front of our first objective, Pine Lane Trench.

The artillery programme preparatory to the attack, which included the cutting of this wire, was already in progress. Consequently, permission to send out an officer's patrol to inspect it could not be obtained as that would have entailed the suspension of the shelling of this wire for three hours to enable the patrol to do its work. Of this, more hereafter.

On the night of the 3rd, the Battalion was relieved by the 4th London Regiment (Fusiliers) and retired to Achicourt for the 4th, 5th and 6th to rest, with the exception of providing parties for work in the assembly trenches on the nights of the 4th and 5th.

It was whilst we were at Achicourt that the Quartermaster made a discovery which produced far-reaching results.

Strolling round the village one evening, with one eye open for unconsidered trifles, he discovered four tanks hidden beneath a tarpaulin. On further investigation they proved to be the four detailed to co-operate with our Division in the attack.

Their C.O. was sought out and invited to partake of the hospitality of Headquarters' mess. He did so, and was shown our plan of attack, which was explained to him in detail.

In return, he described the action to be adopted by his tanks, and produced maps showing the tracks to be followed by the two which were to move diagonally across the Rangers' line of advance. The result of this " liaison " will appear later.

On the evening of the 7th, the Battalion relieved the Kensingtons and London Scottish in the line.

Earlier in the day, the enemy's wire in front of Pine Lane Trench was carefully inspected through field-glasses. It still had the appearance of a formidable obstacle.

Permission was obtained to send out a patrol to examine it, and a break in the artillery night programme was arranged to enable this to be done.

Shortly after 2 a.m. in the morning of the 8th, Lieut. F. O. Baron and three men made a close examination of the enemy's wire in front of Pine Lane Trench, and found it to consist of two very thick belts about breast high on iron stakes. It had sustained very little damage from our shell fire.

The patrol searched for a passage and found one where the tramway crossed the wire at the foot of Telegraph Hill. They were able to enter here and got into Pine Lane Trench. After inspecting that trench about 50 yards northwards, without meeting signs of the enemy, they patrolled southwards of their point of entry for about 40 yards, and, on climbing out of the trench, could see smoke arising from a point about 50 yards further south.

They then returned along the top of the trench to the tramway. Whilst getting through the wire at this point, they were fired on from the direction where the smoke was seen, and when clear of the wire a machine gun opened on them from the north. They reached our trenches unharmed, having performed a very difficult and hazardous task, and not only acquired the information they went out for but a good deal more.

Special attention was directed to Pine Lane Trench wire by our artillery throughout the whole of the 8th, and up to zero hour on the 9th, but even weeks afterwards, when the battlefield had become a back area, it was still a difficult obstacle. All honour to the men who forced it in the face of a murderous fire from the enemy machine guns.

On the night of the 8th the Battalion closed up to the left into their own assembly area, the Kensingtons coming up on their right into the assembly trenches allotted to them, and all ranks settled down to get all the rest they could before the great events of the morrow.

At 5.30 a.m. on the morning of the 9th, the Battle of Arras commenced with the attack of the Canadians on Vimy Ridge far away to the north.

At 7.34 a.m., the 43rd Brigade on our left advanced to attack Telegraph Hill supported by tanks. From our assembly trenches we could watch their advance as though we were sitting in the stalls watching a pageant on a vast sloping stage.

Long irregular lines of heavily-laden men trudging slowly forward close up to our barrage. No perfectly-formed ranks dashing madly forward led by accurately dressed young officers brandishing stick-bombs, as depicted in the posters of the military tailors.

Meanwhile, some of the Ranger officers could be seen walking about on top behind their assembly trenches giving final instructions to their men.

At 7.45 a.m., the Rangers rose to the surface like the crop from the Dragons Teeth and went steadily forward. Down came the enemy artillery fire on our empty trenches.

A Company reached Pine Lane Trench to find the wire in front of them impassable, and it was here that the majority of their casualties occurred. All four officers were wounded and the C.S.M. killed. Then it was that our liaison with the Tanks bore fruit, for the nearest tank, seeing the situation, diverted from its allotted route, trampled along the belts of wire and thus enabled the Company to go through and capture thirty prisoners. The name of the Tank officer has, unfortunately, been lost sight of. May he still be alive and well and should these lines ever meet his eye he may rest assured that A Company of the Rangers owe him a debt of gratitude they can never repay.

The Company Commander, Captain Barrett, was the only officer left on his legs and, although severely wounded in the head, collected fifty men on the enemy side of Pine Lane Trench. It was then found that all sergeants and corporals were down.

The Company pushed on to the Second objective and after placing his men in position under the command of Lance-Corporal Drew, Captain Barrett was forced to return to the Regimental Aid Post.

B Company having garrisoned the strong point known as Flank North Post in Deodar Lane advanced to Pine Lane Trench where the wire was found to be impassable, except at two gaps. Many casualties from machine-gun fire began to occur, whereupon 2nd Lieut. Cunningham rushed ahead with his platoon and, jumping into the trench, personally shot and bombed the gun team, all of whom were killed, except one who was wounded.

The construction of Flank Central Post was commenced by the party detailed as garrison and the remainder of the Company pushed forward to the Second objective and occupied Sunken Road from Fork Road Post (which they proceeded to construct) to the junction with Trump Trench.

C Company following in support of A Company passed through the gaps in Pine Lane Trench wire, captured several prisoners who had escaped the clutches of A Company, pushed straight on to the Third objective, which was reached about 9.30 a.m., and commenced to dig in on the road there.

D Company followed in support of B Company. At about 8.30 a.m. it was apparent that the 43rd Brigade on our left were temporarily held up by the wire in front of them so a defensive flank was established in accordance with the rôle laid down.

By 9.30 a.m. D Company were nearly up to the Third objective but the check to the 43rd Brigade was still delaying them to some extent. By this time the Kensingtons were in possession of the village.

At about 10.30 a.m. D Company was on the Third objective in touch with the 43rd Brigade on their left and the work of consolidation was proceeding.

The London Scottish passed through at about 12.30 p.m. and thus ended the most successful attack ever carried through by the Rangers, the whole programme having worked out " according to plan."

There is always an element of " comic relief " in the sternest battle, and humorous incidents were not lacking on this occasion.

An officer and N.C.O. looking for a convenient dug-out for Company Headquarters descended a likely-looking shaft and, on opening the door at the bottom, found a party of the enemy sitting down to tea. There was a moment's embarrassment at the unexpected meeting, but the enemy decided that discretion was the better part and discreetly put up their hands. The tea was not wasted.

A M.O. discovered a German aid post in the Sunken Road and proceeded to re-open business there. When the work was well started a trap door opened in the floor and a scared head appeared adorned with short bristles and ornamented with Pickwickian spectacles. It disappeared instantly like a Jack-in-the-box. Peremptory commands produced the crestfallen personnel of the original aid post plus some priceless bandages and medical stores, also a wounded man of the Middlesex Regiment, who had been taken prisoner on patrol a few days before.

The German personnel were told to make themselves useful, and it is only fair to say that they turned up like sportsmen and were of great assistance in tending our wounded.

Many welcome "comforts" were found in the German dug-outs and a certain C.O. who visited his companies smoking a Woodbine to show his sang-froid, found the effect somewhat marred by the fact that nearly every man he met was smoking a cigar.

To turn to the sadder side—our success cost us in officers 2 killed and 5 wounded, and in other ranks 63 killed, 125 wounded and 4 missing.

We were able to collect all our gallant dead who were interred side by side in a plot of ground close by the trenches from which they started out to make the great sacrifice. A burial service was conducted by the Chaplain and the place was subsequently railed off with white posts and rails. In addition to a cross for every officer and man a large white cross with the regimental crest and an inscription was erected at the entrance to the little graveyard.

During the period from the 10th to the 14th the Battalion remained in reserve on the captured positions employing their time in clearing up the battlefield and reorganising. A considerable quantity of valuable material was salved during this period.

On the night of the 14th, the 168th Brigade relieved the 169th Brigade and the Rangers moved up into Nepaul Trench in support.

From now onwards we experienced the most trying conditions we had ever been through since the early days of 1915.

The weather was vile, the nights were pitch dark and the ground had been pounded by shell-fire into the consistency of a newly-turned flower-bed.

The average rate of movement across country, even for small parties, was about one mile per hour and that was good going.

On the night of the 17th, the Rangers relieved the 4th London (Fusiliers) in the front line. Here the conditions were about as bad as could be. The only approach practicable to parties in the dark lay through a deep sunken road which was a veritable shell trap. This road crossed the Cojeul Valley at a level crossing which was the object of continual hatred on the part of the enemy, as also were the cross roads by Heninel Cemetery where Battalion Headquarters was situate.

The enemy had abandoned his usual practice of "programme shoots" by his artillery and was indulging in "mad-dog" shooting of a most irritating kind.

It was impossible to foretell when, where or what he would send over next, and the Battalion suffered a steady drain of casualties from his artillery fire.

There were times when attack seemed certain and imminent and yet he never came on. Evidently, the mauling he got in the earlier days of the battle had taken the offensive spirit out of his infantry.

On the morning of the 19th came the welcome news that the Battalion would be relieved that night by the 17th Manchesters. This was one of the best conducted and quickest reliefs we ever experienced. The support companies of the relieving battalion arrived at 7.5 p.m. and the front line companies and battalion headquarters arrived at 9 p.m., having started earlier than arranged and having met our guides on the way.

Mutual compliments flowed like water. Never had we been relieved by a battalion which had mastered so thoroughly the details of what was required. In the whole of their experience they had never been met by guides so intelligent, so well organised, or with such clear and precise instructions, &c., &c.

By 12.15 a.m. the relief was complete and the long weary march back to Arras via Neuville Vitasse and Beaurains was commenced.

It had been realised at the outset that the

condition of the men, the state of the weather and the ground and the enemy's artillery activity rendered it not only impossible but undesirable to attempt to collect into any larger formation than platoons until we were clear of the unhealthy area.

Accordingly, orders were issued that each platoon, on completion of its relief, should make its way independently to our old jumping-off place on the 9th, and that the companies should collect their men there and form up before continuing the march. The Quartermaster undertook to have " something hot " at the rendezvous.

Two officers, whose doubtful privilege it was to be the last to leave on relief nights, were plodding along the road towards Beaurains. They had done about two hours trekking, during which they had overtaken parties of mud-plastered men reduced almost to the limit of endurance by the terribly heavy going.

In silence the pair moved on, each wondering how long a rest the Battalion would require to recover from the fatigue and strain of the past week. Suddenly, one of them exclaimed, " Am I going ' dotty ' or do I hear singing ? " His companion, after an anxious look at his face, murmured something about " the wind in the telephone wires," and silence descended on them once again. A few yards further came another exclamation, " Listen ! I am certain I can hear singing." They halted and between gusts of wind the unmistakable strains of " My old Kentucky Home " came faintly to the ear. " They *are* singing, bless 'em ! come on ! " Another 200 yards and the scene unfolded itself. Two " cookers," each surrounded by a knot of men, were doling out hot tea.

On the rain-sodden ground small groups of men and officers grasping tin mugs containing the steaming liquid, smoking contentedly and singing away like frogs in a marsh. Once again the Q.M.'s department had saved the situation and, in the early hours of the morning when the companies marched into the sun-kissed streets of Arras, going slowly, maybe, but none the less steadily, it was difficult to realise that they were composed of the weary groups of the previous night. Next day, a fleet of our old friends, the mobilised London buses, conveyed the Battalion back to the peaceful valley of Couin for a well-earned rest.

CHAPTER XIV.

THE CARRYING PARTY.

APRIL 9TH, 1917.

THE cannonade that has been rising in a steady crescendo during the past eight days, has now reached a stage of double-fortissimo that proclaims to the world at large—both friend and foe—that the overture is coming to an end, and that the curtain is about to be rung up on Sir Douglas Haig's great Spring Drama—" The Battle of Arras."

It is the evening of Easter Sunday, in the year of Our Lord nineteen hundred and seventeen. A small party of us are waiting in the shadows by the cross-roads at Beaurains, watching the everlasting stream of traffic pass to and fro—guns, limbers, pack mules, infantry, ambulances, working parties, engineers—all congregating and working on the final preparations for the " show " to-morrow. It is our duty to meet at this point the Battalion transport with the rations, and to carry the said rations from here up to our pals out yonder in the assembly trenches, where already they are awaiting the fateful moment when they shall go up and over into the mysterious No Man's Land beyond.

There is plenty to interest us as we wait ; one has the sensation of being behind the scenes on the eve of the production of some tremendous drama. But for all the interest, time passes slowly ; our thoughts keep wandering away, wondering what the morrow will bring forth.

*   *   *   *   *

At length the familiar form of B—— looms up through the darkness. The transport has arrived, and we must attend to the matter in hand. Swiftly the limbers and the pack ponies are unloaded and the Battalion's rations dumped up against the wall of the cemetery, that ghastly cemetery at Beaurains in which every grave has been uprooted and thrown abroad by bursting shells. There is a big load—assaulting troops need something extra on such a night as this—and we realise that we are in for two or three journeys before our little party can get this lot out to the boys in the trenches, while an occasional crash away down the road suggests that our task may be none too easy. Anyhow, the job must be done, so every man to his load and off we go !

    *   *   *   *   *   *

The trenches seem somewhat unfamiliar—even though we have spent many weary nights during the preceding week digging them and improving them, and preparing them for the morrow's show. Down here, everything seems strangely quiet ; there is scarcely a murmur to be heard among the men, while the roar of the guns is not so overwhelming as when away back there among the batteries. Here and there we stumble across a friend and exchange a few meaningless phrases, but on such an occasion there is not much to say that is worth saying, and so we carry on with our work.

Three journeys do we make on the weary road to and from Beaurains, and at last all the rations are distributed and we are assured that, whatever happens, no man need be hungry when he plunges into the Great Adventure at dawn. But one thing is still lacking—and as we set off again on the return journey we make to all and sundry one solemn promise ; that they will see us again ere zero hour arrives and that we shall bring with us then the one absolutely indispensable commodity—the Rum !

Another weary wait by the roadside—already it is well past midnight, and the traffic has died away, while the guns are comparatively silent as though they were already drawing in a final deep breath before giving vent to that vast roar that will betoken the start of the great offensive. A figure appears out of the darkness. It is the Brigade-Major. Good fellow that he is, he knows what the rum issue means to the boys, and busy as he is, he can spare time—God knows how !—to come out to investigate the cause of the delay. . . .

It is three o'clock when at last the cart arrives. Rapidly we unload it ; each man shoulders his burden (a rum jar is damned heavy when you have a mile and a half to carry it at three o'clock in the morning after working all night !) and off we go. A subdued murmur of approval goes round as we arrive at the trenches and perform our final duty of distribution. We feel very much inclined to linger —it seems absolutely mean to sheer off and leave our friends—but orders are orders, and we must obey. A last handshake—a few banal remarks— " Best of luck. Meet you at Millbank ! "—and we scramble off.

*   *   *   *   *

Well ! P——, old boy. Thank God I stayed just for one last handshake. We didn't say much, but I think we understood what was in each other's minds. The next time I saw you, you were lying at the bottom of a shell-hole—and you were very, very cold. But I dare say we shall meet again— Some Day !

Dawn is already breaking as at length we stumble down the steps of our dug-out at the conclusion of our night's work. Even as we fall into our respective corners to rest our aching limbs and to close our weary eyes, the thunder breaks out anew overhead and somebody murmurs, "They're off." . . . . But already we are asleep.

*   *   *   *   *

I awake with a start and look at my watch.

Nine o'clock ! For good or ill the great offensive has been launched—for good or ill our own boys have again gone " over the top "—the great game for which we have been training so strenuously during the past six weeks has been played. And we have slept right through it !

With a sense of shame I scramble up the steps of the dug-out and out into the village. Everything seems strangely quiet. The guns that were all around us the night before seem to have disappeared— the first clue we get that the affair has been successful, for already those guns have gone forward, and are now firing from positions just in front of those assembly trenches where we last saw our pals.

The panorama on the road bears evidence of the magnitude of the success. Streams of prisoners pass down *en route* for the Divisional cage a little further down the road.

At the corner, the Padré—good old Bick !— has organised a sort of supernumerary dressing station, and is in charge of a scared crowd of Boches who are acting as relays of stretcher-bearers.

And down the road also come our own boys— the wounded—all terrifically cheery and full of wondrous tales of the victory they have just helped to win. A few figures stand out very prominently. Dear old B——, O.C., A Company, a little unsteady on his feet, and his face streaming with blood (I believe he fainted twice before he reached the dressing station), but tremendously braced with life. " I got this early, old boy," he says, " but we went right on, and the Company was on its objective when I left 'em." Cyril M——, with a smashed shoulder and a huge grin, " joy-riding " down to Arras on a staff car. . . . And there was a huge Hun who had received a bayonet in his right eye ! . . . :

* * * * *

A couple of hours later we are ourselves traversing

the battle-field. A forward dump of ammunition and water has to be formed up in the " Green Line," and we, as Brigade carrying party, have to do the job. Those assembly trenches where last night we spoke in whispers, are now a scene of bustling activity. Out beyond them we go in broad daylight, and only a very occasional shell bursting on the rising ground ahead, up by Neuville Vitasse, indicates that the battle is still in progress. And then we come to the wire ; that awful bit of wire in front of the first objective. How the boys ever got through that wire is a mystery to me to this very day. It takes our party a full five minutes to scramble through it in clear daylight with no barrage or machine-gun fire to hinder us ! . . . . And round us are those sad, pathetic little figures who had faced that seemingly impenetrable barrier with lion hearts earlier in the morning, and had cheerfully paid that last dreadful price that had enabled others, equally fearless, to win through. . . .

Our task accomplished, we make our way back to Battalion Headquarters which is established in the trenches from which we had kicked off that morning. Standing there, wreathed in smiles, spick and span as though on parade at home, is the C.S.M. He salutes enthusiastically. . . . " A glorious day, Sir," he says, " A glorious day ! The Guards themselves couldn't have gone over better than the boys did this morning ! "

*   *   *   *   *

When last I passed that way there was a neat little cemetery on the right of the road as you go from Beaurains to Neuville Vitasse. And right up against the road was the large composite grave where our boys who died that day were laid to rest. A hundred or so little wooden crosses—glorious in their simplicity—and a little notice proclaiming to all who passed, that these were " Rangers " who fought and died on April 9th, 1917.

I don't know whether in the backwash of Spring, 1918, this sacred little corner was destroyed. I sincerely hope not. I should like one day to go there again and pay homage to the boys who fell that day. And may we not hope that, could the wind, whistling round the desolation there, bring with it an echo from those voices that were stilled that day, then the message borne upon its wings would be : " A glorious day, Sir. A glorious day ! "

CHAPTER XV (I).

SIMENCOURT.

MAY–JUNE, 1917.

I OFTEN think that the first fortnight in May, 1917, was one of the most unpleasant periods that the Battalion ever endured. We were doing nothing of interest, nothing that inspired Mr. Beach Thomas or his friends to sound our praises in the public press ; but the whole fortnight was a prolonged sort of " morning after the night before " business, the intoxication of victory during April being succeeded by the dull, heart-breaking work of holding our own up there by Guemappe, during the " morning after," when most of our supporting artillery had already forsaken us for reasons to be disclosed later, but not totally unconnected with Messines Ridge.

But though, as a result, it was a very weary and tired Battalion that made its way back to Tilloy when we were eventually relieved, nevertheless, a few days in Arras and a few more days at Bernaville soon gave us the rest we required, and by the time we marched back to Simencourt for a further three weeks' rest, we were all beginning to sit up and take a little nourishment.

Simencourt was by no means one of the most charming places that we struck in France, and " Nissen Huts " were not exactly the most comfortable or picturesque billets of our acquaintance ; but for all that, after the trials and troubles of the previous six weeks, life there seemed to be almost a heavenly existence, and those who still survive will have, I am sure, none but pleasant memories of the days spent in that peaceful little camp among the trees.

I am afraid that in these degenerate days of the Armistice, one would look with horror upon our daily programme during those weeks : Reveillé about 4.30 a.m. ; Training from 6 a.m. till midday on a training area 5 miles from camp ; lectures or interior economy work during the afternoon, and sports and games during the evenings—but, at the time, it seemed an ideal sort of life and none of us looked with a favourable eye upon the orders to move, when eventually they came.

Of course, there were one or two flies in the ointment, but when one is accustomed to an existence that is all flies and no ointment, one can afford to laugh at the little fellows when, for the nonce, they are few and far between.

For instance, there was the route march in full marching order on the first day's full training when the personnel of C Company fell out by the wayside in ever thickening numbers till at length the Company consisted solely of the Company Commander and his horse ; or, at any rate, so every other Company was prepared to swear.

Of course, the rest of us were not so very much better ; it was the first day's training, and full marching order on a blazing hot day is a terrible strain when you are out of condition ; but none the less, it was C Company's " day out," as everyone who was in the other companies will tell you.

Or, again, there was that rotten fatigue for which A Company " clicked," when after doing a full morning's work (as per above schedule) we were suddenly ordered to proceed forthwith to Dainville, about 10 miles away, to shift a huge dump of heavy trench mortar ammunition—the " fly fellows"—for which dump the unspeakable Hun had been searching that morning with 12-inch shells ! We *were* happy ! For nine solid hours did we work, heavy, heart-breaking labour all the time, so that it was nigh

on midnight when eventually we staggered back to
camp.

*   *   *   *   *

But little things like these could not spoil the
general effect, and there is no doubt that, on the
whole, our " morale " improved enormously during
that time.

The culminating fun, of course, was the Grand
Sports Day, on June 6th. I have before me,
as I write, the " Secret " programme, and the
nobbly little green rosette worn by the " Committee
men." The programme bears on it a notice that
" This Programme must be treated as a secret
document and must not be allowed out of the
possession of the owner." Well, I have kept the
" secret " up till now, but I take it that no great
harm can be done in these days by divulging that the
56th Division were at Simencourt on June 6th,
1917, or that the " London Scottish " were in the
same Brigade as the " Rangers," or that Headquarters
Company won the Relay Race ; or that the Officers
won the Tug-of-War, or that the Padré sold enormous
quantities of tea and lemon-squash and things at
his little stall ; or any other of the interesting little
items that are called to mind by this crumpled
souvenir of the " Great War." I should like to
reproduce the whole lot of it here, with the list
of prize-winners in full, but perhaps it is better
not to do so. But, so long as I live, I shall keep
that programme by me, and in days to come when
old " Rangers " foregather together—as I trust they
will—I shall produce it, and we will talk together
of the days that are gone.

*   *   *   *   *

The officers, too, will have pleasant recollections
of Andy's little " Glee Party." How we used to
foregather quietly and steal gently round till we

reached the window of Headquarters' Mess, when we would serenade the C.O. sweetly with soulful renderings of "Sweet and Low," "Good-night, Ladies," and other tuneful melodies. Of course, the *pièce de resistance* at all these concerts was the "Rangers'" Hymn, especially composed by Andy, Backhoff, and other malefactors. It went to the tune of "Little Brown Jug," and dealt faithfully with all the leading members of the Officers' Mess, I forget most of the verses, but here is a sample :—

" Our Intelligence Officer gives no maps
With ' C.T.'s ' where they are, perhaps !
He worries a whip as a matter of course,
But has anyone here ever seen his horse ?"

and then would come the chorus :—

" Ha, ha, ha ! Rangers we,
Toddle up and down the old ' C.T.'
Ha, ha, ha ! Rangers we,
And Fritz we strafe with our ' H.E.' "

And then the doors would be thrown open and the Glee Party would be entertained by Headquarters' Mess to such liquid refreshment as seemed advisable, and the programme would be augmented by bagpipe selections from the Doctor, and, occasionally, by a song from the C.O. himself.

Yes ! They were jolly days for all concerned, and when we eventually went on the war-path again we were all the fitter for our three weeks' rest.

CHAPTER XV (II).

"THE BATTALION FAIR."

THE following is an account of a "Fair" held just behind the firing line in France. The 12th London Regiment and a well-known Poly. boy took a very prominent part in the proceedings.

I was asked to rig up a "water chute" for our "Battalion Fair," and, in a weak moment, I consented. That was six days ago! Next morning, I had two wagons and went off with the Chaplain to a large wood, where a Canadian detachment have a wood-cutting plant. It looks quite like a settlement somewhere out West, built up of wood shanties all in among the tall trees, with the old machine saws whirring away, and the Canadians in their slouch hats. The Chaplain interviewed the sergeant in charge, who said we could have what we wanted, and who, with the usual colonial hospitality, asked us to have some breakfast; we were very pleased to accept, as we had started out on our cycles very early. I chose the wood I wanted, and managed to cadge a sackful of nails. By ten o'clock we were back at our Fair Ground, and the job started. The people in power had chosen a splendid site for the fun, and they let me put up the Chute where I liked. It was among a very deep avenue of tall trees, leading up to a large château. The trees being very tall, and not too close together, made the place ideal, and so I started with the help of three prisoners and a regimental policeman. The first day I built the tower, twenty feet up in the air; that was soon done, so we set to on the first down slide. It took three days' hard work to finish it, getting up at five in the morning and finishing up when it was too dark to see, sometimes working alone, at other times having the assistance of three prisoners (not Huns) and their keeper, and often two or three friends, indeed, anyone I could lay hands on to help. The thing promised well, and so help was easy to get, but too many unskilled men get in the way, and I never had more than half-a-dozen at a time.

We covered the rail lines with tin from petrol tins, and scrounged hoop iron for the boat runners. I used cart grease for a lubricant—dirty, black, thick stuff—and oh, horrors ! the trial boat would not go over the first bump. It would get nearly to the top, and then slide back to the hollow. I sent a man for some paraffin ; we cleaned the runners down, and tried dubbin, and oh, cheers ! the boat went over just nicely, and when I got in and tried it, it seemed nearly perfect, and I went to bed feeling that all was well ; next day, however, the boat again would not go over the bump, as the dubbin had congealed. I could not obtain any other grease, and right to the end the anxiety was there. The pond was dug 20 feet long and 15 across, lined with a tarpaulin, and with an average depth of 18 inches, but where the boat went through it was only 5 inches. They would not let us use the water carts to carry the water (I don't blame them, for it was reeking and it stank), so I used a limber, which is shallow, boxed-in shape, and lined it with a waterproof cover ; it made quite a good tank. We filled the pond in an afternoon in about eight journeys from the village pond to our ocean. In the evening I changed into footer shorts and tried coming down. It was a glorious ride, and the boat dashed into the water fine, but I got wet through, and, even with the help of two ground sheets, the effect was about the same, a soaking for all comers. I went to sleep on that, and not over cheerfully, for every man does not want to pay a penny to get wet through. In the morning my batman suggested using a tin lining for the boats. It worked a treat, and with a hood on the front of the boat, like the cradle of a side-car, our boat was good enough even for ladies. I meant to make five boats, but on the last day, after getting up at 4 a.m. and working hard until 3 p.m., I only just finished in time, as the show opened at 3.30, with a procession through the village. The top was disguised with sacking and daubed with dark creosol to make it look like rockwork, which it did. An archway was cut where the boat came through, which made it appear as though the boat came out of a cave. The rest of the framework was hidden by green branches scrounged from the trees and hedges. The night before the show the thing looked ideal, and I went home wishing to goodness I could get some lanterns to light it up at night. I lay in bed wondering how it would all work ; about midnight I suddenly had an inspiration about lanterns, so jumped out and proceeded to make one. I could not find any empty meat and vegetable tins, so I had to waste two full ones, which cost the Government about 3s. I easily found some wire, and in a few minutes had an ideal lantern, covered with white muslin. The trouble was to get the candle in, so I made a hole just large enough to push the candle through from underneath. It worked a treat. I went into the room where the C.S.Ms. were sleeping to show them how it worked, but they are a churlish lot, and seemed to resent being awakened. Next day I got someone to make a dozen similar ones.

Just before 3.30 everything was ready, and I had my small staff of ten all ready. One to take the money, two in the pond to take the boat out and place it on the back slide ready for the next customer to push it back to the tower end, when another of my men hooked it on to the pulley rope. By means of two pulleys and three prisoners, plus one policeman, the boat was soon raised above the chute, and then lowered into position. The (meat) hook released, slid to the ground again by means of a

pepper tin filled with clay for a weight. Two men
on top helped the victim in, and gave him a shove
off. As the band struck up in the bandstand we
sent the first boat down the chute. A large crowd
watched, and oh, horrors ! the boat stuck on the
first bump, and refused to move until the victim
pulled it over on to the second slope down. Of
course I had watched it eagerly, and you can imagine
my remarks when the thing failed. No. 2 boat just
crawled over ; No. 3 failed. No. 1 again failed.
No. 2 went over, and after that they went to perfection. Once the grease got soft they simply
ripped over and dashed into the water with as good
a water effect as I have ever seen.

It was jolly hard work for the staff, but they stuck
it like trojans, and the whole thing was a great
success. We had to pack up at 9.15, but up to then
we had sent two hundred and eighty victims down
the hill, including one Major, one Adjutant, two
Chaplains and a great many officers, to say nothing
of fancy birds, nurses, cowboys and old hags. Two
hundred and eighty journeys for 28 francs. At home
it would have cost £100 to put up and run the show
at least, but fortunately it did not cost us a brass
farthing. The 28 francs are nothing save as a
register to numbers, but the thing was a great success,
and so I felt duly elated.

The Menagerie Procession at the opening of the
Fair was really great, and I had a splendid view
from my perch on high. The whole transport were
out, led by the Transport Officer, disguised as a
Sultan. The limbers were rigged up like cages
with wire netting, and inside were stuffed animals
borrowed from the cottagers. On one of the water
carts, a girlish figure was rigged up as a mermaid.
Top hole he looked too, reclining gracefully on some
hay in lieu of seaweed, and clorinated water instead
of salt. About a dozen men were rigged up as Rough-
riders, Red Indians, with their bodies painted, and

Highwaymen with pistols ready. A fine body of riders, and they just about went mad galloping through the trees. Another spectacle was a Beauty Show. Each Company had dressed up their suitable fellows as girls, and when they got among the crowd, you could not distinguish between " Get-up " and Mademoiselle, and the boy who won the 50 francs for First Prize was a real stunner.

Of the side shows I cannot say much, as I was too busy with my own, but they did a roaring trade, and attracted thousands. Our own brass band (an embryo effort) played sweet music in the bandstand. There were no cocoanut shies owing to a scarcity of nuts, but they had a pipe and mouth shy, and a very ingenious moving target with a wire netting screen, behind which a man slowly walked from side to side, having a high tin hat which stuck up above the netting and made a fascinating target. A Company ran a Maddatic Society, producing " 'Amlet." B Company did the " Beer Boys." Both very success-ful side shows ; and C Company had a screaming " Coster throwing the ring " stall with dud watches as prizes, and also a " 'aunted House," which was a delight to the men, when they saw spick-and-span Subs. diving into their pockets for a penny to go in, and saw them emerge covered all over with flour. I did not have time to go in that. It seems the place was pitch black inside. Once in, you stumbled over tins, fell down holes, knocked your head against flour bags, and got beaten out by very enthusiastic flour baggers.

Another interesting show was the old-fashioned punching machine, with the mallet. A strong man would punch lustily, taking a mighty swing with the mallet. The strength indicator was not in connec-tion with the punch, the former being controlled by a lazy attendant. If he felt energetic when the mallet struck, he would pull a string, and the indi-cator (a tin of bully) would fly up and ring the bell.

When he felt lazy, he would only pull the tin up about a foot, much to the disgust of the would-be strong man. One other show deserves mention, and that had a very gaudy exterior, and a very noisy group outside touting for people to enter, and talking of all the wonders of their show. Fellows flocked in and beheld two notices, the first "Silence," which they observed for about five minutes, and then, glancing at the other, they read "Exit," and followed out the meaning conveyed, realising that they had been "had"!

There, that is all that I remember, but not having seen much of the shows, I cannot do full justice to them.

MAY, JUNE AND JULY, 1917.

ON the afternoon of May 2nd we left Arras and moved up into the trench system which had formed the old German Front Line before his retirement in March, where we remained in Reserve for the operations for the following day. The weather was bright and clear and very invigorating on the high ground.

Zero hour was at 3.45 a.m. on the morning of the 3rd, and from our commanding position we could watch the vast semi-circle of flashes where the shells were bursting. We were much puzzled by the fact that it was still very dark, as we had understood that our assaulting troops were to attack at dawn, but whether it was really intended to attack in the dark or whether the "Clerk of the Weather" played us false or the Intelligence Department were out in their calculations we never heard, but the assaulting battalions declared afterwards that the absence of light and the consequent loss of direction was the main cause of their want of success.

At 8.30 a.m. we moved up into the Harp, which was the old German trench system north of Telegraph Hill and near Tilloy, where his front line had been when we attacked on April 9th.

The next evening after dark we moved up into the support trenches in rear of Guemappe, and about half a mile in advance of Marliere, which is an offshoot of Wancourt.

Whilst here we were in support of the 4th Londons, and assisted them to improve a somewhat "sketchy" front line by furnishing working parties for that purpose.

On the night of the 7th we took over the front line, where we spent the following four days working on the trench system under continual shell fire.

About 11 a.m. on the 9th the enemy artillery became unpleasantly active and kept it up all day. Among other acts of misplaced zeal he put three direct hits in rapid succession on Battalion Headquarters, closing up one of the two entrances and wrecking the other, and ruining a pair of socks (the property of the C.O.) which were airing in the sun.

The next morning, at 10 o'clock, the hostile artillery started again, and gave us a day's gruelling which put the previous day's performance quite into the shade. Unfortunately the enemy kept it up far into the night whilst our relief by the 4th Londons was in progress, with the result that we suffered casualties during the relief amounting to ten killed and nineteen wounded.

On the night of May 13th, the 4th Londons and London Scottish were relieved by battalions of the 167th Brigade, and on the following night we and the Kensingtons were relieved by the same brigade.

The enemy had left the Rangers in peace from dawn on the 14th until 5 o'clock that afternoon, but at that hour and punctually at every clock hour for the rest of the evening until 10 p.m. he put down 20 minutes shelling with 5.9's all round Battalion Headquarters, past which our companies had to go on their way out that night. It was an anxious time as the hour for relief approached, but fortunately, the enemy's hourly programme ceased before the companies began to move out, and we got away without heavy casualties. We arrived back at Tilloy in the early hours of the 15th, and after resting until 2.30 p.m. the Battalion bathed and moved back by companies to the Schram Barracks in Arras.

Here we remained from the 16th until the 19th, resting and refitting and carrying out company training.

Leaving Arras in the morning of the 19th we arrived in billets at Bernaville that afternoon and remained there over the 23rd, on which day the entire Brigade paraded for inspection by the G.O.C. Division.

On the 24th we marched to Simencourt and settled down in a hutted camp in an orchard for a fortnight of welcome peace and glorious weather.

May 2nd was a Saturday, and was celebrated in true peace-time fashion with a Brigade Drill Competition in the morning and Brigade Sports in the afternoon. We had a perfect spring day, and both events were unqualified successes.

D Company of the Rangers managed to win the Drill Competition, and the Copper Shield presented by the Brigadier now hangs in the Officers' Mess at Chenies Street. This shield is of peculiar interest, as the piece of oak on which it is mounted was originally part of a ruined church near the line, the copper for the shield was bought in Amiens, and the shield was engraved and mounted by a private in the London Scottish.

On the evening of May 10th the Brigade moved to Montenescourt, about 1½ hours march to the north, and remained there for one night.

The next morning at 5.15 a.m. we started off in a downpour, which lasted all the morning, to march to Arras, arriving there at 9.30 a.m., and billeting in the barracks.

The 13th saw us on the move again, and at 10.30 a.m. we arrived in the hutted camp southwest of Beaurains where we remained until the 20th and carried out company training daily.

Whilst here we had a great cricket match—Officers v. Sergeants. The Officers played in pyjamas and both sides wore tin hats because of the dangerous state of the pitch.

On the night of May 20th–21st we relieved the Q.V.R., in the trench system on the high ground south of the Cojeul River, opposite Guemappe (where we were last in the line), the relief being completed at about 4.30 a.m. on the 21st. The trenches here were very patchy. In some places they were deep and good, but in others only about 4 feet deep and not continuous. The soil varies considerably, being very loamy in some places (this was particularly the case with the communication trenches), and in others, where the system ran across the crest of the high ground, mostly chalk and flint.

The whole system had been well pounded by our artillery during the fighting in April, and there were several disabled enemy guns lying about, also a couple of our tanks. Battalion Headquarters was a wrecked German gun emplacement, the guns (a couple of Russians presumably captured on the eastern front) were lying wrecked in the emplacement and down below at the bottom of a deep shaft were the dug-outs formerly used by the teams.

Our first full day in these trenches (May 22nd) opened somewhat eventfully.

At 3 a.m. that morning a party of the enemy (estimated about 6 or 8) approached our bombing block in a portion of the front line known as Spoor Trench, and opened rifle and machine gun and rifle-grenade fire on our Blocking Party. Shortly afterwards, as it was growing light, the enemy were seen withdrawing, whereupon Lewis Gunners and Rifle Bombers opened fire on them. A search party went out and found a wounded German who was brought into our trench in a dying condition. He belonged to the 458th Infantry Regiment but had no papers or identifications upon him except the numerals on his shoulder straps.

That night, an officer of the 5th Cheshires (our Divisional Pioneer Battalion) was out in front of our line engaged in the taping out of a new trench when another Hun of the 458th Infantry Regiment strolled up to him. Fortunately, the Cheshire officer was the first to recover from their mutual astonishment, and brought his man in and handed him over to us.

Subsequently, we made a search for the bodies of further enemy believed to have been killed in the early morning scrap in Spoor Trench, but none were found.

Nothing of importance occurred during the rest of our tour of duty, and on the night of the 26th–27th we were relieved by the London Scottish and went back into the support trenches on the same side of the Cojeul River opposite Wancourt.

About 10.20 a.m. on the morning of the 27th a hostile plane flew over Battalion Headquarters (in holes under a bank, overlooking the river valley) and dropped four bombs. One bomb failed to explode, but one man of a Machine Gun Company, which was living under the same bank, was unfortunately killed.

We were lucky to escape so lightly, as practically the whole of our Headquarters Company and the Machine-Gun Company were lying out below the bank enjoying the sun when our unwelcome visitor arrived. The hostile artillery was unusually active on Buzzard Trench on the night of the 27th, and from 1 a.m. until 2.15 a.m. on the morning of the 28th, they shelled the vicinity of Wancourt Tower (then a heap of ruins).

June 29th and 30th were uneventful, and except for desultory shelling by the gunners on both sides nothing much occurred on the first two days of July, but at 2 a.m. on July 3rd the enemy suddenly barraged the area occupied by the forward Battalion (London Scottish) and everybody stood to. At 2.24 a.m. up went the S.O.S. from the front line and was repeated at Wancourt—our batteries opened fire and both sides proceeded to make night hideous. The enemy shelling was very local—nothing falling in our trenches, the unfortunate Scottish getting it all.

The enemy fire slackened about 2.35 a.m., and our artillery followed suit ten minutes later about which time a few enemy gas shells fell in Lion Trench (occupied by us), but did no damage. By 3 o'clock everything was quiet again and at 3.10 a.m. we received the welcome permission from Brigade to " stand down." (It may be of interest to record that although you might " stand to " on your initiative, you could not " stand down " again without permission from higher authority.)

At 11 p.m. on the 3rd the relief of the Rangers by the 6th Durham Light Infantry commenced, and was completed by 1 a.m. on the 4th, the Battalion arriving in our old camp on the outskirts of Beaurains two hours later.

Early on the morning of the 4th, the Transport started for Lignereuil by march route, and at 9 a.m. the Battalion left by march and bus route for the same place. The embussing took place at the point on the Arras–Doullens road on the south-east outskirts of Dainville where the road to Achicourt joins the main road. The place was always known to the older members of the Battalion as " Jones's Billet," as D Company under Major Jones were billeted in the buildings there when the Battalion first went to Dainville in the early part of 1916.

Lignereuil is the next village south of Ambrines, where we were billeted in the early part of 1916, and the three weeks that followed were looked back upon for long afterwards as one of our pleasantest memories of the war.

We enjoyed lovely summer weather amid delightful country, and it was the first real rest we had had for months.

It was during that period that the Rangers' famous Fancy Fair was organised, and it is still remembered by the 56th Division.

Another writer has done justice to that really first-class and original show, which was also the occasion of the birth of the Rangers' active service brass band.

The most important piece of training done during that period was to teach every officer, N.C.O. and man the art of rapid wiring, thereby preparing the way for many successful wiring parties in the future.

The pleasant weeks sped all too quickly, and the 23rd saw us on the move once again, marching north-westwards to Monts-en-Ternois, where we remained for one night, and on the following day we entrained for St. Omer, marching thence to billets in Houlle, north of Calais–St. Omer road. We remained there until August 6th training (chiefly musketry), and employing our leisure in fishing and bathing in the river.

CHAPTER XVI.

YPRES, 1917.

ON August 6th, we left our billets in the pleasant neighbourhood of Houlle and proceeded by train from Watten to Abeele, whence we marched to the Steenvoorde area. Here we spent a week at company training, paying particular attention to wood fighting.

We left this area in buses which took us to Busseboom on the morning of the 12th, and arrived in camp at Dickebusch soon after midday.

Next morning, another move took us to Ouderdom which the Battalion had last seen in the early days of 1915.

The Rangers' share in the attack of August 16th was not a very active one, since the 168th Brigade, for once in a way, was in divisional reserve.

Nevertheless, we did not avoid unpleasantness altogether as we were placed at the disposal of one of the Assembly Brigades (the 169th) during the progress of the battle.

The nature and state of the country round Ypres is so familiar to most soldiers and many civilians that yet another attempt to describe it would be superfluous.

Suffice it to say that recent rains had reduced it to its worst condition at this period when we renewed our acquaintance with it after an absence of two years.

The task allotted to the 56th Division was the capture of the western half of Polygon Wood and the formation of a defensive flank facing south-east between Glencorse Wood and Inverness Copse.

The Rangers became involved in the attempt to capture Polygon Wood.

On the night of the 15th the Battalion moved up

into dug-outs built into high banks containing the reservoir known as Zillebeke Lake.

The battle commenced at 4.45 a.m. on the 16th and, although we were so close up, we might have been miles away, except for the noise, as no enemy shell fell near our billets all the morning, the enemy being too busily engaged with matters up in front.

Owing to all wires forward of the 169th Brigade Headquarters being cut early in the battle we remained without news how the battle was progressing until about 8 o'clock, when conflicting messages reached the signal station of some neighbouring gunners, and left us in some doubt whether the objectives had been captured or whether the attack had been beaten back to Glencorse Wood.

At about 11 a.m. the Battalion was ordered up to Half-way House, a rabbit warren of deep water-logged dug-outs which, when we arrived, already contained two brigade headquarters, one battalion and various other odds and ends.

That we succeeded in getting there with scarcely any casualties seems nothing short of a miracle, when one reflects that the intervening ground was under direct enemy observation and became a veritable inferno whenever he shelled it. Fortunately for us he was too busily engaged with other targets to give us his unwelcome attentions.

It was a brilliant summer morning, and once again one experienced that intensely vivid appreciation of beautiful weather which seems to come with the near approach of deadly peril.

The scarred trees, the waters of the lake, the rare green patches on the banks, and even the scarred and pitted countryside seemed to take on something of the beauty of the morning, whilst ahead of us, on the ridge, were the five tall trees which formed a landmark for miles round by day and night and around which the enemy artillery would play with harassing uncertainty at all hours.

They were our guide to Halfway House which lay some little distance on the far side of them.

Would all the platoons succeed in passing them or would any of them " walk into something " ?

Luckily for us the former contingency happened and by 1.15 p.m. the Battalion had arrived in comparative safety.

On arrival we found that the attacking battalions of the Division had caught it rather badly. The assaulting waves had met with considerable opposition, most of which came from pill-boxes and machine-gun nests, and, although the remnants had succeeded in reaching their objective, they did not arrive in sufficient force to be able to withstand the enemy counter-attack.

The result was that, having no intermediate objective on which to rally, they were forced back to their original position on the western side of Glencorse Wood—a wood in name only, as the collection of water-logged shell-holes and charred stumps of trees bore little resemblance to anything meriting that name. At 7.30 p.m. we received orders from our own Brigade to place the Battalion at the disposal of the 169th Brigade, from whom we received instructions to move at once into support trenches astride the Menin Road about midway between Château Wood and Clapham Junction. Again we had to face the unpleasantness of a move in daylight in view of the enemy, though for some time it looked as if we were to have another lucky avoidance of casualties.

Unfortunately, as the last platoons were arriving the enemy put down one of his lightning barrages on the trenches we were proceeding to occupy, and the last arrivals caught it rather badly and the Regimental Aid Post also suffered. It was with sincere regret that we learnt afterwards that Sergeant J. E. Davis, of the R.A.M.C., who had done such excellent service with the Battalion from the beginning of the war, received a wound necessitating the amputation of his foot, whereby the Rangers lost the services of a hard-working and conscientious medical N.C.O. and the football world was deprived of a very promising player.

By 10.50 p.m. the units of the 169th Brigade had become so intermixed that the Rangers were ordered to send up a company to hold a portion of the front line system whilst the various units were withdrawn for reorganisation.

Owing to the condition of the Line and the fact that it was constantly subjected to shell fire it was considered undesirable to put in more men than absolutely necessary so, with the approval of the 169th Brigade, two platoons only of B Company were sent up. They started at midnight and at 2.30 a.m. on the 17th they were reported in position, where they remained until relieved by a party of Q.W.R. at 4.45 p.m. in the afternoon of the same day.

That night the Rangers were relieved by the 5th Oxfordshire and Bucks, and at 5 a.m. on the morning of the 18th the Battalion arrived in Ottawa Camp at Ouderdom, where we remained until the 24th, on which date we returned to our Headquarters at Houlle.

CHAPTER XVII.

THE BACK OF THE YPRES FRONT.

I HOPE that some other hand than mine is penning an account of the Battalion's experiences on the Ypres sector, during August, 1917. It so happened that I was rejoicing in a spell of " Battle Surplus " during those operations, and, as these are intended to be merely personal recollections, I do not propose to give a hearsay story of the affair ; but will content myself with a few vignettes of life at the back of the front.

    *   *   *   *   *

The little farm that served as Battalion Head-quarters during that damp but delightful fortnight at Houlle (down behind St. Omer) was bearing a very festive air on the night of August 5th. The barn that had done duty as the Scouts' billet had been specially cleared and decorated and was to be the scene of the Private View (for officers only) of the first performance by our very own Pierrot Troop—the " X.L. Boys." Every officer was present, including a few extras. Our Mr. Heath, and little " Miss " Cheney—arrayed as butler and parlour-maid respectively—had served coffee and lemonade, and sandwiches and biscuits ; and the curtain went up, amid considerable applause, to reveal Our Very Special " Miss " Green, and her crowd of attendant satellites. The programme went with a marvellous " swing " from the very beginning, and very few noticed the unobtrusive runners who at irregular intervals crept quietly up to the Adjutant with sundry messages. The Company Commanders knew, however, for every message arriving resulted in hurried " Orders "—written more or less legibly on the Adjutant's knee in the semi-darkness of the auditorium—being passed to those concerned, and the tenor of these was that the Battalion was to move forthwith to immediate reserve, somewhere behind Ypres ; and that valises were to be packed and ready for collection (*a*) at 6 a.m., (*b*) at 4 a.m., (*c*) at 1 a.m., (*d*) at midnight ! And so, in the intervals of shrieking with laughter at Hallett's "Same soldier backwards" absurdities, and of restraining ourselves with difficulty from responding to Green's invitation to "Come and Cuddle " " her," we were engaged in rapid mental calculations as to the possibilities of obtaining any rest during the night. We eventually got back to our respective messes about midnight, just in time to issue orders, and to get our valises ready to await the arrival of the transport.

That late lamented, but enthusiastic, monarch, Nero, has been commonly maligned for giving vent to his musical proclivities at a time when a severe conflagration was raging in the imperial city ; yet I think no one will blame us for thus "carrying on" with our comedy up to the very moment when a greater and a darker curtain was about to "ring up" on the tragedy that should follow.

Laughter and tears ; comedy and tragedy ; sunshine and shadow ; and if, through the light incidental melody of the Concert Party, one could always hear the deep basic theme of the artillery duel—well ! surely that was no reason for abandoning the lighter theme altogether.

*   *   *   *   *

We moved from Houlle to Steenvoorde by "Tactical Train"—more tactical than train—I will draw a veil.

*   *   *   *   *

After spending half the day in admiring the "tactics" of our worthy train, we arrived at a station sufficiently remote from Steenvoorde (which was our immediate objective) to make it a natural rail-head for that village, in the eyes of the gilded staff. We accordingly detrained, and marched off, through the blazing heat of the August afternoon (there were not many such during that August, but this was one of the few)—under the guidance of a couple of worthies, who, like all the guides one ever suffered under in France, were either suffering from incipient insanity, or else were in an advanced stage of shell-shock. Anyhow, they took us carefully round three sides of a square—a distance of 7 or 8 miles instead of 2—doubtless for the reason that the course we followed, after starting off boldly as a real road of ordinary *pavé*—(tiring enough in all conscience when you are in full marching order—very full!—and have spent half the day in a Tactical Train)—tired of life after the first few miles and degenerated into a mere track of first-class Belgian mud, which eventually became so narrow that for some while the whole Battalion was draggling along in single file!

All things—even battalions in single file—come to an end, but it was late in the afternoon when we arrived at what was reputed to be our destination. We heaved a sigh of relief, and, being rear company patiently stood by while Headquarter Company, B, C and D, were marched off to their respective billets. And then came the "last straw." The Quartermaster came up with a long face and generally apologetic air—a very unusual disguise for a quarter-master!—and with sickening apprehension, we waited to hear our fate. "Awfully sorry, old man!" he said to O.C. Company. "But I haven't been able to find any billets for your Company at all!"

* * * * *

The British Army has always been famous for the cheery way in which it rises superior to all misfortunes, and I think, in a small way, this habit was never exemplified more successfully than by the way A Company triumphed over this Mystery of the Missing Billet ! True, no grave interests were at stake ! It was not a matter to attract the majestic attentions of Mr. Beach Thomas or his fellow scribes. But just picture the circumstances. Reveillé had been at 3.30, and since that moment we had marched 3 miles to the entraining point, spent six or seven hours in a crowded, stuffy troop-train, and then marched another 7 or 8 miles, mostly through mud ankle deep ; the whole in F.M.O. and with no meal since breakfast, and with the temperature at about 86 degrees in the shade— and, then, on arrival to be told that there was no billet, and no prospect of one ! Dejecting ? Well ! . . . And yet, when we had " piled hipes " and dumped kits, and been told to stand-by till further orders, what did we do ? . . . Answer No. 1 : Robbed a neighbouring orchard till Madame came and chased us away ! Answer No. 2 : Started playing football ! About 40 a side ; Nos. 1 and 3 Platoons versus Nos. 2 and 4, the game lasting till the Cookers arrived and we were able to get a meal at last.

I don't think I was ever more truly proud of the boys than I was on that occasion. How could the Hun ever hope to win against people animated by that spirit of incurable optimism ? It may seem all very trivial, but am I wrong in suggesting that that little incident in that sun-baked Flanders field, was typical of the whole spirit that lead the British Armies through all their misfortunes to the final triumphant victory ?

Anyway, Fortune favoured the fair on this occasion, for when late in the evening we were eventually provided with a home, we found that it was easily the best billet of the lot.

OUDERDOM.

It is about two o'clock in the morning. The calm serenity of the August night is broken only by the growl and rumble of the guns—but then this is merely the normal accompaniment of life behind the lines in the Ypres area, and we scarcely notice it— except when it occasionally ceases ! Away to the west, the darkness is continually broken by the flashes of light from the active batteries and the occasional rise and fall of the ghostly Véry lights along the line of the " Front." Our Battalion is being relieved from up there to-night, and those of us who have been on Battle Surplus at the Transport Lines have been hard at work all the evening preparing the new camp for the reception of our tired friends. Candles have been placed in every hut ; rations issued in bulk ; the cookers are aglow and a hot meal is awaiting everyone ; the officers' valises have been unpacked, and everything is ready for the weary, mud-stained boys that will shortly be returning.

*　　*　　*　　*　　*

Three o'clock. The other companies are back now—all except A, and we have heard all the news. Though we have been the luckiest unit in the Division during this show, we hear, none the less, of several gaps in our ranks. Poor old H—— has been killed, and we roll up his valise again—it had been laid out awaiting his return, but he won't need it now, poor boy. Corporal B—— will also be among those whom we shall miss—though he is only wounded, fortunately. . . . And there are rumours of gas during the relief, and altogether I am anxious as to the welfare of the missing company. I stroll out of the camp and away through the village out on to the road that leads to Ypres. All is very quiet now—the guns, as is usual at this hour, are silent before the impending storm at dawn. I sit down by the roadside and wait . . . And, at last, out of the darkness, I catch the sound of men whistling. In a few moments the sounds are con-

fused, but soon the melody rings out shrill and
clear—a march, our own march, " The Silver Hunt,"
and down the road swings A Company, battered
and tired, it's true, but marching well ; heads up,
arms swinging ; whistling away at the familiar old
tune as though their lives depended on it.

And whenever, in these later days, I hear the
strains of the Regimental March, I am reminded,
not of any great ceremonial march past, but of that
night at Ouderdom, and of that Company returning
from a troublous tour in the line, weary and war-
worn, but indomitable in spirit, forcing—to quote
Kipling—

> " Your heart and nerve and sinew
> To serve your turn long after they are gone,
> And so hold on when there is nothing in you
> Except the will which says to them ' Hold on ! ' "

    *   *   *   *   *

One more picture of Ouderdom : It is nine
o'clock at night, we have been here two or three days
now and have accustomed ourselves to the routine
of the place, so that we look at our watches, and
there is a general air of restlessness, of expectancy.
We have finished dinner in the little Company Mess,
and are waiting before settling down to the usual hand
of " Solo." " Time he came over, " says someone.
" Yes, he should be here by now, nine o'clock's
his time," says another. We wait a few seconds,
and then through the silence a steady hum, somewhere far up in the blackness of the skies, gradually
forces itself upon our attention. . . . " Ah !
here he is ! " we say : all lights are douched, and
out we go to see the nightly firework display. Three
shrill whistles from the anti-aircraft guard and the
whole camp is instantly plunged in darkness ;
searchlights spring into being from all directions,
and thin pencils of light begin tracing complicated
patterns, as they search to and fro for the intruder.
The indefatigable genii who preside over the various

A.A. batteries start loosing off into the blue—or rather the black !—machine guns rattle ; lines of tracer bullets fly upwards, even our own Lewis gun at the bottom of the camp, fires off a few pans—and the nightly " Brock's Benefit " is in full swing. Through it all, with an irritatingly complacent hum, the visitor can be heard getting nearer and nearer, quite unmoved by our attentions—possibly scarcely aware of them. Suddenly, there is a fresh noise to add to the pandemonium—a swishing whistle, followed by a dull roar and fierce red flash—quite close enough to be pleasant ! Another and another, getting closer and closer, the last one giving us all a thoroughly good shaking, and causing an ominous glare up by the Transport lines. But look ! There he is ! The searchlights suddenly give up their frantic waving to and fro, and concentrate upon a point near above our heads, and there, focussed in the light, is the little chap that is causing all the trouble. The A.A. batteries and the machine guns burst out anew in a fresh frenzy : many shots are well on the mark, and Jerry, doubtless relieved at having accomplished his task more or less success-fully, turns eastward and speeds away, slipping and diving, and twisting and climbing, to escape this unnecessary publicity. Five minutes pandemonium, and then he is gone, far out of range. The guns cease firing ; the searchlights give a final waggle and disappear ; the machine-gunners give a last tattoo ; and the anti-aircraft guard gives one whistle, as a signal that all is clear. The nightly air raid is over, and we go back to our Mess for a final hand of " Solo," before turning in, in a silence unbroken save by the usual rumble " up the line." Only one man appears to be in the least put out by what has just occurred. He is our mess cook and he has indeed a terrible tale to unfold. " Please, Sir," he says, putting a sorrowful face round the blanket that does duty as a door to our Mess, " Please,

Sir, you won't get no breakfast to-morrow, 'cos the explosion of that last bomb has smashed all the eggs " ! Those eggs, the acquisition of which had cost the Mess President a good deal of the available funds, most of his spare time during the preceding day, and the whole of his available stock of the " patois." All smashed at one fell blow by " le sale Boche " ! Truly it was a horrid war !

CHAPTER XVIII (I).

LAGNICOURT.

IF Ypres had been the acme of abomination, Lagnicourt was, undoubtedly, the last word in desolation. When the Hun had retired " according to plan," during the spring of 1917, he left behind him, everywhere, the unmistakable mark of the kultured hoof ! There was just enough left of everything to enable you to realise what beauty these little Picardy villages must have held before the war. To my mind, those places that were utterly obliterated, were more mercifully treated that these roofless, ruined villages that cried aloud of the beauty of the might-have-been.

The little church, ruined and desolate, with a huge mound of bricks as evidence of the tower that once stood " four-square to all the winds that blow," with the pathetic little images (garish and ugly in the cold light of day, but doubtless full of hidden beauty in the eyes of the simple worshippers of bygone days) lying strewn among the litter in the roofless chancel ; the tragic little gardens, uprooted and torn, littered with *débris* from the wreck of the neighbouring estaminet—here a jug, there a child's pinafore, there the remains of a bed ; the tottering bits of walls still standing in the village " place," with here and there an old faded notice in French, more frequently with an arrogant, flaunting superscription in German —all these seemed to protest so pathetically of the tragedy at the very heart of war, that one often felt that it would have been better if they could have been swept into utter oblivion, so that the horror that had visited them might be the more easily forgotten.

As one looked back over the parados from the front line trenches, one could see nothing but this barren desolation—a country bare of every tree, of all vegetation; a desert, in the undulating folds of which there lay rotting these poor skeletons of villages.

But as one looked—with due caution—over the parapet and viewed the land that had yet to be regained, the land that, as yet, had not suffered the devastation of battle, the little villages of Quéant and Pronville nestling among their trees—looking clean and unharmed as compared with Lagnicourt or Doignies, in spite of the frequent attention of our own guns—then one realised how pretty this country-side must have been, and what systematic savagery must have been necessary to have reduced it to its present state.

It was really quite a good war at Lagnicourt. True, eighteen days in the trenches was rather a long spell; eighteen days during which one could get no change of clothing, no bath, no proper wash, and no particular rest; but there was a fair amount of shelter, quite a number of decent dug-outs, rations and the post arrived with perfect regularity, and the Hun was very inclined to adopt a policy of "live and let live."

Patrols were more or less peaceful breaks in the monotony of existence, and though there were the usual trench rumours of huge German patrols having been seen, with company commanders on horse-back, we never saw any trace of these circus processions. Wiring, though a vastly overrated past-time under any circumstances, was a comparatively easy and uneventful sport, except on the occasion when the Hun's 4·2 batteries caught A Company wiring that nice new trench, which inquisitive aeroplanes had spotted the morning before. And the village of Lagnicourt itself gave the ancient and honourable Corps of Scroungers the opportunity of a lifetime. Another month, and I am perfectly certain the R.S.M. would have built himself a four-roomed cottage!

But, of course, the best part of the proceedings was when, having completed our eighteen days, we used to make our way back to Fremicourt for that blessed period of six days in Brigade Rest. Those were really good days, and many of them were actually restful! There was a pleasing absence of fatigues during these periods ; just a little useful training during the mornings ; football in the afternoons, and the " Bow Bells " in the evenings. The nearest civilisation was 30 miles away, but every now and again about twenty-five of the lucky and righteous (?) ones among us were able to avail ourselves of twenty-four hours leave to Amiens—Amiens, which seemed so far from the war in those days, as far removed as London—and yet which was, within a few months, to know what it meant to have the enemy hammering at its gates, and which came very near to sharing the fate of these poor little wrecks of villages !

*　　*　　*　　*　　*

But, really, the outstanding feature of those times at Fremicourt, was the wonderful performance by the " Bow-Bells." Their " Maid of the Mountains " was a Thing of Beauty and a Joy for Ever. In these later days I have seen a praiseworthy effort on similar lines at Daly's Theatre, but I am sure all those concerned will forgive me for saying that even their wonderful successes have been as nothing compared with those of the 56th Divisional Concert Party. Personally, I used to go at least three times in every six days we spent at Fremicourt, and I fancy most of us could tell the same story. And even to this day, whenever I hear " Live ! Oh ! Live for To-day," or " Love will Find a Way," or any of those tuneful melodies, I think, not of the palatial theatre in Leicester Square, but of that knocked-about old barn, with tarpaulins to make good the deficiencies of the roof, and sandbags to hold up the battered walls—that old barn crammed to suffocation with row upon row of eager, jovial faces, snatching this hour of enjoyment during a brief interval in the business of fighting Huns.

How every topical allusion was appreciated! What yells of delight greeted Harry Brandon's description of the Robber Chief as " The Scrounger in Chief," or Mark Leslie's " posh salute," or any sally of a similar nature. A wonderful audience, and a wonderful show ; and if ever the " Bow Bells " should be revived, and should bring their show to the London stage, I think we should meet many old friends among the audience. I am told that, on the occasion of the march past of the London Troops held recently, " Count Ozzle-Gozzle " was to be seen among the crowds who were cheering the procession. But surely he, and the other members of the party should have had an honoured place in the procession itself ?

CHAPTER XVIII (II).

THE GUY.

I DON'T know who first thought of the scheme, but I think it was the Adjutant, poor old boy! Anyhow, there can be no doubt that " Hindenburg " first saw the light somewhere in the purlieus of Headquarters Dug-out. He was a jolly little chap, was "Hindenburg." Dressed more or less in the ordinary field grey uniform of our attractive neighbours, he, nevertheless, had a certain *distingué* air, that marked him out as something superior to the ordinary brand of " cannon-fodder." His moustache—of burnt cork—had that upward tendency at the tips always associated with the more aristocratic members of his Fatherland, while on his breast he wore an enormous iron cross—of tin-foil—which proved him to have been no feather-bed warrior! He filled out well, too, during his short stay with us (I wonder where they obtained the straw), and altogether he was quite a smart little soldier by the time that the night arrived when he was destined to do his bit.

Nobody can complain that the party that escorted him to the scene of his life work was unworthy of the dignity befitting one who bore such an honourable name. The party that crept over the parapet and out into No Man's Land on the night of November 5th, 1917, consisted of one Adjutant, one Intelligence Officer, three Company Commanders, three Platoon Commanders, one Officer " attached for instruction " (I will not describe him more fully, lest international complications might ensue), one Regimental Sergeant-Major, one Company Sergeant-Major, and one Scout, who acted as Chief Bearer to the principal member of the expedition. It was not exactly a silent patrol, that made its way towards the opposite lines. Too many cooks are said to spoil the broth—a proposition which I should be prepared to dispute—but, undoubtedly, it is a fact that too many Officers spoil a Patrol, and if " Hindenburg's " brothers in arms did not hear the arguments that were proceeding the whole time—by no means *sotto voce*—as to the ideal location for the hero to be erected, then the discipline and alertness of their sentries must have been of a very low order indeed.

However, no mishap occurred at that stage of the proceedings. An ideal site was at length agreed upon and with loving care Hindenburg was placed in position. A screw-picket served to support him on his lonely vigil—and there we left him, with arms upraised in the true " Kamerad " fashion, his iron cross shimmering in the moonlight, his face pale, but his moustache as fiercely triumphant as ever— as nice a little " Guy," as any Bosche who was well trained in his History of England could possibly desire.

Over the adventures that befel certain members of the party on the return journey I will draw a veil. It will be sufficient to say that certain members of both the opposing armies got severe shocks, and a good deal of perfectly good ammunition was exchanged. However, no casualties ensued on our side, and even if a certain Hun sentry did get a rather surprising reply to his challenge, I doubt if he were very much the wiser as a result !

And when the cold grey dawn arrived, and Brother Bosche, beholding there upon his very own wire this gross insult to the hero of the Fatherland, opened up, thereon, a fierce fusilade from every machine gun, trench-mortar, and even every " whizz-bang " battery in the vicinity, then our cup of joy was indeed full, and we felt that

> " Something attempted, some one done
>   Had earned a morning's Repose ! "

CHAPTER XVIII (III).

SEPTEMBER, 1917, TO JANUARY, 1918.

SEPTEMBER 1st, 1917, found the Rangers at Beaulencourt, about 2½ miles south-east of Bapaume on the road leading from that place to Peronne. On the night of the 3rd they marched to Fremicourt Camp (tents), and came into Divisional Reserve. The following night the Lagnicourt Sector in the front line was taken over from the 13th King's Liverpool Regiment, our companies occupying the line as follows :—A Company, right front company ; B Company, left ditto ; C Company, right rear company ; D Company, left ditto.

The enemy welcomed our arrival by shelling the Intermediate Line with 4·2 and gas shells mixed, an unusual proceeding on his part, as this was an exceptionally quiet sector and all those who served with the Battalion during the autumn of 1917 are agreed that it was the pleasantest time we ever spent in the line.

The weather was exceptionally fine, and our casualties for the whole period up to the Battle of Cambrai were unusually small.

The front line was found to be well wired. The front line trench contained a series of " posts " with a connecting trench which was very narrow all along and shallow between the posts.

The country here is a rolling down land of chalk, the valleys and ridges running at right angles to our front.

Our position lay across one of these ridges with our left resting in the valley in which Lagnicourt lay, and in front of that village, our right resting in the next valley on the other side of the ridge.

The top soil of the ridge was fairly deep and the trenches did not go down into the chalk, but on either flank they were mostly all in chalk with about a foot of soil on the top of the parapet.

The intermediate line was good with revetted fire-bays but much damaged on the left owing to the shelling with which the enemy had greeted us.

There were several deep dug-outs in the trench system for the garrison.

Battalion Headquarters with the Aid Post, Magazines and Stores and also Headquarters of the two rear companies were in a sunken road. They consisted of sand-bag structures built close up under the bank nearest the enemy, and there were also some deep dug-outs under the bank for use in the event of shelling, but we never required to use them on that account.

Cooking could be carried out here so long as no smoke was shown, and consequently we were always able to provide the companies with hot tea at midnight, the companies in the intermediate line getting it for breakfast also. There was a cookhouse for the Right Company in the front line when we arrived, and afterwards another one was constructed for the use of the Left Front Company.

Water was scarce, and had to be brought up nightly from the Transport Lines in petrol tins and water carts, but the unique feature of this trench system was that the rations were taken up nightly to the front line on pack animals.

We did a great deal of work on the front line during September, the daily time-table being as follows :—

Stand down	5.30 a.m.
Rifles cleaned by ..	6.30 a.m.
Washed and shaved by	7.0 a.m.
Breakfast	7.15 a.m.
Trench Inspection ..	8.10 a.m.
Work	9.0 a.m. to 12.30 p.m.
Dinner	1.0 p.m.

Afternoon Rest   ..
Tea   ..   ..   .. 4.30 p.m.
Work ..   ..   .. 9.0 p.m. to 12 midnight.

Constant patrolling took place nightly in No Man's Land, which was about 400 yards across at the narrowest part, and 1,200 at the widest, and on more than one occasion the opposing patrols played " cat and mouse " with one another, although neither side secured a " bag " by this means.

The Rangers' first capture was effected under unusual circumstances and disclosed an interesting side-light on the German officers' methods of dealing with their senior N.C.O.'s.

The early morning of September 10th was very misty, but about 8 a.m. the mist suddenly lifted, and two Germans were seen out in front of our extreme left post. They were fired on and fell to the ground.

The post Commander with two N.C.O.'s and two Riflemen immediately went out and found hiding in a shell hole two unwounded young Germans of the 86th Reserve Infantry Regiment, one of them being a Company Sergeant-Major, who was carrying a valuable map of our front, with our trenches and posts accurately marked.

The C.S.M. stated that he had already been over once and reported that our trench was not complete, but that his officer had refused to believe him and had sent him over again to see with the other man as witness !

On the 25th the Battalion was inspected by the G.O.C. IVth Corps. The only criticism was that some of the horses looked thin. His remark on the men was " A fine regiment."

About this time the enemy began to get rather troublesome at night with small trench mortars and machine-guns.

A young officer, fresh from a course at an Army school, demonstrated the effect with which a Lewis gun, skilfully used, could deal with the latter kind of pest. After studying the position of the flashes from the enemy machine gun for a few nights, and taking careful bearings he was able to post his Lewis gun so successfully that, after a little practice, he got the enemy's range to a nicety, and could always take him on whenever he opened fire, and shut him up very soon.

Towards the end of September our splendid Padre was promoted Divisional Chaplain, much to every-one's regret, although we were all very glad, for his sake, that his excellent services had received such recognition.

During September and October the Rangers and London Scottish relieved one another in the line every six days, and each period out of the line was spent alternately in support and in Divisional Reserve.

At the beginning of our tour in this sector the Battalion used to go up to Lagnicourt by train on relief nights, but this was discontinued afterwards as more trains were required for carrying up material, and it was found more convenient and often quicker to march up.

During October the Scottish, assisted by one hundred and fifty Rangers, dug a fine new trench (Edinburgh Avenue) connecting the Intermediate Line and Front Line so as to form a flank defence in the case of an attack, and also a new support line between the Front and " Intermediate " Lines.

The task of wiring this new line fell to the Rangers, who succeeded in putting up a belt of 750 yards long, three " bays " thick, with an " apron " back and front and so full of loose wire as to be impenetrable, at the rate of 250 yards a night. This was held to be a record, the secret of which was the employment of just enough men for each task and no more, thus avoiding a common mistake of employing large wiring parties, who get in one another's way.

We were credited with having employed a special

party of highly trained wirers, but this was not the case as each company took a turn at the job.

The material was carried up in limbers the night before the task was commenced, and dumped in shell holes behind the front line.

To enable the limbers to get up on the track used by the pack animals at night a ramp up from the sunken road by Battalion Headquarters was constructed. The bridges across the trenches between these and the front lines were fortunately wide enough to take limbers.

The details and organisation which produced the success were worked out by the Second in Command, and the Adjutant, and to the latter is due the credit for the bold conception of using the limbers instead of carrying parties.

On November 5th some frivolous Rangers constructed a " Guy " out of an old German uniform, with a sandbag face painted in a colourable imitation of the " All Highest," and wearing an enormous Iron Cross cut out of a biscuit tin. They carried it out into No Man's Land and erected it there.

Next morning, as it began to grow light, the enemy spotted the object, and opened machine-gun fire on it at once, but soon spotted their mistake. They turned the laugh against us that night by capturing the effigy.

From now onwards it became increasingly evident that there was " dirty work " of some kind afloat. The visits of " brass hats " became more frequent, all telephones to the front line were removed lest any indiscreet conversations should be overheard by the enemy's listening apparatus.

Strictest orders were issued against any discussion in masses of any unusual occurrences behind our lines, and officers were absolutely forbidden to mention anything they might happen to notice. Our aeroplane activity increased. Deserted villages near the line sprouted guns like mushrooms during a single night, and thus events gradually worked up to the great " Hush Battle."

CHAPTER XIX.

THE BATTLE OF CAMBRAI.

THE Rangers took no active part in the first phase of this historic battle. Their turn came later.

On November 18th the Battalion was relieved in the front line by the 7th Middlesex and withdrew into Divisional Reserve at Fremicourt, where we completed our final arrangements for the forthcoming operations, as far as we were allowed to know the nature of them.

The sector vacated by the 168th Brigade was taken over by the 1st London Regiment Fusiliers, and the 7th Middlesex, whose rôle was to hold it in sufficient strength to prevent the enemy from discovering that the garrison of the sector had been reduced, and, at Zero hour, to attract the attention of the enemy by the use of some life-like dummy tanks supported by small groups of stuffed figures and groups of " head and shoulder " targets placed out in No Man's Land the night before.

So successful was this ruse that the enemy wasted some minutes and a considerable quantity of ammunition in shelling the tanks and dummies.

At 6.20 a.m. on the 20th the bombardment started. The morning was very misty and swarms of our small 'planes were constantly flying to and from the battle just over the trees in which the Battalion billets lay. It was a revelation to see what a large concentration of 'planes had been effected, and the noise of our bombardment gave a clear indication of the very large increase in artillery which had taken place.

At 10 a.m. the veil of secrecy was lifted, and the C.O. was able to call the officers together, and tell them, for the first time, the details of the plan of the battle.

At 2 p.m. we received orders to detail working parties amounting to two hundred and twenty men for various jobs, which we took as an indication that we would not be put into the battle on that day.

During the morning and afternoon the intelligence wires came flocking in with news of successes everywhere, and we began to have visions of British cavalry in the streets of Cambrai.

At 5 p.m. the weather turned very wet and stormy and got steadily worse until a heavy rain was falling when we turned in to get a good night's rest in view of the possibilities of the morrow.

The morning of the 21st was still wet and stormy, but the weather began to improve later in the day. At about 7.30 a.m. a very heavy bombardment was heard to the north. We ascertained from Divisional Headquarters that this was a counter-attack against our 3rd Division, and that it had been completely repulsed.

At 11.45 a.m. a warning message came of a possible move forward. This was followed at 2 p.m. by a wire telling us that the 109th Infantry Brigade (36th Division) were attacking the villages of Moeuvres and Inchy, and the trenches between— that the 169th Brigade of our own Division had been ordered to get into touch with the 109th Brigade, also to send patrols to gain touch about Moeuvres, and to ascertain progress made—that, as soon as possible the 169th Brigade would get into the Hindenburg front line and clear it between Demicourt and Moeuvres.

The rain stopped at about 9.30 p.m., and a fine clear night followed. At 11.15 a.m. on the morning of the 22nd (the weather being still wet) the Company Commanders met the C.O. at the Headquarters of the right battalion of our Brigade, which were situate in dug-outs under the bank of the road leading from the Bapaume–Cambrai road to the village of Louverval (in ruins).

Here the situation was explained and orders issued as to the parts of the line to be reconnoitred.

The Battalion moved, at 2.30 p.m., from Fremicourt to Lebucquiere, arriving there at 4.30 p.m., and shaking down in the dark to the best of their ability.

When morning came, on the 23rd, the weather was brilliantly fine with a touch of frost in the air. Orders came at 7.30 a.m. to move to Doignies and at 8.15 a.m. the Battalion was on the move. Progress was slow, as we were on the heels of the Guards Division all the way, they being bound for the same place, where they bivouacked in the fields on the south side of the village.

The Rangers arrived at 10.30 a.m. and found temporary accommodation amongst the ruined houses of the village, which afforded concealment from enemy aircraft, and battle stores were issued. Some of us spent most of the day watching the battle from the top of the ruins of Doignies Church, which had been blown up by the enemy in his retreat, leaving a pile of *débris* about as high as a two-storey house.

At 5.40 p.m. we received orders to relieve the 1st Londons as right battalion of the 167th Infantry Brigade (under whose orders we were placed), and were once more on the move at 6.30 p.m. The companies began to arrive in their trenches at about 7.30 p.m. when a warning order was issued that a patrol of the 1st Londons was out searching for one officer and sixteen other ranks missing off patrol, and that our sentries must be prepared for wounded men trying to regain our line. Since the battle the enemy had " whizz-banged " the front line, and also shelled Robin (support) Trench.

At 9 p.m. a message came from Brigade Headquarters to cancel our wiring parties and carry all available wiring material to London Scottish Headquarters. The Brigade stated that the Scottish were being heavily counter-attacked. Orders were issued to A and B Companies accordingly and they spent a busy night.

Next morning (24th), at 6 a.m., Brigade Headquarters rang up and ordered our 4th Company to be sent to the front line to reinforce the Fusiliers but, in view of the approaching daylight and our reluctance to part with our Battalion reserve, it was suggested that the three companies already in the front line could extend, if required, without impairing the defence, and the Brigade agreed to this course being adopted.

Early in the afternoon, the Rangers received a warning order to be prepared to relieve London Scottish that night. News came through, at about 3 p.m., that the enemy were counter-attacking over the open from Inchy.

The " fog of war " then descended upon the situation until 3.45 p.m. when a telephone message passed through the Artillery Exchange at Battalion Headquarters stating that the enemy had regained possession of a considerable portion of his trench system, that the situation was very critical, and the enemy were bombing down towards the portion of the Hindenburg Line held by our troops and down all the C.T.s. All our companies were ordered to " stand to " and to report progress of events.

From reports received from O.C. our right company, between 6.40 p.m. and 7.15 p.m., it was apparent that the enemy's efforts had been checked and the situation was quietening down.

A message came through from Brigade Headquarters telling us that the relief of the London Scottish would be carried out to-night, and that written orders were on their way. These arrived at 11 p.m. and half an hour later the relief was in progress and was finally completed at 7 a.m. on the morning of the 25th.

Orders came from Brigade Headquarters at

8.15 a.m. for an attack on the Hindenburg Line westwards, the 4th London (Fusiliers) being placed under the orders of the O.C. Rangers for the purposes of this operation.

The general plan of attack was divided into two phases. First phase—To secure the C.T.'s. running from the Hindenburg Front Line to the Hindenburg Second Line and also a portion of the latter. D Company of the Royal Fusiliers (4th Londons) were to bomb westwards and A, B and C Companies of the Rangers were to bomb up the three C.T.'s., and in the case of C Company to consolidate their C.T. so as to face west.

Second phase—A Company Rangers were to bomb westwards along Hindenburg Second Line, blocking all C.T.'s. running northwards from that line. As things turned out, the second phase was not reached.

Our artillery bombardment opened at 12.20 p.m. and at 1 p.m. the companies commenced bombing up the trenches allotted to them.

Our C Company met with considerable opposition all the way, and finally came up against a barricade about 50 yards from their objective, which they repeatedly tried to carry with the bayonet, but without success. Finally, at 3.15 p.m., the enemy counter-attacked C Company's left flank over the open and down the Hindenburg Front Line, driving the Company back on to B Company, and inflicting many casualties including all C Company officers.

The experience of B Company was very similar. After forcing their way almost to their objective they were held up by opposition, which they were unable to overcome.

A Company succeeded in reaching the junction of their C.T. with the Hindenburg Second Line, at about 2.30 p.m., where they waited a long time for D Company of the 4th Londons, who were delayed by having to clear two German dug-outs *en route*.

An officers' patrol of that battalion managed to make their way to a considerable distance westwards along the Hindenburg Second Line without encountering any parties of enemy, who were apparently only holding the " trench blocks " in the C.T.'s. up which our companies were attacking.

Unfortunately, the patrol did not bring back this information in time for it to be acted on. By 6 p.m., the situation was all quiet again.

The morning of the 26th passed without incident, and we seized the opportunity to consolidate the positions held by us and to organise the Lewis gun defence. At 3.50 p.m., a party of the enemy suddenly raided a post of D Company in Tadpole Lane and captured their Lewis gun. So neatly and unexpectedly was it done that under any other circumstances it would have been laughable.

A quiet night followed, during which A Company, who were now holding our left flank, succeeded in pushing out our westernmost trench block in the Hindenburg Front Line to a point 50 yards nearer the enemy. At 6 a.m. on the 27th, our artillery became very active on our left front in the direction of Quéant, and, just as we were all wondering what was up, a message arrived warning us of this activity and ordering us to take no action.

II.

DEFENCE OF TADPOLE COPSE, NOVEMBER 27TH, 1917.

At about 8 a.m. on the 27th, the enemy artillery became unusually active with 4·2 and 77 mm. on the area around Battalion Headquarters and the trench junction in Tadpole Copse. This shelling continued, except for a break between 11.30 a.m. and 12.15 p.m., until 3.10 p.m., when it suddenly became very intense and took the form of a " box " barrage around the above-mentioned areas, and a steady barrage on our trench system in Tadpole Copse.

Simultaneously with this barrage the enemy attempted to rush our trench blocks, which were held by A Company.

The enemy's first rush carried the new block which had been pushed out the previous night, and reached our original block.

As a result of the determined action of A Company the enemy was beaten back beyond the new forward block and held there.

The Company Commander (Captain Harker) made a gallant attempt to press home this advantage by leading a flanking movement over the open with Lewis gun and bombing sections. He was hit almost immediately and fell, mortally wounded in the head, but the movement had a measure of success owing to the very gallant action of the Lewis gunner who accompanied the Company Commander. This man's performance was described by an eye-witness as nothing short of marvellous, for he stood up in the open without a scrap of cover firing his Lewis gun from the hip. A fine piece of work for which he was deservedly decorated.

The bombing efforts of the enemy continued unabated, but A Company was more than equal to the occasion, for not only did they keep the enemy at bay but eventually outbombed them.

One young officer (2nd Lieut. Knight) backed up by another (Lieut. Beer) held our principal trench block until he was too exhausted to continue bombing any longer. It is stated that the latter was removing the pins from the bombs and quietly handing them up to the former to throw, a fairly good example of cool nerves when one remembers that the enemy bombers were doing their best to " out " both performers.

At about 3.45 p.m., a message was received from the forward companies that reinforcements were needed, and at our request the O.C. Kensingtons placed two platoons at our disposal, which were sent forward to report to A Company.

By this time the reserve of bombs and rifle grenades at Battalion Headquarters had been depleted and D Company of the Queen Victoria Rifles on our immediate right (who had previously offered to furnish carrying parties if required) were asked to lend two platoons to fetch more bombs, rifle grenades and S.A.A. from the Brigade dump at Houndsditch.

Great praise is due to the officers in charge (Lieuts. Malcom and Hall, of the Q.V.R.), and all ranks of these two platoons for the promptitude with which they responded to this request and the rapidity with which they brought up fresh supplies. The supply forward of Battalion Headquarters was maintained successfully under Battalion arrangements by Headquarters personnel, the buglers, headed by their sergeant bugler, doing great work in this respect.

(Certain irreverent Rangers are rather fond of making merry at the expense of Battalion Headquarters over the generous way in which bombs were rushed up to the threatened points, where they state that the garrison was standing " knee deep in bombs " (sometimes it is " up to their necks "). The retort is that messages kept coming back, " Send more bombs," and, when events were moving so rapidly, it was hardly the time to " reason why " until definite news came in that the supply was sufficient.)

At about 4.15 p.m., we were in a position to report to Brigade Headquarters, by wireless, that the enemy attack was held and half an hour later that the situation was well in hand and no ground had been lost.

A very valuable and gallant piece of work was performed by the Signal Company, R.E. (Wireless), who erected their masts during the barrage at considerable personal risk.

Next morning (28th) we received a message from the Divisional Commander congratulating the Battalion on the defence of the previous day. The 28th and 29th were spent in resting, bathing, cleaning kit and reorganising.

At 9 a.m. on the 30th the Battalion received orders to relieve the London Scottish in the line that night, but at 11 a.m. a message came that the enemy was counter-attacking and the Battalion was to be ready to move at 15 minutes' notice.

Ten minutes later came the order to move at once and by 11.30 a.m. all the companies had got well away.

Our first destination was Louverval Wood, not a very pleasant spot, as the enemy was rather given to bombarding it with gas shells and faint traces of previous bombardment were still tainting parts of it when we arrived.

Then followed several hours of waiting, the tedium being relieved by many orders and counter-orders as the fortunes of the day changed with the progress of events down south where the luck was going all in favour of the enemy, and it was thought probable for some time that we should be drawn into the fighting south of the Canal du Nord to help stem the tide of his advance.

Towards midnight the situation began to clear up and finally the order came to carry on with the relief of the London Scottish.

On arriving in the trenches held by them we found they had had a very rough time indeed, and had suffered many casualties, and, to the sincere regret of all Rangers who knew him, we learnt of the death of their gallant young Adjutant, who had always been a very strong link in the chain forged by the many months of mutual endeavour which bound the Scottish and the Rangers together.

The relief of the Scottish was completed by
2.30 a.m. on December 1st. Two Companies of the
1st Londons (Fusiliers) remained in the trench system,
and came under the orders of the O.C. Rangers,
and before daylight a third company of that battalion
arrived.

The remainder of that night was very quiet.
During the hours of daylight there was a good deal
of artillery and machine-gun activity on both sides,
and after dark the enemy gave a great exhibition of
fireworks, sending up lights of all colours and com-
binations of colours and several fine bursts of golden
rain.

We had many casualties during the course of the
1st, and as our numbers were sadly depleted the
remaining Company of the 1st Londons was moved
closer up in support.

From 5.30 p.m. everything was quite quiet, and
nothing occurred to spoil the beauty of a perfect
moonlight. The morning of the 2nd was very misty,
but later on it lifted, and a fine day followed which
was spent in comparative peace. Orders came in the
morning for a relief that night by the Gordons (51st
Division) and by 10.40 p.m. the relief was completed,
and we marched back to the Transport lines at
Fremicourt.

The 3rd was a brilliant day of sunshine and at
1 p.m. the Battalion entrained for an unknown
destination.

Whilst the bulk of the Brigade was waiting in the
neighbourhood of the siding to entrain, two Bosch
'planes came over, an incident which did not make for
comfort as we were in no mood to be bombed.

However, they cleared off without dropping
anything, and no artillery action followed.

At 4.15 p.m. the Battalion detrained at Heaumetz
and marched into billets at Warlus (about 5½ miles
west of Arras).

December 4th (which was very fine and frosty)

was spent in resting and refitting and that afternoon we received a warning order that the Brigade would move on the morrow.

At 11.25 a.m. the Battalion started to march to Mont St. Eloi. The weather was fine and cold and just right for route-marching, and the march was a grand tonic to all ranks after the hardships and dangers of the previous fortnight.

We reached St. Eloi at 2.20 p.m. on the 5th, and remained there resting and bathing until the morning of the 8th, when we marched to Ecurie (at the foot of Vimy Ridge) where we were allotted billets in Springvale Camp.

Ecurie was a very good example of an " up-to-date " camp behind the lines.

There were self-contained groups of hutments, each capable of holding a Battalion ; the main road was given over to " institutes " of all kinds, and there seemed to be a canteen, cinema or Y.M.C.A. hut every few yards. The side roads were transport lines each with good horse standings, wagon lines, and huts and cook-houses for the personnel.

We remained at Springvale Camp carrying out company and platoon training until December 15th, when we relieved the 4th Londons (Fusiliers) in the Oppy Sector, the relief being completed by 10.45 p.m.

On our way up we made the acquaintance of the largest communication trench we had ever seen, namely Ouse Alley, which was 3 miles long.

From now until the end of December things were very quiet. Relief took place every five days between the Rangers and the 4th Londons. All our activity was concentrated on the work of repairing and improving the trench system, which was in a very bad state, and putting up wire, of which there was none to speak of when the Brigade took over this sector.

Wiring operations were very difficult, as a hard

frost lasted the whole time, and the state of the
ground was such that it was next to impossible to
screw in the pickets.

On Christmas Day there was a fall of snow and
the artillery on both sides exhibited their " Peace
and Goodwill towards men " by shelling one another's
infantry, with the result that the Rangers suffered
two casualties (one officer and one rifleman),
the first they had sustained since arriving in this
sector.

There was another fall of snow at dusk on Christmas night, and then a full moon and the official
diary describes it as " one of the lightest nights of
modern times—wiring quite impossible."

On the 28th, the 7th Middlesex relieved the
Rangers, who travelled by light railway to Marceuil
into billets which were probably the worst they were
ever in. New Year's Day, 1918, was celebrated by
eating Christmas dinners, followed by company
concerts.

On January 3rd, 1918, we moved to Wakefield
Camp, near Roclincourt, into Brigade Reserve.

Another move to St. Aubin took place on the 6th
and next day saw the Battalion in Stewart Camp,
near Roclincourt, where we remained until the 16th,
finding working and carrying parties. The working
strength of the Battalion during this period was
two hundred and seventy men, owing to one hundred
and fifty-five being on leave.

On January 16th, the Battalion moved back to
join the remainder of the Division in General Headquarters Reserve by train to Tinques, which was
reached at 4.30 p.m., and marched thence to good
billets at La Twieuloye, about 6½ miles north-east of
St. Pol.

Here we remained resting, training and bathing,
little dreaming of what the near future held for us.

Rumours were afloat that brigades were to be
reduced to three battalions, and later on another

battalion in the Brigade received a warning that they were marked for elimination, but, on the 24th, the blow fell, and the 1st Battalion of the Rangers, after three years' service as a unit of the British Army in Flanders, received orders to divide the bulk of the Battalion between the L.R.B. and 23rd Londons (47th Division), and to send the remainder (including Battalion Headquarters) as a nucleus to the amalgamated 1st and 2nd Battalions.

On the 29th, the party for the L.R.B. left by march route and the party for the 23rd Londons left by bus.

The nucleus entrained at Tinques early on the morning of the 30th, arrived at Villers Bretonneaux (then untouched) about midnight, where they billeted for the night, and next morning proceeded by march route to Corbie, where the 2nd Battalion were billeted, and thereupon the amalgamated Rangers came into existence.

To face page 165.]

COLONEL A. S. BARHAM, C.M.G., V.D.

PART THREE.
· The Second Battalion.

CHAPTER I.

FROM THE FORMATION OF THE BATTALION TO MARCH, 1915.

AT the end of August, 1914, when the First Battalion was earmarked for Foreign Service, authority was given for a Reserve Battalion to be raised. This Reserve Battalion was intended to fulfil a double purpose. It had to take the place of the First Line Battalion in the scheme of Home Defence, and it was to find drafts to reinforce the Service Battalion as casualties thinned their ranks.

The Second Battalion, or to give it its official title, the 12th (Reserve) Battalion, was formed on a nucleus of Officers and men detached from the Service Battalion, and these returned to Chenies Street on September 4th, 1914.

Recruiting began at the beginning of that month, and Captain K. R. Wilson took charge. Within a very few days the numbers were complete. Men were signed on for Home as well as Overseas Service, and in a remarkably short time the Battalion was full up—over 1,200 men having been taken on.

Lieut.-Colonel Wilton, who had relinquished the command of the Service Battalion on being found medically unfit for Active Service, now arrived and took over, while Captain Wilson became the O.C. Depot.

Between September 1st and 10th large numbers of applications for commissions in the new Battalion were received, and on the 16th the completed list of Officers was sent to the Territorial Force Association.

In addition to the Commanding Officer, Major A. G. E. Syms and Captain C. Hardy were transferred from the Service Battalion. The former became Second in Command, and the latter Adjutant.

Captain Tucker also came back from the Service Battalion to become the Senior Captain, while Captains W. H. Wellsman, D. Matthews and E. F. Webster came from the Reserve, having served in the old Paddington Rifles. Captains S. Chart and G. W. Monier-Williams, both old Rangers Officers, rejoined, while the London Scottish supplied Captain V. L. Burnside. The list of Captains was completed by M. Spencer-Smith, who came from the Inns of Court.

The following gentlemen were given Lieutenancies —G. R. Stuckey, F. Waller, R. H. J. Delmé-Radcliffe (from the Inns of Court), T. D. Wakefield (late of the London Scottish). Later on, Lieut. H. O. Perkins was transferred from the Service Battalion.

The 2nd Lieuts. consisted of—L. C. Benns (from the London University O.T.C.), the brothers F. P. G. and S. G. Telfer, the former by a curious freak being gazetted Senior to his brother, who was several years older, Frank Farnham, the famous 'Varsity Soccer Blue, H. B. Longhurst, J. A. R. Reeves of Clifton, the Hon. Bryan B. Buckley from the Cambridge University O.T.C., A. V. Wheeler-Holohan, of Cheltenham, for many years a Sergeant in the Service Battalion, who had been transferred to the Reserve Battalion with a Commission, A. E. Ellis, another old Cheltonian (who had served in the Oxford University O.T.C.), and W. F. Amsden, also a recruit from the Inns of Court.

Major Ehrmann was the Medical Officer, while Sergeant Scott, late of the Permanent Staff of the First Battalion, became the R.S.M.

With the exception of the Officers, the Battalion were entirely without uniform, and were all billeted at home. Parades were held in Alfred Place, and training, which took place in Regent's Park, consisted of drill entirely.

At the end of September, about 150 men left for Crowborough to replace a number of men who were unfit or who had not undertaken the Foreign Service obligation. Eventually, on October 21st, the Battalion moved into the White City, the Officers being billeted in the Fine Arts Hall, while the men slept in the Machinery Hall.

Quoting from the notes of one of the Officers—
" The 2nd Battalion started its corporate existence amid grotesque surroundings. A 'Palace of Fine Arts' accommodated the Officers, who were apt to complain that they found little of the palatial or the artistic in their surroundings ; and in fact the place was chiefly remarkable for a lasting draught such as the rigours of overseas campaigning never reproduced ; the men, on the contrary, found their quarters named appropriately enough, for they were in the 'Machinery Hall,' and what newly-enlisted soldier but has passed through that early stage of thinking he was being converted into a machine ? Physical drill (before breakfasts in those hardy and unscientific days) might be enlivened by a scaling of the wiggle-woggle, or a humble lecture on the care of arms be delivered from a gilded rostrum built for the measured words of a crowned head. Army rations were cooked and carried by dis-gruntled men orderlies from kitchens whence had issued sumptuous fare ; you could sit for nothing in a 10s. seat in the stadium and watch the most diverting novice at his arm drill. You could come into the Exhibition for nothing, but you needed a pass to go out. Thus does war turn human things inside out."

Training was carried out at Richmond Park, Wormwood Scrubbs, Regent's Park and Hampstead Heath. The Battalion marched out daily and carried out physical jerks, drill and certain field-training. The training was greatly handicapped by the lack of any equipment. Practically no musketry could be taught until the end of December, when rifles were drawn.

To quote again : " The Battalion suffered much from having no barrack square and so no rigid drill in its infancy. Our parade ground was a quagmire, and a small quagmire at that. Wormwood Scrubbs, the nearest open space, was little better, and at least one company commander had it in mind to get himself and all his men made convicts, with a right to the asphalt of the prison yard ! Hampstead Heath, Richmond Park, Wimbledon Common, Putney Heath, were manœuvre areas where we first heard of the use of cover, fire and movement, advanced guards, rear guards and all the mysteries of F.S.R. Many a Londoner learnt the intricacies and the vast extent of the highways and byways of his village from the long marches to these places and will ever connect the Castlenau road with ' What cheer, me old brown son, how are you ? ' and Brondesbury Station Railway Arch with ' Here we are again,' prohibited for one memorable excess of vociferation beneath its resounding walls. Rifles came to us as the result of an invasion scare, which also produced an improvised equipment of beer bottles slung with string, and school satchel haversacks. The rifles were fetched by route march from the Tower,* and it is a long way from the Tower to the White City when you are carrying two rifles, or perhaps three. What, by the way, is the detail for dealing with a colour party of the Guards or a Buckingham Palace sentry if encountered by a detachment thus doubly or trebly armed (and in bowler hats) ? For uniform was not issued until shortly before our move to Crowborough, though many Rangers supplied themselves with it at their own expense."

---

* It is interesting to note that, when the C.I.V's. were being armed for the South African Campaign, the " Rangers " Company drew their rifles from exactly the same place, Capt. Chart (then a Lance-Corporal) being present on both occasions.

During one of these trips to Richmond, and as the Band was passing the Shepherds Bush Empire, the first and most celebrated horse possessed by the Battalion—" Sleepy " to wit—decided to visit this theatre of varieties, regardless of the hour and of his duties. He turned sharply to his left, and in spite of desperate efforts on the part of his stricken rider, boldly mounted the steps, and presented himself at the pay box in the booking hall ! ! !

Another form of recreation beloved of the authorities was " trench-digging." Parties were detailed daily for some considerable time, and after an early breakfast and a hurried march to Wood Lane Station, entrained in the Metropolitan Railway for Liverpool Street. Here another change was made on to the Great Eastern Railway, and a special train proceeded to Loughton or Ongar, remaining there until the evening. Sometimes an excursion was made to Rayleigh—on these occasions the parties being granted the boon of a special train all the way from Wood Lane and back without any change.

Quoting again from the notes of one of the officers who frequently made the trip :—

" On arrival, the civil engineers who were in charge of these works of the London Defences would meet the troops. Often they brought a message of trenches water-logged with rain so that no work could be done, and the day was spent as best it might be in training or less laudable occupations. When fine, good work was indeed done, the traces of which may perhaps survive—like the Martello Towers along the south coast—to remind a peaceful population that England has known the fear, though never the presence, of an invader.

" When darkness fell, our special, lightless, heatless, train reappeared. Those wise virgins who had bethought them of candles, settled down to bridge or nap for the three hours that separated them from home. Few battalions can ever have reduced entrainment and detrainment to the science which the Rangers then evolved. No bugle, no shouting of orders, but a deft partition of carriages by expert officers, a swift hustling of ' in-fours-right-turned ' troops by vigilant N.C.Os., and platforms emptied as noiselessly and rapidly as camp lines will empty when a fatigue party is required. Such were the circumstances in which the 2nd Battalion discovered the organising genius of Colonel Chart.''

During the days at the White City, the first football match in which the Battalion—as the 2nd Battalion—participated, took place. A match was played between the officers of the 2/11th and those of the 2/12th.

The game was remarkable for two things—the tremendous enthusiasm evinced by the rank and file of the two battalions, who, on each touch-line, roared their acclamations from start to finish, and the wonderful goal-keeping of Colonel Grant for our opponents and Captain Spencer-Smith for ourselves. The latter, indeed, with his long, six-foot figure bedizened in a bright yellow sports coat, repeatedly brought down the house.

A goal-less draw was the result. In this we were fortunate, for our opponents were faster, and much more experienced players. It must be mentioned in our favour, however, that four of our team, although Rugby players, had never played the Association game before ! ! The eleven consisted of :—

Goal : Captain Spencer-Smith.

Backs : Captain Hardy and Lieut. Waller.

Half-backs : Second Lieuts. Buckley, Ellis and Farnham (Captain).

Forwards : Second Lieuts. Benns, Reeves, Wheeler-Holohan, S. G. Telfer and F. P. G. Telfer.

A few days before Christmas, the Battalion passed Roehampton House where the Service Battalion lay fitting out, and on December 23rd the news came that they were under orders for France. They left the same night, and, to the sorrow of the Battalion, the rigid orders issued by the authorities cancelling leave, prevented any of us from seeing them off or to wish them God speed and Farewell.

Christmas, 1914, can best be described by an extract from the Diary of the Officer of the Day :—

"December 24th. All leave stopped. Rumours of a projected landing by the Hun. Eh bien, c'est la guerre! If the stories of what Messrs. Lyons have in store for us to-morrow be true, we shall, anyhow, be in a position to march and fight rationless for several days once our Christmas dinners are consumed.

"December 25. What a life! At 6 a.m., Rifleman X deems it right to cut his throat—being in the Guard-room for some malpractice or other. But two months' training in the art of killing seem insufficient, and his attempt is far from satisfactory— a mere piece of child's play for Ehrmann, Major, R.A.M.C., who, by his lectures, is proved to know all there is to be known of pressure-points, tourniquets, and such, as well as of the correct position of the hands of the soldier at attention! At 11 a.m., Church Parade being dismissed, a brave show of sports and games : two tug-of-war teams stuck fast in the mud of the parade ground and despaired of : Colour-Sergeant Henley borne off fainting to the den of Ehrmann, Major, R.A.M.C., his arm broken in a boxing bout, and with it all hopes for the solution of the pay tangles of F Company abandoned. 12.30 p.m.—Dinners. Corporal Y. (who is a *bon vivant*), complains that he cannot negotiate his mince pie without an oyster-knife, but in general 'no complaints.' 5. p.m.—All still sleeping. 7.30 p.m.—Officers' Mess. No complaints again.

Still less complaints as the evening wears on. 12 midnight (?)—To bed. 12.15 a.m.—' Alarm to arms.' Officers at a hard double to the lines severely conscious of (1) being perfectly unaffected by anything which has taken place since 7.30 p.m., (2) loaded revolvers, (3) hatred of the disturbing Hun. It turned out to be an imagined fire and the bugles blew the wrong call. P.S.—I forgot to mention that at 12 noon, the German Fleet entered Portsmouth Harbour and the Imperial Ensign was hoisted on the ' Victory.' "

Looking back upon those days, the mystery of these alarums and precautions seems more and more inexplicable. One of the officers (who afterwards served on the staff at General Headquarters, Home Forces) is able to give a reason, which may be regarded as correct, and which will interest all those who, then and even now, wonder at the cause of those Christmas panics. Our Naval Authorities, aware always of the identity of Hun spies in our midst, caused a rumour to be spread in the enemies' midst that the British meditated a surprise landing. Great wind up on the part of the Boche, and consequent massing of divisions towards the coast. End of Part I ! Unfortunately, the Admiralty omitted to warn the War Office of the rumour spread by them, and the resultant action of Jerry. End of Part II ! Part III. The War Office hears through its agents that the enemy is massing divisions near the coast. Why ? Brains under Brass Hats busily working. Ha ! They mean to invade us ! " *Stand to* " the troops at the White City. Good-bye, Rangers, to your Christmas leave ! (Curtain.)

Towards the end of December, the weird and wonderful rumours as to the ultimate destination of the Battalion were set at rest by the definite statement that Crowborough was to be the new training station, and those members of the Battalion who had trained under canvas there with the Service Battalion were eagerly questioned as to their impressions of that place.

Towards the end of the month an advance party left for Brown Knoll Hutments. The reports received from them indicated that we were bound for a desert island set in a sea of mud. One particular rumour had it, " on very good authority," that the huts were gradually sliding down the hill !

To quote again from the notes of one of the Platoon Commanders :—

" The Battalion spent its remaining days at the White City in various pursuits preparatory for the more advanced stage of soldiering it was entering upon. Company Commanders were mounted—the Transport Section (equipped with horses and vehicles discarded by the First Battalion) mobilised, and uniforms were issued. The Band was returned to the Depôt ; farewell leaves were granted to friends in town. In particular, equipment was issued—a matter which sounds simple enough but which, since very few souls in the unit knew the solution of the puzzle of assembly, and these founts of knowledge could not be everywhere, was a cause of much intricate trouble, and formed, as it turned out, the foundation of that great three-year-long controversy between Company Commanders and Authority, whose details the Censor will never allow to be related."

To this period belongs the first of two famous jokes in Battalion Orders. When we came to move the Orderly Room typewriter was indisposed, and it could no longer distinguish between its " e's " and " o's " ; consequently, an order for the stocking of bed boards was published to us as an injunction that " Beards should be piled in tons," the success of which operation was assured by its being put under the supervision of Captain " Wobster."

At last, the day of the move, January 19th,

arrived. Matters were complicated from the outset by the fact that the caterers had chosen that day to move out, and their successors to move in. The old love was off, but the new love was certainly not on. Some breakfasts were provided for the men, certainly not enough to go round. The officers broke their fast on cold sausages and preserved cream. At about 8 a.m. the main body marched off to Addison Road Station.

A rear party was detailed, and this party, as it transpired, had an exasperating and also amusing experience. Second Lieut. Wheeler-Holohan, who, by service in the First Line Battalion had been in several moves, was placed in command. It was an honour no one else envied him, and his unfortunate platoon perforce had to remain with him.

This party " stood easy " in the empty, echoing Machinery Hall, ruefully eyeing a large pile of kit-bags. A motor lorry had been detailed to fetch these bags to the station. This motor lorry eventually arrived, but, alas, was too small to hold them all.

Time was too short to allow of any fresh arrangement being made, and the heroic party decided to carry these remaining bags to the station. Accordingly they set out, each bearing two bags. By the time, however, the corner of Wood Lane was reached, the compact military ranks had given way, and the procession had begun to lengthen. By the time the famous green by the Empire came into view, the Platoon were spread out in single file, and the last man was not in sight. An enormous party of small boys surrounded them on each side, and many of them, charmed into politeness by the promise of a magic " tuppence," were carrying some of the surplus kit-bags on their heads.

It was evident, however, that the party would never reach the station in time ; at the psychological moment a ramshackle laundry cart, dragged by a brilliant yellow horse, hove into sight. This was commandeered, the bags were loaded in, and the cart, rattling hideously, accelerated its pace, with Sergeant Smith, with the mien of a D'Artagnan, perched on the dicky with the driver. A steady double brought the rest of the band of heroes to the terminus with half a minute to spare.

It can be said that training started in earnest at Crowborough and the Great Adventure had really commenced. Shortly after our arrival there the first overseas draft was detailed, and, numbering 60, they left under the command of Lieut. Wakefield, embarking on April 22nd for France.

About February 15th, the expected news came through that the Service Battalion had gone into its first big action, and the seriousness of a fighting soldier's life was emphasised by the dread information that three officers and nine gallant men had gone to their last rest. A Memorial Service was held in Crowborough Church, and, as the echoing notes of " The Last Post " resounded through the building, all realised that a stern and grim experience lay ahead.

On March 1st, the vacant command was filled. The new Commanding Officer, Colonel A. S. Barham, was a Volunteer Officer of long experience. He came to us from the 9th Battalion, and was known by them as a soldier of energy and capacity, not hide-bound with tradition or fettered by red tape.

Again drafts were needed by the Service Battalion, and a draft of 120, with Captain Tucker and Lieut. Stuckey, went out. Then officers were needed, and the second reinforcing officer, 2nd Lieut. Wheeler-Holohan , followed Lieut. Wakefield over-seas. Five weeks later, Lieut. H. O. Perkins, 2nd Lieuts. S. G. Telfer, Bentley, Whitehouse, and Benns crossed. The Service Battalion at this time (May 1st to 8th) was making its great stand at Ypres. Second-Lieuts. S. G. Telfer and Whitehouse reached the Regiment before the end, and were, unfortunately, both killed. The other officers were in time to meet the remnants of the Regiment as they came out of the line, and found that no combatant officers were left.

In the meantime, we were training very hard at Crowborough. Night operations had been instituted. Of all forms of training, this, although not the most popular at the time, affords the most amusing recollections. Compass marches across the heath led to sudden and unforeseen encounters with streams, water holes, and prickly gorse bushes. Perhaps the climax was marked by the assault of a certain tree clump. This was delivered, under the direction of the Scout Officer (Lieut. Farnham), with the full effect of silence and the correct amount of dash and noise at the right time, and the finishing touch was provided by an enterprising rifleman, who, meeting the General Officer Commanding the Division in the tree clump (whence he and his staff were endeavouring to witness the operation) per-emptorily called upon him to " put his hands up " at the point of the bayonet.

In these early days of mobilization the idea of turning out to meet a German invasion was regarded as quite likely—a feeling not entirely free from the desire that the Battalion might be called upon for that duty. Mobilization parades were a species of entertainment beloved by the C.O. and regarded with mixed feelings by everybody else. Practices were frequent and most ranks became quite skilful in foretelling the times when such a parade was likely to be called. Gradually the time of turning out was reduced to a minimum. This culminated in a Brigade Practice when the time allowed was really too short and the battalions were consequently late at the rendezvous. The Rangers were in time partly because of previous practice and partly be-cause they forgot to issue the ammunition ! At the ensuing Brigade Route March the fine bearing

M

and marching of the Rangers were much commented upon, a result not surprising considering that each man carried nine pounds less weight than those of the other battalions. These congratulatory remarks were the source of some anxiety lest they should lead to the discovery that the ammunition had been left at home.

It might be mentioned in passing that the designation of the Battalion had been changed shortly after its arrival at Crowborough. The formation of the Third Line Battalion, which was really the Reserve Unit, made the name of 12th (Reserve) Battalion incorrect, and the Unit was henceforth officially described as the 2/12th London Regiment.

CHAPTER II

FROM MARCH, 1915, TO FEBRUARY, 1917.

THE 58th Division moved to the East Coast in May, 1915, where it formed part of the defensive force, and the 2nd Rangers were billeted in private houses on the Eastern outskirts of Ipswich.

Major Syms having proceeded to join the 1st Battalion, the vacant position of Second in Command was filled by the promotion of Major Chart, who rendered devoted and most valuable service in that capacity until he succeeded to the command of the Battalion in November, 1917.

The first great step towards preparing for foreign service was taken. All home service and medically unfit officers and men were drafted from the Battalion and for the last time a reinforcing draft was sent to the 1st Rangers. The periodical loss of a number of the best officers and men upon their transfer overseas was always a melancholy event.

In August, 1915, the Battalion moved into Grove Farm hutments on the outskirts of Woodbridge, shifting in October to billets in that town, and passing on in April, 1916, to a camp on Broomeswell Heath.

The Transport Section received with mixed feelings its first draft of mules, and a new excitement was added to life in the morning search for those animals which, thanks largely to their appetite for head stall ropes, broke out of the horse lines during the night. An understanding between men and mules was soon arrived at and developed into mutual respect.

The chief excitement during the stay in the Eastern Counties was connected with Zeppelin raids. At the first of these, the Battalion having done its best to carry out the Brigade Order which specified that all rifles were to be fired at the airship, in doing which men were, if necessary, "to lay on their backs and continue shooting," the resulting retaliation by bombs unfortunately caused destruction and loss of life in the town, and made the Rangers' efforts in doing battle with Zeppelins extremely unpopular. As a result of this, the approach of Zeppelins led to a machine gun being sent to an outlying and desolate spot from which it came into action if possible, and the hasty mustering of the detachment and its despatch from the pitch dark High Street in a limber was quite an exciting event, especially on the evening when, owing to a misunderstanding between the driver and the mules, it carried away the window of a corner shop.

In addition to Zeppelins the Battalion suffered from " Periods of Vigilance," times when everything was held in a state of readiness because the German Fleet was either at sea or there was reason to suppose that it had the intention of coming out. Nothing resulted from these beyond the cancellation of all leave and a few nights spent on the Headquarters floor by the Battalion Staff.

During the winter the Battalion was brought up to full strength, chiefly by contingents of men enlisted under the Derby Scheme, the Battalion being fortunate in securing men of exceptionally good physique and character.

This influx kept recruit training very busy, and many a good soldier learnt the rudiments of his profession on the field in the rear of " Deben Gate," the empty house which served for Headquarters.

A defensive position between Ipswich and the coast was surveyed for occupation by the Division, the portion allotted to the Rangers extended to the north of the Woodbridge–Hollesley Road near a cottage called " Gobblecock Hall "; here trenches were dug and wire obstacles prepared; the place was some miles from billets and the following rhyme which went to a favourite tune of the bugle band happily expressed the feelings of the Battalion towards this position :—

Gobblecock Hall !
Gobblecock Hall !
We're going to march out to Gobblecock Hall ;
With spade and with maul,
Wire cutters and all,
We're going to march out to Gobblecock Hall !

And when we get there,
When we get there,
Trenches to dig, revet and repair,
Britons prepare !
Germans beware !
Trenches to dig, revet and repair.

And that isn't all,
That isn't all ;
We've got to march back from Gobblecock Hall,
Oh ! Peter and Paul !
King David and Saul !
We've got to march back from Gobblecock Hall !

This rhyme has been preserved in the columns of *The Jab,* a Battalion journal which recorded many incidents, brightened the life and encouraged the *esprit de corps.* It continued to appear until the Rangers left England.

The Battalion football team won its way to the final in the competition for the Divisional Cup presented by Brig.-General Cooper, commanding the Division, and secured the trophy by defeating the 2nd London Brigade, R.F.A., by four goals to one on the Ipswich Ground.

A dinner to the team at the Bull Hotel was one of the entertainments with which the winter evenings were enlivened ; others took the form of concerts, dances and plays.

An inspection by the Inspector-General of Overseas Troops raised hopes that the desired day for foreign service had arrived, but, alas ! it proved to be one of those days when everything went wrong— including the temper of the distinguished General upon whose verdict hung the realisation of the hope of going to France. It was soon apparent that the Division was to remain upon the waiting list, and the inspection day was long remembered as " Black Friday."

In August, 1916, the Division was transferred to the Western border of Salisbury Plain in the neighbourhood of Warminster, and the Rangers occupied huts at Longbridge Deverill. Here the final polish was put on preparatory to proceeding overseas. General H. D. Fanshawe took over the command of the Division, and the greatest good fortune befell the Battalion in that the command of the 175th Brigade was taken up by Brigadier-General H. C. Jackson, D.S.O., who remained until appointed to command the 50th Division in March, 1918. General Jackson had returned from the front suffering from severe wounds, from which he had not entirely recovered. His untiring example, in which he never spared himself, kindly consideration for the comfort and welfare of his troops, strictness against faults and encouragement of good work, could not fail to call forth the most ready and loyal response that it was possible to give any leader, and his presence in command of the Brigade had the greatest possible effect in influencing the progress of the Battalion to the high state of efficiency which it reached and maintained.

In November, the Brigade was camped near Imber to dig trenches for an artillery practice range. The day of arrival at the camp was the last of a spell of fine weather and that night it blew and rained, and many tents were levelled. Wet weather continued during the stay and the ground became muddy enough to be worthy of Flanders ; indeed this period was regarded by some as being as uncomfortable as any experienced during the war. On the completion of the work the Battalion returned to the comfort of its permanent quarters, wet and weary, but with an enhanced reputation for good work and soldierly conduct under discomfort.

Hard training continued in all the details of general and specialist warfare leading at last to another inspection by the Inspector-General, who could find no fault this time and gave his official benediction. Final leave followed about Christmas time, and only the order to move was awaited.

CHAPTER III.

FROM FEBRUARY, 1917, TO THE AMALGAMATION.

EARLY on the morning of February 5th, 1917, a very cold morning, the roads heavy and slippery with snow, the 2nd Rangers marched from the huts at Longbridge Deverill, which it had occupied since the previous August, and entrained at Warminster station for Southampton.

The departure for overseas, so long awaited, was welcome to all ranks. It was an efficient and keen Battalion which started on the great adventure, not fearing comparison with any other, and lacking only the actual battle experience which awaited it.

On arrival at Southampton a party of about three hundred, under Major Chart, was detailed as escort to the Divisional Ammunition Column, which they accompanied by steamer and train, rejoining the Battalion in France some days later. The remainder of the Battalion embarked on the " Viper " and sailed at 8 p.m.

Shortly before sailing thirty-seven prisoners were received for delivery on the other side ; this detachment was composed of examples of a type of humanity of which the Rangers had very little experience, and they were inclined to give trouble until two or three of the ringleaders had been placed in irons, and the remainder were effectually quieted by a rough sea.

The ship was very crowded, men, rifles, kits, were packed in every available corner.

In accordance with orders a guard was detailed for duty on the boat deck in order to shoot at any submarine which might appear, but the open sea quickly reduced the guard to a condition quite past all possibility of hitting a submarine. Indeed, it was a night of misery and not a few would have rather welcomed a submarine or any other deliverance from their sufferings.

The " Viper " arrived at Havre at 3 a.m. on February 6th, and some hours later the Battalion disembarked and marched 5½ miles to the Rest Camp over roads which were hilly, heavy with snow, and very slippery. Everybody had had enough by the time they reached Camp, which consisted of old tents pitched on a high and bleak plateau across which the north-east blizzard swept with icy coldness. It was an exceedingly chilly spot, conditions which somewhat reconciled the Battalion to a rapid progress through the Rest Camp, which ill fitted its name and was the cause of some sarcastic remarks.

On the next day the transport went off at 5 a.m.; the Battalion at 6 marched to and entrained at the Gare du Marchandaise, having been warned that the journey would take 12 hours, and without any idea as to its destination.

In the train the Battalion made its first acquaintance with the French box trucks which carry eight horses or thirty-six men, and agreed that whilst they may be excellent things for horses they were sadly uncomfortable for men.

The pace of the train never exceeded six miles an hour and it was no uncommon sight to see men running alongside the train for exercise and warmth. There were numerous stops, at one of these the whole Battalion being turned out for exercise.

Having been 24 hours instead of 12 hours *en route*, the Battalion detrained at Auxi le Chateau, and marched a short distance to Wavans, where it settled into billets for the first time in France, remaining there for three days.

Numerous troops had passed through *en route* for the front and the village was found to be extremely dirty, containing much refuse. The Battalion commenced the reputation, which was afterwards maintained everywhere it went, of leaving all places where it stayed much cleaner for its visit.

Considerations of discipline, *morale*, and the health of the Battalion as well as of other troops demanded the strictest attention to sanitation and cleanliness. This was well maintained, bringing frequent messages of appreciation from civil and military authorities.

Major Chart and his detachment of three hundred arrived at 3 a.m. on the 9th and the Battalion was once more complete.

The welcome arrival of the mail from England was first experienced here. The weather continued extremely cold.

On the 11th the Battalion proceeded by route march to Beaudricourt, passing on the way through the area where the remainder of the Brigade was billeted, and being played along by the band of the 10th Londons for about two miles.

Sundry articles of equipment were issued during the stay of three days here, box respirators (which were regarded with real affection later on when their value had been tested in German gas), waterproof capes, &c., each of these was received with some amount of pleasure which was greatly qualified when the owners realised that all their possessions had to be carried on the back for many a weary mile, a condition which has a powerful effect in simplifying one's needs.

Later, on the 14th, London men renewed their acquaintance with London 'buses, the Battalion being " embussed " for transit to the front.

Neither the vehicles nor the roads were so good as when they ran to the " Bank," and it was not uncommon for all the occupants to turn out and walk, or perhaps push, on bad pieces of road.

The 'buses were left at La Cauchie and the Battalion was divided amongst various units of the 146th Infantry Brigade, then occupying a trench line from about Berle-au-Bois to Wailly. This was a very quiet sector and there were no casualties during the four days' stay, although sickness began to make itself apparent.

On the 19th the Battalion proceeded to Halloy to rest billets. It was intended that the Battalion should move by 'buses, but because of the break up of the frost the roads were so soft that 'buses were not permitted and the distance was therefore covered by route march.

The Divisional General and the Brigadier were on the road and saw the Battalion pass. They were both very complimentary on its appearance and marching.

On arrival the Battalion was billeted in barns, and found the village a very dirty and insanitary one, reeking with the smell of rotting straw, &c., and deep in mud, but the cleaning was taken in hand, and, aided by brightening weather, a great change was effected in a few days. Some sickness here, but less than in other units quartered in the same village.

During this time training of all sorts was in progress and rehearsals of trench assaults of various patterns were a regular occupation.

The great institution of the Battalion Canteen was started, and thanks to Major Chart's energy and devotion it became a great convenience, and followed the Battalion almost wherever it went.

Early in the morning of the 25th intimation was received that the Germans had retired their line along the front, and the Battalion was warned to be ready to move in pursuit by 5 a.m. However, nothing came of this, and it was not until March 2nd that the Battalion proceeded by route march to Bailleuval, where it remained in Brigade reserve until 5th, two Battalions being in the line.

On March 5th the Battalion relieved the 2/11th Londons in trenches in front of Wailly; it was snowing hard and was very cold.

This was the first experience of the Rangers in accepting the responsibility for barring the road to the Hun, and altogether the conditions were such that in the light of later experience the Wailly trenches would have been regarded as a health resort, yet there were conditions which made them trying to inexperienced troops, green not only to the dangers, but to the discomforts of trench warfare.

The front had previously been held by two Battalions, but the Rangers had for the first five days three Companies in the front line, afterwards only two. The system of holding the line by Platoon posts separated by stretches of empty trench was just beginning, and it left an eerie feeling of isolation. The weather was at first so cold that few men could sleep, and when the frost thawed the trenches were soon in an appalling state of mud, which it was quite beyond the strength of the small garrison to cope with. Shelters were few and poor, the platoon posts had little or no preparations for defence.

The disposition was two Companies in the front line, each having two platoon posts in the first and two in the second lines, one Company occupied the third line, having a Platoon in Keeps on either flank—Petit Chateau and Wailly Village—and two Platoons near Battalion Headquarters. These two Platoons had to carry supplies to the front Companies and they felt the strain most. The fourth Company was resting in Battalion reserve in cellars in Wailly. A move round took place every four days.

There were very few casualties but the hard conditions of the life were too much for many men and much sickness resulted.

No Man's Land was in a curious position here, occupying the crest of a slight rise, the opposing front line trenches being on either side of the rise so that neither British nor German could see the other's front line. The Germans had, however, dug several saps which reached the crest, one of these saps in particular, distinguished as " Z9A," was driven to within 40 yards of the British front line and was the source of considerable interest to the Rangers.

To clear the situation, " Z9A " was raided one night by a party under Lieut. George and found to be empty.

It was known that the Germans were about to retire from their position in front. Indication of this intention was given by numerous fires and explosions. Lieut. Nunn led a party over one night as part of a demonstration to gather information.

During the night of March 17th–18th the German lines were very quiet, and being entered by a Patrol under Lieut. Foucar were found to be abandoned. The Battalion advanced and occupied the third line of the German trenches at 6.30 a.m. D Company, under Captain Waller, led the way.

Later on two Platoons of A Company and two of C were sent forward to reinforce this new position, and the whole was placed under Captain Burnside. Outposts were pushed forward but no touch was obtained with the enemy, who had withdrawn to a considerable distance.

The outposts were taken over in the early morning of the 19th by the 10th Londons and the Rangers concentrated in Ficheux at 9.30 a.m. This village had been utterly demolished by the retreating Germans, who had left it a complete wreck with not a wall or tree standing. Such shelters as were possible were improvised amongst the ruins but they were of little avail against pouring rain.

The first draft arrived on this day—a reinforcement of four officers and thirty-one men.

On the following day the Division was withdrawn for a much-needed rest and re-fit, and the Rangers marched to Bretencourt where they went into billets. The casualties since the 5th inst. were three officers and seventy other ranks, of these one was killed, twelve wounded, sixty sick.

Two days later the Battalion proceeded by route march to Lanerliere and Bavincourt, where it was only four miles away from the billets of the 1st Rangers, and the opportunity was taken to exchange visits between some members of the two Battalions, being the first time they had met, and the only time, until the two were amalgamated later on. At these billets Captain Lockett, C.F., joined the Battalion and commenced a service and friendship which were highly appreciated, but did not continue for nearly so long as both parties desired.

On the 25th the Battalion proceeded by route march to the old quarters at Halloy, and remained there until the 31st, training and refitting, especially troubled by a shortage of boots and leather in consequence of which a large proportion of the Battalion was imperfectly shod for some time.

Whilst here, owing to the premature bursting of a rifle grenade during practice, Sergeant Simmonds, a very efficient Battalion Bomb Sergeant, was killed, and Lieut. Willett and two riflemen wounded.

Captain Shepherd, late of the 9th Londons, took over charge of the Transport from Lieut. Solomon, who was transferred to the position of Quartermaster, taking the place of Lieut. Pearce, who returned to England.

Lieut. Solomon was a great acquisition in the position of Quartermaster, and his efficient and painstaking work contributed largely to the comfort, good feeling and welfare of the Battalion.

At 10.45 a.m. on April 1st (Palm Sunday) the Battalion marched out of Halloy and it was noticed that the Chaplain left a notice attached to the School room door announcing that service would be held at 11 a.m. and 7 p.m. It was never determined whether this was a joke appropriate to the day or a deeply laid scheme to mislead German spies.

The route lay through Doullens, a large and busy town, to Neuvillette, the cleanest village in which the Battalion had so far been billeted.

The question of weight of baggage had begun to receive consideration, as roads were hilly and the tendency to accumulate impediments had become manifest, and the Doctor suffered some little personal inconvenience by reason of an impromptu inspection of the contents of the Medical Cart. The rigid enforcement of limits of weight is more popular with the transport animals than with the officers whose luggage is concerned, but thanks to it the Battalion Transport was never overloaded or broken down and was always at its appointed place.

The following day the march was continued to Neux and during the latter portion of this march, after reaching the main road at Frohen le Grand, a very bad road was struck, great holes practically filled with brushwood, and mud and water often over boot tops. Near the end of the march the Battalion passed through Wavans, the village at which it had been billeted on February 8th. The Divisional General saw it pass near here and was very pleased with its appearance.

Two days were spent in billets at Neux, training.

On the 5th the Battalion proceeded by 'buses towards the front once again, passing through Doullens to Bus les Artois where it went into a hutted camp and passed under the command of the 5th Corps and the 5th Army. In this village the whole Brigade was brought together again for the first time since leaving England.

On Easter Sunday, April 8th, the Battalion was again on the march, as it had indeed been on the four preceding Sundays, but this was exceptional, as the route left the French population behind and passed through the battlefields of Beaumont Hamel, along the valley of the Ancre to Miraumont and for the first time the Battalion saw the actual conditions of severely contested battlefields. It was a quiet and determined battalion that noted that the villages had entirely disappeared (the only sign of them being that the road was composed of the bricks which had once been houses), trees were reduced to blasted stumps, there was not a blade of grass or a green leaf to be seen, and parties were collecting the shattered débris of the battles.

The quarters at Miraumont were such as men could find or make for themselves amongst the ruins.

On the 9th all available men were sent to help on the repair of the railway ; this was a duty which continued very frequently whilst the Battalion remained in this district, parties often being at work helping the Canadian Railway Reconstruction Corps.

Whilst here Captain Malkin, R.A.M.C., took over the duties of Medical Officer and commenced a connection which, with the exception of a short interval, lasted through the remainder of the Rangers' war service, and was greatly appreciated by all ranks.

The next day the Battalion moved by short route march to Achiet le Petit, where it went into billets until May 3rd in buildings which were still standing, and found much better quarters than those left at Miraumont. The time was divided between field training and work on the railway. The billets were good, the village was sweet by comparison with those in which the inhabitants were still living, the weather to start with was very cold and snowy, but it afterwards became springlike and, on the whole, the time spent here ranked with many of the Battalion as the pleasantest time since September, 1914.

An old shed was soon converted into a Bath House, and with the help of three coppers, a certain amount of clay, trench ladles and a trench pump, quite an elaborate bathing establishment was in full swing, of which other units availed themselves. Battalion Sergt.-Major Chatfield was the leading spirit in this excellent institution.

A mine left by the Germans in the railway embankment at Achiet le Grand exploded twenty-three days after the Germans had left and gave some little work in filling up the hole. A somewhat

similar crater was found in the village of Achiet
le Petit itself. It was an enormous affair, considered
by those who had experience on service to be the
largest they had ever seen, and as numerous 9-inch
shells were strewn about the neighbourhood it was
surmised that it marked the site of an ammunition
dump which the Germans had blown up. The
crater was afterwards terraced, a wooden platform
was erected at the bottom and it made a magnificent
theatre which was in frequent demand for boxing
matches, concerts, &c.

The Transport lines were thrown into consterna-
tion one morning by the discovery that two horses
had disappeared in the night, and it was generally
thought to be more than a coincidence that some
Australian troops had marched through that night.

One of the horses was recovered a few days afterwards, being seen passing through the village in the
transport of another unit, but the other was never
traced.

On April 15th the Brigade was warned to stand
by, expecting an order to retake the trenches at
Lagnicourt where the Germans had penetrated the
Australian lines early on that morning and over-run
many of the artillery positions. However, the warning was shortly afterwards cancelled, the position
having been restored by the Australians themselves.

The general position to be taken up by the 175th
Brigade in the event of an attack in force was on the
line Hamelincourt to Ervillers, and opportunities
were taken of reconnoitring and occupying this line.

Provision of green vegetables was the one thing
in which the rations, so excellently issued, were
deficient, and in the endeavour to remedy this
experiments were made by trying various remains of
cultivated crops which were found in the field.
Dandelion spinach never became a very popular
dish, but the great discovery was a field of artichokes from which the Battalion drew in regular

instalments, until, it being apparent that some other unit had also discovered the field, the limbers were sent and artichokes were available for some time.

A rifle grenade accident happened here by which Lieuts. George and Willoughby and one rifleman were wounded.

On May 4th the Battalion marched to the neighbourhood of Vaulx and after dark proceeded through the ruins of that village and took over from the 8th Australian Infantry a support position in shelters along the side of a road south-east of Bois de Maricourt. This road ran along one side of a valley, in which were numerous heavy guns, and it proved to be an exceedingly noisy spot.

By 10 a.m. on the 5th the 2/10th Londons having taken over the support position, the Rangers advanced towards the front line, where they relieved the 6th Australian Infantry, holding the position between the Lagnicourt–Queant Road and l'Hirondelle stream. The front was occupied by two lines of platoon posts furnished by two platoons of B and by the whole of C and D Companies. The posts were isolated and communication was only possible by night. A Company and two platoons of B were in Battalion Reserve in shelters along the Lagnicourt–Noreuil Road. Headquarters were in a lane near the Crucifix at Lagnicourt. Although subject to bursts of heavy shelling the casualties during the four days were light, totalling eleven, mostly the result of patrol encounters.

The Battalion was relieved on the 9th by the 30th Australian Infantry and moved back to the same support position that it had occupied on the 4th. While here parties were employed nightly in wiring the platoon posts in the front line.

Early on the morning of the 11th the Rangers were relieved from support position and retired to a line of old trenches and shelters west of Vaulx. There was a well in the immediate neighbourhood,

and with the aid of canvas sheets the Quartermaster's staff had prepared a number of baths, which
were welcome after eight days and nights of dirty
trench life.

Later on in the day the Battalion marched to a
standing camp of tents west of Favreuil where it
remained until the 15th, training and refitting.

An Observation Balloon was located in the village
and its antics when attacked by enemy aeroplanes
formed a frequent entertainment.

Whilst here the great event of leave to England
was commenced, and Company Sergt.-Major Part-
ridge, by reason of his long service with the Rangers,
had the privilege of being the first man home.

On the 15th the Battalion marched into Brigade
Camp at Bihucourt and just before reaching camp
defiled before Brig.-General H. C. Jackson, D.S.O.,
Commanding the Brigade, and received his description as " the best marching Battalion in the Division."
About this time the 58th Division passed into a fresh
Corps which included another second line Territorial
Division and the renowned 7th Division. It was
commonly reported that the latter expressed their
opinion that as there were two second line Territorial Divisions in the Corps they, the 7th Division,
would now be up every night. They soon found,
however, that such an idea was mistaken, and when
the time came for the 58th to leave the Corps they
took with them the profound respect not only of the
7th Division, but also of the Australians with whom
they came in contact at Bullecourt.

On the 19th the Battalion marched forward to a
position one mile west of Vraucourt, where the
transport lines were permanently pitched and from
whence the Battalion proceeded after dark to take
over from the 2/3rd Londons the position in support
of the trenches between Bullecourt and Ecoust.
Battalion Headquarters and C Company were in
shelters on the railway embankment, the other

Companies in trenches in its immediate neighbourhood. This was an old battleground which had
been several times contested, and within view from
the Battalion Headquarters were five aeroplanes,
three tanks, one wagon and horses, and an enormous
quantity of battle débris of the smaller kind, rifles,
equipment, machine guns, &c. The Battalion was
employed on salvage work clearing up this débris,
and in carrying food and water to its own position,
and forward to the front line. Funeral parties were
also busy.

The protection and comfort of the men was much
hampered by the bad conditions and the frequent
shelling, no movement being possible by day.
Casualties whilst in this position were three officers,
Lieut. Weston (mortally), Lieut. Lacey, wounded,
Lieut. Volta buried and suffering from shock, and
forty-four other ranks wounded.

On the 23rd the Battalion relieved the 2/11th
Londons in the front line South of Bullecourt.
It was a difficult relief and many casualties resulted.
The line occupied here was a part of the noted
German Hindenburg Line, the trenches, as a result
of heavy shelling by both sides, were blown to pieces
and consisted of little more than shell holes, in many
places protection was only waist high, but the old
German dug-outs were still in good order. The total
frontage occupied was about 1,000 yards. Each
Company had two platoons in the front line as
detached posts, and two in the support line. Heavy
fighting had recently taken place, the Germans' last
attempt at recapture having occurred only a few
days before, and there was a high degree of tension
on both sides. S.O.S. signals had been of frequent
occurrence. With the arrival of the Rangers things
became more settled and S.O.S. calls ceased, at
least on the British side. The line was frequently
subject to heavy shelling, which greatly hampered
the nightly efforts to improve the trenches, bury the

numerous dead, salve the débris and generally tidy up the place. The atmosphere was very foul, as a result of dead bodies brought to the surface by every burst of shell fire, and conditions of life were distinctly unpleasant. Nevertheless a very large quantity of rifles, ammunition, equipment, &c., was carried to the embankment and cleared away by the ration limbers nightly, and the trenches were left better than the Rangers found them.

Lieut. Hills was wounded, twelve other ranks killed and forty-three wounded. Communication with the support position being only possible after dark, all wounded men had to remain in the trench until then, a condition which greatly aggravated their sufferings.

On the night of the 24th–25th, dispositions were re-arranged. C Company were withdrawn to the third line trench, their posts in the front line being taken over by one platoon each of D and B, and Headquarters returned to the Railway Embankment.

Relieved by the 2/8th Londons on the 26th, the Battalion marched to the Transport Lines west of Vraucourt where the Battalion arrived on the morning of Whit Sunday, the 27th, to find cold baths, breakfast, clean clothes, the hedges white with hawthorn, the fields covered with wild flowers and generally a change very complete from the putrid atmosphere and tumbled ground in which it had been living during the previous few days.

This was a Whit Sunday to be long remembered by those who experienced it. The spell in the trenches at Bullecourt was the severest time that the Battalion had had up to that date. Everybody was steady under the trying conditions and did well. The Battalion now remained in camp at Mory for the usual interval for rest and training.

On June 3rd the Battalion relieved the 2/8th Londons in support position and was located in shelters and trenches along and near to the Noreuil–

Longatte Road with Headquarters in Ecoust. Parties were employed in wiring and trench digging. Whilst here Battalion Headquarters had a visit from a German shell which, fortunately for the Headquarters, did not burst.

On June 6th the Battalion returned to the front line trenches south of Bullecourt which it had occupied from May 23rd to 27th, but the situation had quieted considerably in the meantime, and although there was intermittent shelling, the conditions were much more comfortable than on the previous visit. A new communication trench called " Tank Avenue " had been dug, and the place had generally been cleaned up.

The Patrolling and Sniping by the Battalion was very good and obtained a marked ascendancy over the enemy, and received the special commendation of the Brigadier. As a result of encounters three Germans were brought in alive and three dead, enabling identifications to be made of the 119th and 180th Regiments.

The trenches were taken over by the 9th Devons, a very good and quick relief. Casualties during this spell were : Lieut. Carte (mortally), and Lieut. Nunn wounded, other ranks, thirteen killed, thirty-nine wounded. There were numerous sick resulting from the two tours in this part of the trench line.

On the 15th the Battalion proceeded to Mory Camp from where it was employed on two nights digging a new communication trench north of Bulle-court. In addition to general training special practice was made for an intended assault on the German position north of Bullecourt, but, owing to conditions not connected with the Rangers, the order for this was countermanded and it was never carried out. The officers had been, by casualties and sickness, reduced to one per company.

On the 24th, only a few hours before they were to be vacated, the Horse lines, which had escaped harm all the time they had been established since May 27th, were shelled, and casualties caused to one man and four horses.

The Battalion was relieved by the 2nd Royal Warwicks, who were very appreciative of the condition in which they found the camp, and proceeded to a Camp on the south side of the Bois de Logeast which was taken over from the Manchesters and found to be very dirty. The usual conditions of training were diversified by field firing and competition on a short range, the great event being an inter-company contest for whch the first prize was a Half-Holiday.

Some excitement was caused here by leave being given for one day at Amiens, the announcement of which resulted in Headquarters being snowed under with applications.

The Brigade held a horse show at which the First Prize in the Driving Competition was won by a limber of the Rangers, and Battalion Sports were organised, the most notable occurrence being the Obstacle Race, in which the large number and vigour of the competitors resulted in the Obstacles being carried away bodily.

Although this position was only a few miles behind the lines, the Very Lights being in sight at night, the Battalion was never disturbed by false alarms or warnings. The freedom of the rear troops from alarms being remarkable all through the service of the Battalion.

On July 5th the Battalion proceeded by route march through Bapaume to a Camp near Bullecourt. The Corps Commander watched the Battalion defile by at Bihucourt as it passed out of his Corps, and was very complimentary upon its services during the time that it had been under his command, whilst the Battalion felt that it had gained experience and made good its reputation. The march was continued the following day to Bertincourt, where the Battalion was quartered in shelters in the ruins of a small town, which had been destroyed by the Germans on their retirement.

On the 8th the Battalion marched to Ytres, where it entrained at dusk on a light railway and detrained at Havrincourt Wood at a terminus which was only about 600 yards behind Battalion Headquarters. Here it relieved the 115th Manchesters, holding a line of trenches from the Canal du Nord on the left, where A Company was posted on a conspicuous chalk heap, to the front of Havrincourt Park, where D Company joined the Q.V.R., C Company being in the centre, each of these Companies having two platoons in posts in the front line and two in the support line. B Company was in the third line. Headquarters were in an old chalk-pit about the rear of the centre, partly in shelters and partly in the deep dug-out.

The line here was of an interesting character, along its front were interspersed copses, craters of mines which the Germans had exploded in the roads, and the Park surrounding Havrincourt Chateau containing numerous trees. Within the line was Havrincourt Wood, for the most part recently felled, but still having many trees in places, and overgrown with a profusion of wild flowers. It was, generally, a quiet and peaceful spot, the enemy kept most carefully underground, occupied his advance posts at night only, and was practically never visible.

There was little artillery fire, but trench mortars were rather troublesome on both flanks, especially on the right, where they fired from concealed positions in Havrincourt Park and could not be located.

Much useful patrolling was carried out by both day and night. The M.M. was awarded to Sergeant Palmer for good handling of his Platoon and repulsing a German reconnoitring party which advanced against his post after it had been heavily bombarded.

On the night of the 11th–12th, following upon the shelling of " Dean Copse," about 400 yards in front of the line, Lieut. Galbraith advanced, with a patrol, to make a reconnaissance of the position. It soon became evident that the German post had suffered but little from the artillery fire, and Lieut. Galbraith's Party was met with heavy fire from two machine guns, and from rifles. A little engagement resulted and the patrol returned in good order, the Commander and six other ranks being wounded. It was well led and behaved admirably. Lieut. Galbraith, who handled the Lewis Gun after " No. 1 " had been wounded, received the Military Cross for his good leading on this occasion.

The stay in these trenches was comparatively quiet and enabled the trench organisation and routine to be carefully organised and improved in details, the Battalion benefited very much by reason of this experience, and its discipline and conduct was described by the Brigadier in a Brigade Order as being so good that " in three years' experience he had never seen it surpassed."

The total casualties during the period were— Lieut. Warren and three other ranks killed and eight other ranks wounded.

On relief by the 2/11th Londons during the night of the 16th–17th, the Battalion withdrew to a support position on the West of Havrincourt Wood, close to the Canal du Nord, where it was accommodated in shelters, those of D Company being situated in the midst of a luxuriant growth of wild raspberries of which they took full benefit. Platoons were withdrawn in rotation for baths and clean clothes at Ruyualcourt and working parties were furnished nightly to improve the front line trenches. Numerous details were detached to Bertincourt where a Battalion School for training specialists in Lewis Guns, Signals, Bombing, &c., was instituted and did very good work.

It having been decided that " Wigan Copse," a small Wood held by the enemy in front of the left of the position, should be raided the duty was allotted to Lt. Foucar and a party of A Company, who spent their time making plans and training for the purpose.

On the night of the 20th–21st, the front line was raided by the Germans; two companies of the Rangers were already near the line as working parties, and assisted in repelling the attack, the remainder of the Battalion received the alarm and moved up to support, but the position was restored without their services being required.

The casualties to working parties between the 17th and 22nd were four killed and one wounded.

On the 23rd the Rangers, except A Company, retired to Ruyualcourt, being relieved in the support trenches by the 2/9th Londons. Here they were quartered in tents and a few shelters in the ruined village, and passed into Divisional Reserve.

On the night of the 23rd–24th, the raid on " Wigan Copse " was carried out by Lieut. Foucar and forty other ranks of A Company. The party passed out of the front line along the bank of the Canal du Nord, penetrated the German wire close to the Canal, and, having established a party to cover its rear, the remainder entered " Wigan Copse " from the rear and searched the copse throughout; some Germans were found and dealt with. During the operation the Copse was enclosed in a very effective Box Barrage and no attempt was made by the Germans in the main line to interfere with the operation. The party carried out their programme precisely to time-table and returned without casualties; Lieut. Foucar received the Military Cross for his leading on this occasion, and a Complimentary Order was received from the Army Commander. The Military Medal was awarded to Sergeant Harris.

On the 26th the Battalion quarters at Ruyual-court were taken over by the 10th Argyll and Sutherland Highlanders, and the Rangers marched to Bertincourt, where they stayed until the 27th and then proceeded to Bapaume, partly by 'buses, partly by the light railway from Ytres, the latter portion being considerably delayed owing to the railway being shelled and broken ; the Battalion entrained at Bapaume for Beaumetz where it detrained at 11 p.m. and marched to billets at Dainville, 2½ miles west of Arras. This was an untouched village and the Battalion was once more, after an interval of four months, amidst civilian population and whole houses.

Whilst at Dainville training was carried on partly in the immediate neighbourhood and partly over the old trench line at Vailly, the very position first occupied by the Battalion when it came to France, where much practice in trench assaults in conjunction with tanks, &c., was obtained.

Six months had passed since the Battalion landed in France and there were only two officers who had served continuously without sickness or change during that period.

A Brigade Assault at Arms and Sports were organised on the Aerodrome at Wagnonlieu and in this the Rangers representatives met with conspicuous success, the First Prizes in Inter-Battalion Competitions for Platoon Drill, Physical Drill, Stretcher Bearers, Bayonet Assault, Pack Animals and Reveille Stakes, the Second Prizes for the best turned-out Platoon, Bombing, Yukon Pack Race, and the Third Prize for signalling, were won, being a total of six First and four Second out of fourteen offered. In the Athletic Sports the Battalion representatives scored 20 points against 12 points by the next best Battalion in order of merit. The final of the Officers' Tug-of-War between the Rangers and the Brigade Staff was an event which worked up much enthusiasm.

In order to thin out billets in Dainville, which were overcrowded, the Battalion was moved on the 11th August to Wagnonlieu, where one Company was located in each of four empty aeroplane hangars, and the officers in huts, and a week later to huts near Duisans, where it continued training, devoting special attention to intensive digging, with a view to getting underground in the shortest possible time. The period of rest, fitting and training which it was understood was preparatory to a hard time, came to an end on the night of the 24th August and the Battalion entrained at Arras.

About 8 a.m. the next day, the Battalion detrained at Proven near to Poperinghe, having at last reached the Ypres salient, the place where the soldier " saw life," and the furnace of war through which all units passed in the course of their service.

The Rangers were quartered in Brake Camp, situated in a wood three miles W.N.W. of Poperinghe. At this time the offensive known as the Passchendaele Push, and officially as the Third Battle of Ypres, was in full swing, and the salient bristled with military activity. Adjoining the camp was a large model of the battle area, from which model everyone was familiarised as far as possible with the ground over which the advance was to be made. After a few days the Battalion moved to another camp, " Brown Camp," about a mile further west. The battle surplus of six officers and 53 other ranks was detached and proceeded to Divisional Camp at Houtkerque. This was a routine precaution observed by all units before joining in the battle, its object being to preserve a sufficient nucleus to reconstruct the Battalion in the event of very heavy losses. Later the Battalion marched to Dembre Camp, situated between the two Chateaux of Trois Tours (Brielen) and Vlamertinghe.

On September 6th the Battalion advanced to shelters on the bank of the Yser Canal and furnished working parties for the various work forward of that line, and on the 9th relieved the 2/9th Londons in the front line, Headquarters being in St. Julien, and the line itself being, for the most part, on the ridge east of that town. It was a difficult relief, carried through in the midst of heavy shelling, including a considerable proportion of gas shells, the guides were none too good, and about thirty casualties resulted before the Rangers were settled in. Exceptional steadiness was shown in the trying circumstances by Captain Simms, who was blown up by a shell but carried on, Lieuts. Compton and Lees, Colour-Sergeant-Major Leman, who did fine work in clearing the wounded and reorganising No. 10 Platoon and the Company Headquarters under heavy fire, and Sergeant Owen.

The various Headquarters were situated in concrete shelters which had been captured from the Germans, these varied from the small " Mebus " which would hold four or five men, to an elaborate building known as " Hackney Villa " at St. Julien, consisting of about seven or eight chambers connected by a corridor, but all suffered from the disadvantage that having been made to withstand the English shells coming from the West they presented their weak side to the German Artillery from the East. Jutting into the Battalion's front line was a " Mebus " still held by the Germans from which they overlooked the British position and caused considerable annoyance. This had been the object of an unsuccessful attack by the 2/9th Londons on the night of 7–8th. It was then decided that it should be destroyed by heavy artillery fire and an attempt was made to do this on the 10th but without success. As a result of this, orders were then issued for the Rangers to capture it by a flank attack in a manner similar to that tried by the 9th, and this operation was intended to take place on the night of the 12th, but as a

result of reconnaissance made on the night of the
11th the attack was not carried out.

C Company had its Headquarters in "Janet
Farm," A Company, at "Springfield"; B and D
were in support in St. Julien.

On the 13th the Battalion was relieved by the
2/1st Londons and moved back to the Canal Back,
its casualties during this period being 14 killed and
70 wounded, including gas. The next day the
Battalion returned to Brake Camp.

On the night of 20th-21st the Rangers relieved the
2/11th Londons and some Companies of the 173rd
Brigade in the reserve trenches west of St. Julien,
the Battalion Headquarters being in "Cheddar
Villa." Whilst here, there were frequent S.O.S.
signals from the front line and consequent drum fire.
The line had been in a state of agitation for months,
and conditions were unsettled. The Battalion returned to the Canal Bank on the 23rd for two or
three days' special training and fitting preparatory
to participating in the attack, which was specially
rehearsed on ground near to "Gold Fish Chateau."

For some time the battalions of the 58th Division
had been successively engaged in a series of attacks
upon the German lines, and the Q.V.R. and the
Rangers were selected to represent the Division
in its last assault before being withdrawn for a rest.

The attack was planned for the morning of
September 26th, and it extended from Steenbeek
Stream, as its left flank, to the north-west for a
considerable distance. The left flank, from the
Steenbeek to the Hannebeek, was entrusted to the
175th Brigade, the starting line being about "Tirpitz
Farm," and the centre of the objective "Aviatik
Farm" with a possible advance as far as Boetleer.
The advance thus lay along a spur which to some
extent commanded the remainder of the line in
lower ground to the north-west.

The 175th Brigade was divided into two attacks,

the left portion to start at 5.30 a.m. under Lieut.-Colonel L. Parry, commanding the Q.V.R.'s, who had in his front line the four companies of his own battalion, and B Company of the Rangers (Captain Best), which Company was to revert to the command of Colonel Barham (Rangers), when all objectives had been taken ; this Company advanced with its left resting on the " Triangle "—Boetleer Road. C Company of the Rangers (Captain Hardy) connected from the right of B Company to the Hannebeek Stream, where it joined the left of another Division ; this Company was under O.C. Rangers, and was not to advance until 6.11 a.m., conforming to the main attack. A Company (Captain Simms) and D Company (Captain Waller) were in support about " Tirpitz Farm " under Colonel Barham's orders, for use only in case of counter-attacks ; the 10th Londons were in reserve, two companies in St. Julien, and two about " Cheddar Villa," the Brigade Headquarters being at Alberta. Headquarters of 9th and 12th were in separate " Mebus," not far from " Tirpitz Farm." Battalion Aid Posts were established by Captain Malkin for the Rangers near the " Cluster Houses " and by Q.V.R. at " Janet Farm."

At dark on the night of the 25th–26th the Rangers advanced from Canal Bank heavily laden with food and water for 48 hours, extra ammunition, bombs and spades, progress being hindered by shelling, and a burning ammunition dump near " Janet Farm " giving a bright light which would gladly have been dispensed with. However, the allotted positions were taken up well before the time for the assault.

At 5.30 a.m. B Company went " over the top " following a heavy artillery barrage and, overcoming the resistance of the enemy, it reached its ordered objectives with the loss of both of its subaltern officers, Lieuts. Rose and Hooper ; the latter was first wounded, but continued to lead his Platoon and set a fine example until killed. Several prisoners were captured.

Being unable to gain touch with any party of the Q.V.R. on his left, Captain Best withdrew some distance to line with a party of the Q.V.R. so as to secure his left flank.

At 6.11 a.m. C Company advanced, also preceded by a heavy artillery barrage ; it was magnificently led close up to the barrage by Captain Hardy, and after a sharp fight captured the German Mebus together with numerous prisoners. It secured and held all its objectives, the limit of its advance being the Mebus marked " Nile " upon the official map.

For their gallant leading Captain Hardy, who was wounded but remained on duty, received the D.S.O., the first one awarded to the Brigade, and Captain Best the Military Cross.

Sergeant Dunstone, who had received the M.M. for gallant conduct on a previous occasion, led his Platoon very well and although seriously wounded made a personal report at Battalion Headquarters on his way to the Aid Post.

Sergeant Kerry was awarded the M.M. for good leading ; he was wounded at close range.

Sergeant Miller was in command of the most advanced post held on " London Ridge " and held on splendidly throughout the operations.

Lance-Corporal Baker also gained the M.M. for special bravery in action with Captain Hardy in the assault.

The action of Rifleman Ratcliffe was exceptionally notable ; he found himself in charge of the remnants of No. 10 Platoon, being one of only four survivors, collected a few men who had strayed from another Battalion, including a Company Sergeant Major, a Sergeant and a Lewis Gun party, informed them that they were under his command, took up a position covering the flank of his Company and held it with the aid of a captured German machine gun. He was promoted to Corporal and awarded the M.M.

Lance-Corporal Aldridge, in charge of C Company signals, was in communication with Battalion Headquarters within fifteen minutes of his Company reaching its objective. He was awarded the M.M. but was mortally wounded on September 27th.

Prisoners, numbering 60 unwounded and 12 wounded, and six machine guns were captured.

At about noon a message was received at the Rangers Headquarters from the O.C. Q.V.R., to the effect that he was unable to ascertain the whereabouts of his battalion (except about two platoons) and at the same time heavy rifle fire came over the Headquarters position and the enemy infantry were seen to be advancing.

It being most urgent that immediate steps should be taken to secure the position and fill the gaps left by the missing Companies of the Q.V.R.'s, Colonel Barham immediately ordered D Company to secure the left flank and A to connect with the platoon of the 9th which was in touch with B; he also sent for the two companies of the 10th from Reserve at St. Julien. In carrying out this operation D Company lost Captain Waller wounded and Company Sergeant-Major Smith killed. The action of this Warrant Officer was very fine; he carried a wounded Corporal to a shell hole under heavy fire, then, Captain Waller being hit, he also placed him under cover and proceeded to inform Lieutenant Stone of his succession to the command of the Company. Whilst on this errand Company Sergeant-Major Smith lost his life.

Sergeant Land, the Captain of the Battalion football eleven, was shot through the wrist and thigh but continued to advance with his platoon.

Lieut. Griffith of A Company was killed. Captain Spencer, Adjutant, had three bullets through his clothes.

The 10th companies came up quickly and well,

and the first to arrive, Captain Bowran, was used to strengthen the front line, the other being kept in support.

The remaining two companies of the 10th had not been asked for but came up by Brigade order ; they were not required, the line being now established and strong enough, and they returned to the reserve position.

During the afternoon of the 26th a Brigade Order was received approving the action taken and appointing Colonel Barham to command all the troops of the 175th Brigade in the line.

Whilst these operations had been in progress on the left, Captain Best had beaten off a counter-attack upon his position, and the Division on the right having retired and left Captain Hardy unsupported, he had also retired to conform with the general line.

Between 7 and 8 p.m. the hill was heavily bombarded, especially about Headquarters, which were smothered in smoke and dirt.

During the 27th the position remained unchanged, some deployments of enemy infantry being broken up by artillery, machine gun and rifle fire, the front posts being in more or less continual engagement with the enemy. The troops on the right re-advanced to their allotted objectives, and C Company, conforming to their movements, re-occupied the Mebus " Nile."

Just after sunset, S.O.S. signals went up from the troops on the right, a great artillery battle developed in the valley to the north-west where the Germans seemed to be counter-attacking, but the failing light, obscured by smoke and dust, made it impossible to see what was happening ; the sight of bursting shells and rocket signals through the smoke was wonderful and the noise so great that the troops on the hill could hardly hear each other shout. No attack was made on the hill itself, but the line of communication to the rear was heavily shelled and, the signal lamp being useless because of the smoke and dust, a message was sent by dog runner to Brigade asking that the Artillery would quiet down as there was nothing doing on the Brigade front.

By about 2 a.m., on the 28th, the relieving battalion, 5th Gloucesters, had taken over the position, and the Rangers returned to Reigersberg Camp.

In these operations the losses were 3 Officers and 19 other ranks killed, 3 Officers (including Lieut. K. H. S. Clark, who remained on duty) and 90 other ranks wounded and 6 other ranks missing.

A complimentary message was received from the Corps Commander, and to commemorate the completion of the capture of the hill by the 58th Division, it was called London Ridge, and is so marked on the Official maps.

The total honours given to the Battalion for its action on this occasion were 1 D.S.O., 1 M.C., and 29 M.Ms.

Colonel Barham, who had in the meantime been mentioned in despatches, was created C.M.G. in the Honours List of the following New Year.

During the afternoon of the 28th, the Rangers, having cleaned up after the mud and dirt of the previous 48 hours, marched a short distance to Damore Camp, where a reinforcement of 120 N.C.Os. and men awaited them ; the Brigadier watched the defile and sent the following letter :—

HEADQUARTERS, 175TH INFANTRY BRIGADE,
September 28th, 1917.
My dear Barham,
    Will you please tell your Officers, N.C.Os.' and men how proud I am to have them under my command. They did simply splendidly throughout, and the way in which they marched out of camp to-day was beyond praise. I have never seen a cleaner, better turned out lot of men, which is perfectly marvellous considering that they only came out of the battle this morning.
    What you all want now is sleep.
Yours ever,
Hy. Jackson.

O 2

After one night spent at Brake Camp the Battalion entrained at Vlamertinghe for Audrique and marched from the latter station to billets in and about the village of Zutkerque. The entire division was billeted in the neighbourhood for a rest. Calais was not far distant, and parties were sent there by motor 'buses for a day's leave. A fortunate detachment of 2 Officers and 60 other ranks went to the Rest Camp at Boulogne for 14 days.

During the stay at Zutkerque, General Cotar took over the command of the Division.

The weather was very wet and the billets poor, conditions which somewhat spoilt the enjoyment of this period. The ground for training any larger number than a platoon had the disadvantage of being 6 miles distant from the billets, so that most of the available time and energy was spent in marching there and back. Practice in Attack by Battalion and Brigade was a frequent event.

Two good Officers, Lieuts. Hart and Warrener, left on transfer to the Indian Army; the latter had been Intelligence Officer since February.

The Rangers returned to the Ypres salient once more on October 21st, expecting to participate in the second series of assaults to be made by the 58th Division. The journey was made by rail to a station rejoicing in the suitable name of Houpout, from which a distance of 5 miles was covered by road to huts at St. Jan-ter-Biezen. The weather continued very wet and training was much hampered in consequence. The reserve, or battle nucleus, was again detached to a Divisional Camp at Houtkerque.

During a reconnaissance of the front line made by Company Commanders preparatory to the Battalion moving forward, Captain Simms was killed by a German shell. A loyal Ulster man who had been with the Rangers since 1915, his death was a great loss and was specially unfortunate just before going into the line.

On the 30th the Rangers moved by rail to Reigersberg Camp and marched thence to a group of Nissen huts dignified by the name of " Kempton Park," situated in the midst of heavy guns some distance to the east of the Yser Canal. At the same time the transport moved to Siege Camp, between Vlamertinghe and Kiverginghe. The usual complimentary message upon the condition in which the camp at St. Jan-ter-Biezen had been left followed the Battalion to the front.

On the 31st, A Company moved forward from " Kempton Park " to the Pheasant Trench, acting as support to another battalion of the Brigade which was holding the line.

The continuance of rainy weather, resulting in an awful state of mud and cold, had proved to be an insurmountable difficulty to troops detailed for attacks, and further attempt to advance on this portion of the Front was abandoned. It was difficult to move except on boarded paths and practically impossible to carry stretchers, so that the loss of wounded and the number of missing was very great.

On the evening of November 2nd the Rangers relieved the Q.V.R. in the outpost position in front of Poelcappelle. The ground about here showed only too much and too painful evidence of the losses suffered by those battalions which had been trying to advance over the mud and had been beaten by conditions of wet and cold greater than human strength could overcome. It was extremely swampy and muddy, movement was only possible with great care and difficulty, and the relief, although commenced at 5 p.m., was not completed until midnight. Some men of the 9th Londons were found buried up to their shoulders in the liquid mud and were dug out, as also were some Rangers during the two days' occupation.

The right of the outpost line rested on the Iakkerboterbeek Stream, the left on Requette Farm, and the Line was held by B, A and C Companies in that order from right to left, D Company being in support, two Platoons in the ruins of the Brewery in Poelcappelle, and the others at Gloster Farm. Headquarters were in a concrete Pill Box at the south end of Poelcappelle.

In consequence of the hard conditions of life in the front line, owing to the wet state of the ground and the absence of shelter, and the great difficulty of movement rendering it impossible to bring up supplies, troops at this time remained only two days in the front line and took with them all the supplies that they required for that period.

On the night of the 4th–5th, the 11th Londons took over the outposts and the Rangers returned to the Canal Bank, where the Quartermaster and his staff were waiting with hot tea, porridge, hot water for feet, clean socks, blankets, &c. Apart from the hard conditions due to the mud and cold, there were but few casualties during this tour of duty.

On the 6th, the Battalion marched to Brake Camp, the junction for all troops passing to and from this part of the line, where the transport rejoined and the routine of training was resumed. A reinforcement numbering 120 joined the Battalion; they were all men of good type, continuing the good fortune which the Battalion enjoyed in receiving, on the whole, drafts of men good in both physique and character.

On the 14th, the Battalion marched to tents at Penton Camp, north-east of Proven, where the ground was extremely muddy, as indeed were all camping grounds now.

Captain Spencer was transferred from the Adjutancy to take over command of D Company, in place of Captain Waller, wounded on September 26th, and Lieut. Lyall was appointed Adjutant.

On the 17th, the Battalion marched to Parroy Farm, about 1½ kilometres east-south-east of Elverdinghe, where it was quartered in canvas shelters and in dug-outs.

Colonel A. S. Barham, who had been in indifferent health for some time, left the Battalion, on recommendation for a Home Command, by reason of age, and the conditions of the approaching winter, and Lieut.-Col. Stephen Chart took over the command of the Battalion.

Colonel Barham had served continuously with the 2nd Battalion since its early training days at Crowborough, and that Battalion owed a great deal to his thoroughness and tremendous grasp of detail. Colonel Barham's one idea was to turn out a battalion trained to war to the utmost possible limit, and all ranks realised on his departure what it had meant to be under the guidance of so capable a commander during the difficult days of bringing into shape a new Battalion.

The march from Proven to Parroy Farm was a tiresome one as Brigade Orders had specified a definite route, which route was varied considerably by the instructions given by the traffic controllers, the march in consequence proving to be several more miles than anticipated. On arrival the Battalion (reinforced by one Company of the 2/9th Battalion placed under orders of the O.C. Rangers) took over the duty of providing working parties for the 173rd and 183rd Companies, R.E. Parties numbered from 500 to 600 daily, the work being to repair the damage to the roads near Langemarck, which had been caused by the previous day's shelling. On the 25th, the Battalion returned to Proven and reoccupied Penton Camp, the transport leaving the next day for Semingham.

On the 27th, the Battalion moved by train to a rest area, detraining at Wizernes Station and arriving at excellent billets in the villages of Semingham and

Affringues at about 11 p.m. An official intimation was received that the Division could expect a lengthy stay in this area, and preparations for refitting and training were pushed forward. During this period General Maxse (the Corps Commander) had arranged to hold a three days' conference attended by the Divisional and Brigade Staffs and the Battalion Commanders of the three Divisions in the XVIIIth Corps, which conference was broken up on the third day by the General, who informed the officers attending that he himself was moving south, and that the 58th Division would return at once to the Ypres sector. An excellent range in this neighbourhood had enabled the Battalion to fire the complete practices for classification.

On December 5th, the Transport left for Siege Camp, Elverdinghe, by march route, followed a day later by the Battalion, which entrained at Lumbies Station and detraining at Elverdinghe marched to Siege Camp, one of the many undesirable camps in this neighbourhood, a favourite bombing ground for enemy aeroplanes, and in wet weather a sea of mud.

Leaving the Transport to make itself as comfortable as circumstances would permit, the Battalion on the 8th relieved a Battalion of the North Staffordshire Regiment in a sector of the line immediately south of the sector previously occupied in front of Poelcappelle, D and C Companies (Captains Bell and Spencer) being in the front line with B Company (Captain Best) in close support at Winchester House, while A Company (Captain Foucar) remained upon the Canal Bank.

Battalion Headquarters was at a large Mebus named Alberta, which had been Brigade Headquarters during the attack on September 26th. The ground was exceedingly muddy and movement practically confined to duck board tracks. The sector was difficult to organise satisfactorily, Battalion

Headquarters being too far in rear while the Regimental Aid Post was in the front line itself, and had it been possible to move off the tracks the position of the R.A.P. would have been impossible.

The Rangers were relieved by the 2nd Inniskillings, the relief being completed at 8 p.m. and the Battalion rejoined A Company on the Canal Bank, the occupation of the sector for this short period being to assist a neighbouring division to effect a relief, the sector occupied by the Rangers not being upon our own Divisional front.

The Battalion relieved the 2/8th Battalion (Post Office Rifles), taking over the outpost line in front of Poelcappelle on the night 12th/13th, the disposition of the Companies being as follows : B Company at Tracas Farm and Gloster Farm on the right ; D Company at Noble's Farm and Helles House ; A Company in Poelcappelle and C Company in Pheasant Trench in rear of Poelcappelle. Battalion Headquarters occupied their old quarters at Norfolk House. The tour in the line was generally quiet, and although the state of the ground was still extremely bad, the conditions of the sector had been improved and the area considerably cleaned up.

Relieved by the 2/9th Battalion two days later, the Rangers moved back to the support position at Kempton Park, the relief being complete at 10.30 p.m., and two days later, the 175th Brigade being relieved by the 173rd Brigade, the Rangers handed over Kempton Park to the 2/2nd Battalion, and took over White Hill Camp at Elverdinghe, this camp being one of the best occupied by the Rangers while in this neighbourhood, the only drawback being the fact that three bombs were dropped in the centre of the camp during the Battalion's stay, a few casualties resulting.

On Christmas Eve the Rangers moved up by the light railway to Kempton Park and then took over the outpost line in front of Poelcappelle from the

2/2nd London. The conditions were a complete change from former tours in this sector; the ground was frozen hard and covered with snow and the visibility extraordinarily good, duck walk tracks were no longer necessary and patrols could move unrestricted by ground conditions. Whether the conditions made the enemy nervous of an attack or not, his artillery was exceptionally active during the tour and several casualties were experienced during the relief, A Company being the chief sufferers. The stretcher bearers of the 2/2nd London were of great assistance and, thanks very largely to their efforts, the casualties were quickly evacuated. Considerable work in the way of wiring was put in by the Rangers during this stay in the line, and on December 28th the Battalion handed over the front line to the 2/9th Battalion, returning once again to the support position at Kempton Park, being relieved by the 2/2nd London and returning to White Hill Camp by train on the morning of New Year's Day, 1918, where Christmas Day was officially celebrated on January 5th, arrangements having been made by Major Hardy for a special dinner followed by entertainments which appeared to be much appreciated.

Relieved by the 23rd Manchesters on January 7th, the Battalion moved by train to Proven and thence by light railway to good billets at Herzeele. The billets were somewhat crowded and very scattered, but in every respect a pleasant change from the conditions of the line in the salient or the camps of Elverdinghe. Training was carried on daily and a Brigade Parade was held on January 12th, when Lieut.-Gen. Jacobs, the Corps Commander, presented ribbons to those Officers and men of the Brigade who had gained honours in the recent fighting.

The Rangers entrained on the 20th, and moved by light railway to Proven, arriving at 9 p.m., and at 12.30 a.m. entrained again, arriving at Villers Bretonneux at 2 p.m. on January 21st, marching to La Neuville, where billets were obtained and where the Battalion carried on training pending the amalgamation with the 1st Battalion. On January 30th Major Worthington with 8 officers and 105 other ranks from the 1st Battalion arrived, and the Battalion became officially the 12th London Regiment, Colonel Bayliffe taking over the command upon his return from leave. During the training at La Neuville the Officers of the Brigade carried out a tactical scheme under the Divisional-General upon the identical ground from which the Rangers were to commence their advance the following August, with the victorious 4th Army of General Rawlinson, and the knowledge gained of the ground was to prove its value when this time arrived.

PART FOUR.
The Amalgamated Battalion.

CHAPTER I.

FEBRUARY, 1918, TO JULY 31ST, 1918.

DURING the first ten days of February 1918, the Battalion remained at Corbie. The time was spent in training and a good deal of sport was also enjoyed. The Battalion then entrained at Corbie Station and detrained at Apilly late at night. Hot food and tea were served in the growing darkness—the Battalion being congregated in an open, water-logged field. They then embussed and were conveyed to a camp consisting of large Adrian huts in a wood. D Company went straight forward to Fort Liez; the next day the remainder of the Battalion proceeded by march route to the Bois de Vieuille — where they came into reserve — being located in Adrian huts at the bottom of the reverse slope of a hill, amidst an extent of shrubbery.

For about a fortnight the Battalion remained in reserve. Large parties were sent forward nightly to dig an alternative line of trenches—behind the front line. This work was carried out without casualties. Reconnaisance of the forward area was also undertaken by all. The Battalion then relieved the 10th London in the line. The front occupied was about a mile in length—and was only held by posts, A Company and Battalion Headquarters were in Fort Nendeuil—the other Companies forward with posts on the St. Quentin Canal. Generally the period was quiet and passed without incident.

Towards the end of February the Brigade was relieved by the 18th Division and moved further south. The Battalion marched by day to Tergnier and C Company, coming into view of the Boche whilst crossing a sky line, were shelled, but only suffered a few casualties—plus a broken kitchen.

One night the Battalion lodged in Tergnier,

where the houses, though broken, were quite habit able, and another night rested at the Glass Factory in Chauny Sud. After the Battalion moved out, the Transport Lines and Quartermaster's Stores remained in the Factory until they had to be suddenly evacuated on the night of March 22nd. This Glass Factory was a very large building with numerous outbuildings, also very large. While damaged it was in much better repair than a large portion of the town.

The Brigade held the line just south of the River Oise. The front line, consisting of posts, was established in the Coucy Forest—which was very thick. The French had erected large, strong belts of wire entanglements in front—which took an hour or more for our own scouting parties to pass through. Comfortable dug-outs were found throughout the wood. Battalion Headquarters were at La Fortelle.

The Battalion had generally two Companies in the Line and two at Sinceny, where they were billeted in houses which were in a fair state of repair. For the first part of March everything was very comfortable and quiet.

Then the enemy attacked on the morning of March 21st. The south side of the Oise held by 175th Brigade was not menaced. Considerable shelling took place on the Buttes de Rouy and the village was filled with gas as also parts of the Forest—but no infantry action developed, though an anxious guard was kept for several days. Transport lines had to evacuate Chauny hurriedly, and moved to Manicamp, and on the following day to Besmé, where they remained until the Battalion left the area.

The 173rd Brigade—on the north side of the Oise—and the divisions further north—widely strung out over a long line, without adequate forces to develop defence in depth, were overwhelmed by the

Boche rush. The enemy swept down the salient, but made no attempt to cross the Oise. Simency became front line, and was held by a composite force of stragglers from the 18th Division and 173rd Brigade. Captain Bell and Major Worthington were in command. Further down the Oise a Middlesex Battalion under Lieut.-Colonel S. Chart were brought into the line, extending the flank.

No withdrawal or change in the general position south of the Oise took place during the next week. Higher Command then decided to withdraw from the front edge of the forest. The Battalion withdrew, leaving six platoons to hold our original posts. These were left under the charge of Captain Spencer at the old Battalion Headquarters, and 2nd Lieut. Gurton in the front posts. Although parties of Boche managed to penetrate our wire and roamed about in the forest, this rearguard party was not seriously interfered with, and eventually the whole Battalion was withdrawn to positions around Bac d'Arlingcourt facing the Oise. These were held without serious incident until the whole Brigade was relieved by the French.

After two days' march the Battalion entrained at Villers Cotteret.

The journey occupied twelve hours, and during this time the train came under shell fire near Boves. Detrainment took place at Longeaux, just east and in front of Amiens. The Transport and Stores proceeded to the outskirts of Amiens where they remained for the next six weeks. The journey to the line was from 10 to 12 miles nightly.

The Battalion moved straight forward into a little wood just to the rear of the Bois de Gentelles. On the same night they took up positions in reserve in front of Gentelles village, and the Bois de Gentelles. The aid post was in a cellar in the village itself—the majority of the troops were in trenches and improvised shelters. The weather was bad. The whole of the positions were amongst, or near, our batteries, and were constantly subjected to shelling, although casualties were not heavy.

After a week in this position the Battalion went into the line at Villers Bretonneux. This large village was in a fair state of repair, but constantly shelled with gas. The majority of the Battalion were in trenches—or behind embankments in front of the village. The ground was very flat and open around and in front, and the Boche machine gunners were, as usual, very alert.

Large stores of food, principally tinned, and wine were found in the cellars, and the troops lived well.

After a tour of eight days the Battalion were withdrawn. Coming through Bois d'Abbé, one platoon of B Company was practically wiped out by one shell. The next few days were spent refitting in Glissy—where quarters were found in the houses. A few inhabitants still remained in this village, which was not much shelled. The Battalion then returned to the positions in front of Gentelles. Lieut.-Colonel Bayliffe went on leave and did not again return to the Battalion.

Here the Battalion again experienced a large amount of gas-shelling and one large gas shell exploded on the top of the bank where Battalion Headquarters was situated. The gas did not disseminate for some time, and when all danger was thought to be over a puff of wind blew the gas out of the hole and down the slope. All officers and a large number of signallers and mess staff became casualties—many of whom died at a later date. The casualties included Major Worthington (in command) and Captain Copeland, the Adjutant. Major Cawston was sent to take command. 2nd Lieut. Beer acted as Adjutant—until wounded—when Captain Spencer took over the duties.

The Boche then launched his big attack on Amiens with tanks. The 173rd Brigade were in the line,

P

with the French on the right. The attack was stopped. The Battalion were in reserve, but in the afternoon were pushed forward to make a counter-attack, where a Battalion of the Fusiliers had been obliged to withdraw. The counter-attack was successful, although heavy casualties were experienced from shell fire and enemy machine guns. No further Boche attack took place. One Boche tank penetrated some distance behind our front line, but was unsupported and withdrew.

The following night the Battalion were relieved by the French and moved a little south into the Dumart Valley, where they remained 24 hours. During the whole of this period the valley was very heavily shelled. At night they were relieved by the French and withdrew to a small wood south of Glissy. Next day they embussed at Amiens and were taken back to Bussus.

Bussus was a delightful village, some 15 miles from Abbeville. Quarters were excellent, the countryside was untouched, and there was no night bombing. Training and inspections, with some football competitions, occupied the time.

After a week here the Battalion again embussed and were taken to the Bois Robert behind Baizieux. There they remained a day and then marched to Warloy, where they came into reserve. Lieut.-Col. S. Chart rejoined the Battalion here on May 9th, and assumed command. Major Cawston returned to the 10th Londons.

After a week the Battalion were moved into immediate support in the Maze. This consisted of a series of trenches, so called because of their complicated appearance from air photos. The front line ran in front of Albert. Four days were spent in the Maze and the Battalion then took over the front line.

During the next month the Battalion remained in the vicinity of Albert, periods in the front line alternating with periods spent in immediate support and in reserve in tented camps in woods further back. The periods in the line were generally quiet. Patrols were active—a large amount of constructional work was done—and a certain amount of shelling experienced. The whole front line was kept constantly on the *qui vive* by reason of the strong expectation of a further Boche attack, which never materialised. Weather was generally better, the trenches were rather shallow, and generally the only shelter was in improvised undercuts in the sides. Dugouts were available for Battalion Headquarters. In the second week in June the Battalion were withdrawn. A week was spent in Molliens-au-Bois under canvas, and the Battalion then went back by 'bus to Pissy, where they spent a glorious week. Under the direction of 2nd Lieuts. Williams and Gurton sports were arranged nightly—the quarters were good—and the training was not too strenuous.

The return to the line was again by 'bus. A few days were spent in Molliens-au-Bois, and thence the Battalion proceeded by march to Round Wood, near Baizieux. For the remainder of the month and the first three weeks in July the usual trench life and routine were followed. Periods of six days were spent in the line, in immediate support and in reserve. Lieut.-Colonel Chart spent a fortnight of this period in charge of the 173rd Brigade, and the Battalion was left in charge of Major E. C. Fortescue of the Oxford and Bucks Light Infantry. The front line was in a poor condition although the support lines were better and more shelters were available. Boche shelling and trench mortaring was active and a number of casualties were caused. The periods in reserve were spent under canvas near Round Wood.

CHAPTER II.

AUGUST 1st to 10th, 1918.

IN the first week in August the Rangers were in the front line immediately opposite to Morlancourt, a battalion of the 47th Division being on the left, and an American battalion, in the line for the first time, on the right, beyond them being the Australian Corps. On August 1st the Boche outpost line was about 200 yards from our line but owing to the configuration of the ground it was not visible from our lines. On August 4th, certain indications denoting intentions of a withdrawal seemed apparent, and were reported to Brigade and Division who were very sceptical about it. To clear up the matter daylight patrols were sent out by Colonel Chart under Lieut. Cook and Sergeant Mason, and eventually the Rangers reported the withdrawal of the enemy to the other side of the River Ancre and the occupation of the enemy's front lines by the Battalion. An unfortunate incident occurred, our daylight patrols being fired at by the neighbouring Division and Lieut. Cook wounded in the face and leg. During the day and night patrols were pushed forward and outposts established on the river line, which were handed over to the 12th Division, who relieved us the following night. The Rangers proceeded by 'bus to Vignacourt.

The Battalion was billeted at Vignacourt. The Division had been in the line for 42 days and expected to go out to rest. During the two days at Vignacourt the C.O. was informed that the role of the Division was to form a defensive flank to the Main Fourth Army Advance.

On the night of August 7th–8th the Rangers embussed at Vignacourt for Franvilliers, from which point the Battalion marched to bivouac in the Bois

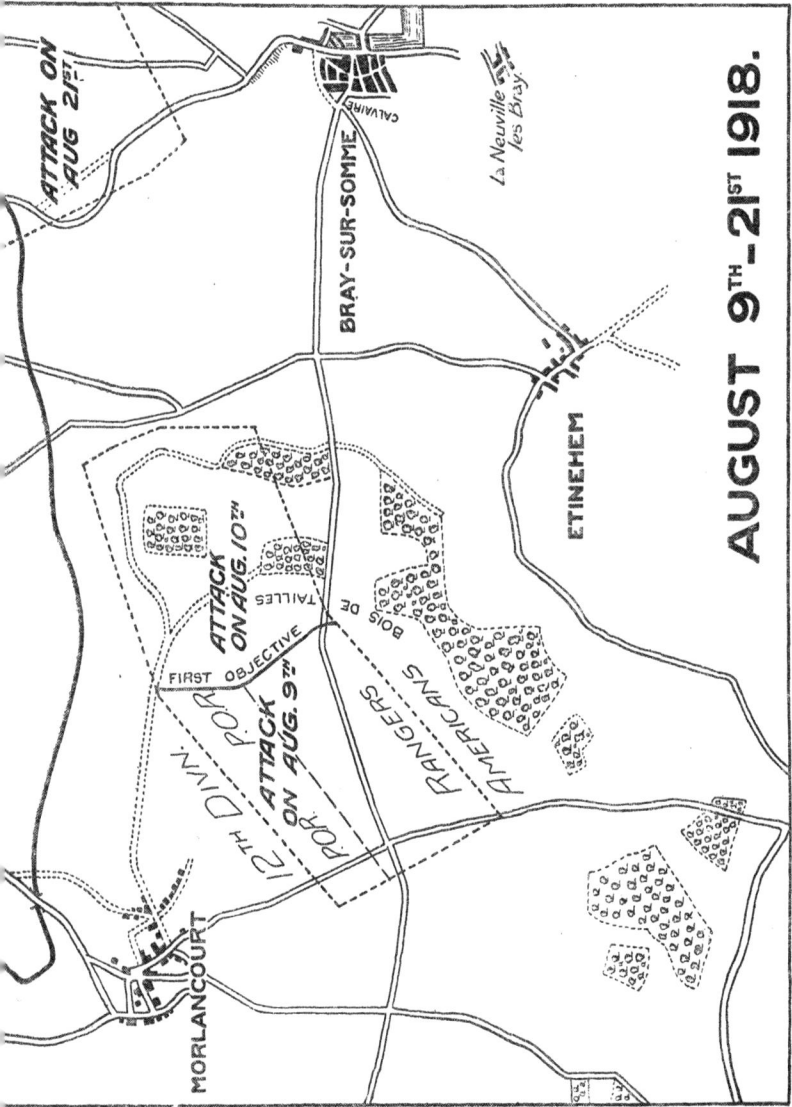

[To face page 228.

AUGUST 9TH–21ST 1918.

BRAY-SUR-SOMME

CALVAIRE

La Neuville les Bray

ETINEHEM

ATTACK ON AUG. 21ST

ATTACK ON AUG. 10TH

FIRST OBJECTIVE

12TH DIVN PL

BOIS DE TAILLES

RANGERS

AMERICANS

ATTACK ON AUG. 9TH

MORLANCOURT

d'Escardonneuse where with the Q.V.R. we became the Corps Reserve (the III Corps consisted of the 12th, 18th and 58th Divisions).

At 4.20 a.m. the attack commenced—the 174th Brigade advancing to the first objective, where after an hour's halt the 173rd Brigade were to pass through them to the final objective. At 12 noon we received orders to stand to and move to Bonnay Church, where guides would meet us with orders. At 1 o'clock we were on the move following the Q.V.R. and on the way up we gathered the news that the 174th Brigade had been very successful and that the Divisional Cage had received nearly 1,000 prisoners. (N.B.—The 2–10th Battalion had taken part in the attack of the 174th Brigade.) We were also informed that the 173rd Brigade had captured all objectives, which information was not reliable. On meeting the guide at Bonnay Church we were ordered to proceed to Ballarat Trench, where we became Divisional Reserve to the 18th Division. We remained at Ballarat Trench until 10 o'clock that night, when the C.O. was ordered to proceed to the Headquarters of the 35th Brigade for instructions. On arrival it was evident that the Staff did not know the position in front and instructions were given for the Battalion to proceed to the head of the valley, and to fill up any gap existing in the front line. The front line given proved to be entirely erroneous, the actual line running round the east and north of the Bois Malard. The C.O. was ordered to report to the 7th Sussex to obtain information and a guide was furnished by the Brigade to show these Headquarters.

The Battalion moved off by companies with orders to assemble at the head of the valley. The night was very dark and without guides it was doubted if they would reach the rendezvous by daylight. The C.O. and the Adjutant proceeded with the guide and, after wandering about for several hours the guide confessed himself hopelessly lost. At daybreak they found ourselves close to the rendezvous, the whole of the Battalion having arrived in close proximity. It was then discovered that the 7th Sussex had moved their Headquarters and no one knew where to locate them. We, however, got into touch with the 6th, 7th, 8th, and 9th London Battalions, from whom we heard that orders had been issued for us to attack at 5.30 a.m. with tanks. A reconnaissance of the line was made, with the result that the C.O. was satisfied that the line was complete and that no gaps existed, and we remained in the valley during the early part .of the day. Meanwhile we were again in touch with the 175th Brigade, under whose orders we came again. During the preceding 24 hours we had been in all three Divisions at different times.

At 5 p.m. Captain Swift, Brigade Intelligence Officer, brought a map, together with orders to attack, Zero hour being 5.30 p.m. The attack was to be made by the 131st American Regiment on the right, the 175th Brigade in the centre, and a Brigade of the 12th Division on the left. On our Brigade Sector the 12th Battalion was on the right, the 8th (P.O.R.) on the left, the 5th Royal Berks in support and the Q.V.R. in reserve. Five tanks were to assist and a creeping artillery barrage was to be provided. Company Commanders were hurriedly summoned, and orders for attack given verbally, and in a quarter of an hour we were on the move. Great credit must be given to the Company Commanders for their quickness in getting off the mark. The C.O. had received verbal communications that both the Americans and the 12th Division were likely to be late, in which case the 175th Brigade were not to wait but to press on. The advance was to be in line of sections in file preceded by an extended screen, B and D Companies forming the front line, supported by C and A. The

Battalion shook out into columns in excellent style and, despite the lateness of the orders, crossed the zero line only about eight minutes late. This eight minutes, however, had meant that the Boche barrage had come down and we had to go through it. The Battalion pressed on and touch with the P.O.R. was obtained and kept throughout, and very soon after our start the Americans were up and in line with us. For the first 500 yards the machine guns of the enemy caused us considerable trouble, but reports soon came in that progress was excellent and batches of prisoners began coming down. Lieutenant Duckett (Battalion Intelligence Officer) brought news that our objective was secured and consolidation was proceeding. On our left, however, the P.O.R. were reduced to about 60 of all ranks, and none of the 12th Division was seen, the left flank being completely in the air. On the right the Americans were very disorganised and both our flanks seemed insecure. The Brigade Major promised to send up the Q.V.R. to support us and form a defensive flank on the right, while the 5th Berks were to come up on the left to fill up the gap between the 12th Division and the P.O.R.

During the night these arrangements were carried out, and consolidation and re-organisation was satisfactory, and at daybreak patrols were pushed forward to locate the new Boche position. Meanwhile the Q.V.R. were ordered to endeavour to push forward of the wood in front of us. This was successfully done, and we were ordered to take over a portion of this line, which we held until the night of the 12th–13th August when we were relieved by the 142nd Brigade and moved back to the Bois d'Escardonneuse. Our casualties during the operations amounted to two officers killed and five officers wounded and ten other ranks killed and 146 wounded.

CHAPTER III.

AUGUST 14TH, 1918, TO SEPTEMBER 20TH, 1918.

THE Rangers on the 14th, on relief by a Battalion of the 47th Division, returned to bivouac in the Bois d'Escardonneuse, again becoming Corps Reserve, and on the morning of their arrival were visited by General Ramsay (Divisional Commander), who expressed himself as delighted with the Battalion's share in the successful advance of the preceding days, and requested the C.O. to make this known to all ranks. A special order was also issued by Lieut.-Colonel Chart congratulating the transport upon their share in the operations. The Battalion was also honoured by a visit from their former Brigadier-General, General H. C. Jackson (at that time commanding the 50th Division), who was exceedingly complimentary as to the work of the Rangers.

A very useful draft of 250 (mostly K.R.R. men) arrived to make good the recent losses in the ranks, and Captain Cubitt of the 4th Suffolks joined the Battalion as second in command *vice* Major Fortescue, who left to take up duties as a special Court-Martial officer. During this stay Colonel Chart proceeded to England on 14 days' leave, Major Sampson of the Q.V.R. being sent to take command during his absence.

Information was received on the 22nd that the enemy were delivering a strong counter-attack upon the position handed over by us to the 47th Division, and in consequence the Rangers were ordered to stand to and at midnight were moved up to Tailles Wood, and on the night of the 23rd-24th the Brigade was attached to the 47th Division, and at 1 a.m. the Rangers moved to an assembly position and attacked the enemy in conjunction with the 142nd Brigade, capturing their objective after a sharp tussle and sending at least 100 prisoners to the rear for incarceration, the casualties in the Battalion being unfortunately very heavy.

On the 25th, Orders were received for a further advance and dawn found the Battalion prepared to move. Preceded by a terrific artillery barrage an advance to Trigger Wood was made, no resistance being encountered, and at nightfall the 7th Battalion London Regiment took over the front line.

On the 28th, the Rangers moved to Bronfay Farm, acting as support to the 173rd and 174th Brigades, who were carrying on the advance, the enemy fighting rearguard actions as they retreated, and on the following day the Rangers relieved the 6th London and pushed forward as far as Marrieres Wood, where the enemy machine guns were found to be strongly posted, and it was deemed advisable to delay any further attempt to advance until a properly organised attack could be made. The Rangers, therefore, contented themselves with occupying a defensive position, and at 1 a.m. on the morning of the 31st the 174th Brigade passed through in the darkness and cleared the wood, the Rangers moving back to Maricourt as Divisional Reserve.

During the period, from August 22nd to August 31st, the Battalion had lost 4 officers killed (Lieuts. Bennett, Johnson, Barton and Sullivan), 6 officers wounded (Lieuts. Glendenning, Garnham, Grosvenor, Veitch, Williams and Dickens), 39 other ranks killed, 210 wounded and 18 missing. On September 1st, Major Sampson returned to his own unit, and Captain Cubitt commanded the Rangers until the return of Colonel Chart on September 8th.

On September 6th, the Battalion moved up in 'buses and relieved a Battalion of the 47th Division near Ainecourt l'Abbé and the following morning an advance of 7,800 yards was made by the 175th Brigade, the Rangers acting as supports to the

9th and 10th Battalions, both of whom were in contact with the enemy rearguards throughout the advance, and on September 8th the Brigade returned to Divisional Reserve, the Battalion moving to bivouac at Gouvencourt.

Since the first great advance commenced upon August 8th the resistance put up by the enemy had gradually weakened, but evidence was apparent that a more vigorous defence would be forthcoming and the operations from this date until the withdrawal of the 58th Division from the Fourth Army area were chiefly undertaken against the famous German Alpine Corps.

At dawn on the 10th, the 173rd Brigade, assisted by the 8th Battalion (Post Office Rifles) attacked the villages of Epehy and Peizieres, meeting with a stiff resistance, and during the morning the Rangers found themselves placed at the disposal of Brigadier-General Corkran, commanding the 173rd Brigade, to be used for supporting, re-inforcing or relieving as thought desirable. The C.O., accompanied by Lieut. Duckett (Intelligence Officer), accordingly went forward to the Headquarters of Lieut.-Colonel Walsh, commanding the 2/2nd London, to obtain news of the attack, and from the information obtainable it was evident that the attack had not met with success. At 9 p.m. orders were received from the 173rd Brigade that the Rangers would take over the front line, relieving all units of the 173rd Brigade including the Post Office Rifles attached. The relief was a difficult one, as reliable information as to the positions held by the troops who had taken part in the attack was not obtainable, but, thanks largely to the exertions of Lieut.-Colonel Walsh and the excellent arrangements made by him to render the task as easy as possible, the relief was completed at 2.30 a.m., and the Rangers could report that a fairly satisfactory line was held. During the progress of the relief orders were received for a further attack to commence at 3 a.m., in order to assist the Division on our immediate left. At the time of the receipt of these orders the chance of a successful relief by the zero hour appeared to be very remote, and the position being represented to the Brigade the order was cancelled. The Rangers had the misfortune to lose Lieut. Gillespie during the relief, this officer walking into a post occupied by the enemy owing to the darkness, and in the fight resulting being killed.

The position occupied by the Battalion was on the outskirts of the villages of Epehy and Peizieres and consisted of an old trench line originally constructed to face the reverse way for the defence of the village, and an isolated post (named Tottenham Post) not visible from the trench line, the post being over the reverse slope of the hill and actually connected with the village itself, which was strongly held by the German Alpine Corps. This post was occupied by D Company under Captain Anderson, whose position was at the best a very unenviable one, no communication being possible by daylight, although Lieut. Williams succeeded on one occasion in reaching it. Representations were made for permission to withdraw from Tottenham Post, and these representations were strongly supported by the Brigadier (Brig.-General Cobham) who realised the risk entailed by attempting to hold an advanced position such as this, but the Corps, anxious to utilise it upon the attack being resumed, declined to acquiesce. The Battalion was disposed with A Company (Captain Peabody) and C Company (Captain Nunn) occupying the front trench system, with two platoons in the front line and two in support, D Company (Captain Anderson) in the advanced post some 200 to 300 yards in advance and entirely isolated, and B Company (Captain Loveless) in Battalion support in rear of A and C, and on 11th September the 9th and 10th Battalions took over a portion of the front line, and the Rangers came again under the orders of the 175th Brigade.

At 9 a.m. on the 12th news was received at Battalion Headquarters that the enemy were bombarding our front line and the parapet was being swept by machine gun fire ; at the same time our advanced post was bombarded, the bombardment in this case being followed up by an infantry attack on the post. A box barrage was put down by the enemy upon three sides of the post and after a stout resistance the garrison were driven out, captured or killed. Sergeant Moore with about thirty men fought their way back to the Battalion, while Captain Anderson, Lieut. K. S. Clarke, and Lieut. A. A. Baker were captured and Lieut. Beeching killed. An attempt to reach the position by a party led by Lieut. Sievwright proved unsuccessful, the enemy machine guns being too strongly posted. It is only fair to the officers and men concerned to state that the position in which by force of circumstances they were placed was an impossible one to hold against a determined attack, and the defence put up against overwhelming odds was a credit to the Rangers.

The Battalion was relieved by a Battalion of the 174th Brigade and moved back to Divisional Reserve.

After a turn in Divisional Reserve the Rangers again took over the front, being relieved in due course by the 173rd Brigade.

At 2.30 p.m. on September 20th orders were received from Brigade Headquarters that the commanding officers of the Rangers and the 2/10th Battalion would at once reconnoitre the front, paying especial attention to Kildare Trench (the enemy front line opposite to the 173rd Brigade front) and would meet the Brigadier at the Brigade Headquarters in the line at 6 p.m. Lieut.-Colonel Chart, accompanied by Lieut. Duckett (Intelligence Officer), accordingly proceeded via Lieut.-Colonel Walsh's headquarters to the front line, whence a view of the ground in front of the position could be obtained, and at 6 p.m. a conference took place at Brigade Headquarters, and preliminary orders were received for an attack to take place the following morning, zero being fixed for 5.30 a.m. The attack was to be in co-operation with the 1st Queens on the left and the 7th Norfolks on the right. The final objective of the 175th Brigade was given as the trench system known as Dados Loop, Kildare Post, and Kildare Avenue. The attack was to be carried out by the 2/10th Battalion leading, with an objective including the trench system mentioned, followed by the Rangers, whose instructions were to form a defensive flank in Kildare Avenue, to garrison Kildare Lane, and to form defensive posts in rear of the 10th, strong enough to resist counter-attacks. The operations were not easy and, with orders issued so late, it was not possible for Company or Platoon Commanders to obtain any first-hand knowledge of the ground over which the attack would take place, and, to add to the difficulty of keeping accurate direction, the Battalion was obliged to form up behind two semi-circular trench lines which would naturally tend to divert the attackers from their true line of direction. An attempt was made to obtain permission to form up in front of these trenches, but the difficulty of altering the artillery barrage table so late in the day proved insurmountable. Orders were issued to the Company Commanders, and a conference of all Officers and Platoon Sergeants held, to explain all necessary details and to give them the benefit of such information as had been obtained in the reconnaissance made by the Commanding Officer and Lieut. Duckett. The Battalion then moved up to the old front line, with which it was well acquainted, and after a few hours' rest moved up to the assembly position to await zero hour.

During the stay at the old front line barrage maps and additional wire cutters were supplied by the Brigade, these reaching the Rangers at 1 a.m. The Platoons were considerably hampered on the way up to the place of assembly by the fact that the neighbouring division were carrying out an inter-Brigade relief, and, the night being very dark, several Platoons crossed and recrossed our line of advance, while in addition the enemy shelled the area considerably and the 2/10th Battalion suffered a number of casualties *en route*, a fact which had unfortunate results in the morning, in some cases both Platoon Officer and Platoon Sergeant becoming casualties.

At 5.15 a.m. the Rangers were on the position of Assembly waiting the zero hour, Battalion Headquarters being in the support trenches. At 5.30 a.m. the advance commenced, and almost immediately the enemy barrage came down, a short distance in front of our leading line. Casualties were frequent and upon reaching No Man's Land the Rangers encountered heavy machine-gun fire from both flanks and it was evident that the task was a heavy one. Every endeavour to push forward was made, but in face of the intense machine-gun fire which our artillery was not successful in subduing, it was impossible to reach the objectives specified. The 2/10th had suffered very heavy casualties, especially among officers and N.C.O.'s, and the remainder of that Battalion had become merged in the Rangers. The attacks made by the troops on our flanks had been less successful than ours and in consequence both flanks were exposed. Messages were received from the leading Companies showing clearly that to reach our final objective would be at such a loss that the position if reached could not be maintained, and Captain Nunn and Captain Peabody on the left decided to hold on to the portion of Kildare Avenue which had been secured, while on the right flank Captain Loveless and Captain Sievwright were holding a ditch line about halfway to the objective.

A reconnaisance was made at great personal risk by Lieutenant Duckett (Battalion Intelligence Officer) and a clear statement of the position forwarded to Brigade, who were informed that a further advance could not be expected and that the Rangers intended to hold and consolidate the positions obtained.

Later in the day arrangements were made for a portion of D Company (Captain Sievwright) to connect up the position held by A and C Companies with that held by the remnants of B and D Companies. A visit from the Brigade Major (Captain Ashmead-Bartlett) brought with it a proposal to renew the attack by means of a bombing party from the 2/10th, but the suggestion was impracticable and was abandoned, and at dusk a working party of the 9th Battalion came to our assistance and completed our consolidation. Our casualties during the day were very heavy, and throughout the night the stretcher bearers worked unceasingly, with the result that by daybreak nearly all casualties were accounted for. Every Sergeant, with one exception, had been hit, and nearly every Officer (including Captain Loveless, whose services during his short period with the Battalion had been extremely valuable).

The attack was resumed the next day by the Q.V.R., assisted by a Company of the 4th Suffolks, and the Dados Loop system was successfully occupied, and on the night of September 23rd-24th orders were received for the relief of the 58th Division, the 175th Brigade being relieved by the 36th Brigade, the Rangers' trenches being taken over by the 5th Royal Berkshires. For the purposes of the relief the 2/10th London (now very much reduced in numbers) were placed under the command of the O.C. Rangers, and after a long and wearisome trudge through the darkness the " embussing " point at Villers Faucon was reached, and, after a hot meal from the cookers, the Battalion moved by 'bus to Trones Wood where Captain Cubitt had prepared accommodation. During this tour in the line Captain Wyatt and Captain Bell had rejoined and were awaiting the Battalion at Trones Wood, Captain Wyatt taking over the command of A Company and Captain Bell the command of D Company. A short stay of two days at Trones Wood concluded the Rangers' service with the 3rd Corps and the Fourth Army, and the Battalion moved to the newly constructed railway station near Derna-court (situated in what had been the No Man's Land of the sector in front of Albert where so many months had been spent earlier in the year). From here the Rangers entrained for the Lens Sector and joined the 8th Corps under General Hunter Weston, moving to an area in all respects the opposite of that from whence the Battalion had come.

Instead of the disorganised back areas consequent on the rapid retreat of March and April, 1918, followed by the equally rapid advance commencing in August and carried on continuously through September, the Rangers found themselves in a district which had remained comparatively quiet for a considerable period, with the back areas wonderfully organised, the whole fitted with beautifully painted notice boards and everything in that state of polish which is to be found when hard fighting is not the main idea in the minds of everyone, and it was generally felt that a haven of rest had been reached.

CHAPTER IV.

OCTOBER, 1918.

DURING the first few days of October the Battalion remained in reserve near Lievin. For two days A Company (Captain Wyatt) were loaned to the battalion on our right—a battalion of K.R.R. (20th Division)—but were only used as a reserve and not called upon. On October 5th the Battalion—less A Company—spent the day in Lens clearing the débris from the main roads and thoroughfares. Otherwise the Battalion continued training. A very convenient short rifle range was found in a big disused chalk quarry, and a large amount of practice was done. Competitions were held between Company teams of eight aside. The winners were Headquarters Company team of Runners and Signallers, and the prize for marksmanship gained by Runner Kitchen of Headquarters Company.

On the night of October 8th–9th the Brigade relieved the 174th Brigade in the line—just in front of Annay—the 12th Londons relieving the 6th Londons. The night was very dark and, owing to the recent retirement of the Boche from this region, roads and tracks were in a very bad state and there was only one passable. There was a long trudge—much confusion with the 10th London and Artillery Transport, but eventually relief was completed.

The front line ran along a deep railway cutting and B and D Companies were posted in this cutting. A little further back there was a big railway embankment, where Battalion Headquarters was located in a tunnel. A and C Companies were in the remains of coke ovens and village and trenches at hand.

Constant patrolling was ordered, as the Boche was expected to withdraw from the Annay switch line opposite. A Company was moved up to assist in the work.

Night patrols on the nights 8th–9th, 9th–10th, and 10th–11th found the enemy still in occupation, but a daylight patrol on the afternoon of the 11th found the trenches empty. While watching the progress of the patrol from our front line Lieut.-Colonel S. Chart was hit in the leg by a machine gun bullet from one of the flanks and had to be evacuated, and Captain Wyatt returned to Battalion Headquarters to take over until at 7 a.m. on the morning of the 12th Lieut.-Colonel A. D. Dervishe-Jones, D.S.O., M.C., arrived and took over command.

In the night A Company had moved forward and occupied the enemy trench system 1,000 yards in front, with B Company in support halfway across the old No Man's Land, and C and D Company in the cutting.

CHAPTER V.

OCTOBER 12TH, 1918, TO THE ARMISTICE.

IN the afternoon A Company made a further advance of 1,000 yards in conjunction with the 10th Battalion, who advanced through the village of Annay on their left, while B Company moved into the position vacated by A Company. That night the Battalion was relieved by K.O.S.B., and moved back to Cité Ste. Auguste, whence it proceeded the next morning further south to billets in Fouquieres. Here the same night Lieut.-Colonel A. Grover, D.S.O., M.C., 1st Bedfordshire Regiment, took command, exchanging with Colonel Dervishe-Jones, who proceeded to the 8th Battalion. Here a few days were spent in resting and cleaning up, until a move forward to billets in Courrieres was made. On the 17th the enemy started a retirement, closely followed by 9th Battalion, who reached Moncheaux without establishing touch. After a long and somewhat wearisome march through Ostricourt and Le Foret the Battalion relieved the 9th Battalion at Moncheaux from whence, early the next morning, the advance was continued until touch was established with the enemy about mid-day on a line in front of Point de Breuvy and an outpost line was established. Considerable shelling and machine gun fire was experienced, and some casualties were caused. The enemy retired at dawn, and the 10th Battalion marched through our line to continue the advance. Billets were found this night in La Planque, and the following in Haut Hameau, in both of which places the civil inhabitants, set free by the enemy retirement, welcomed the British troops with utmost cordiality and warmth. On the following day the Battalion in its turn took up the advance as Advance Guard, passing through

Rumegies. Shortly after both the Companies in the advance, B on the right and D on the left, were hung up by heavy machine gun fire from houses in front and from the enemy position in Fort de Maulde, and the further advance was stayed until nightfall, when a platoon of A Company advanced to clear a group of buildings on the right of the advance, only to find that the enemy had retired. Later, orders were issued, at short notice, for B and A Companies on the right to advance at 1.50 a.m. in conjunction with the Division on the right in an endeavour to reach the canal bank. After an advance of 1,500–2,000 yards heavy machine gun fire was encountered and barbed wire in defence of the Fort de Maulde, and these Companies had to withdraw to the Cense de Choque. During the day and night a fairly heavy list of casualties had occurred, chiefly in B Company. The following day the right sector was taken over by the 10th Battalion, C Company took over the advance Company in the left sector in front of Quesnoy, with the three other Companies in Quesnoy. Here a certain amount of shelling was experienced. The following night the Battalion was relieved by the 9th Battalion and marched back to Rumegies, to find its intended billets occupied by troops of the Division on the right, clearly out of their sector. In the early morning these were induced to leave, and billets were occupied about 6.30 a.m. Here the Battalion remained in reserve a few days, resting, training and playing football, with intervals of being shelled out of billets by enemy long range heavy artillery of, at spasmodic intervals, considerable activity. D Company and the Band were the chief sufferers. On the 27th a further backward move was made to billets at Aix, where a similar pro-gramme was entered upon, with the shelling left out. Battalion schemes, musketry, P.T. and B.T., specialist training, interspersed with lectures and demonstrations by the R.E. on raft-building, and one ceremonial Brigade parade at Rumegies, very much in the rain, were the order of the mornings, while inter-company football matches, Divisional and Artillery entertainment parties filled in the afternoons. Rumours of armistice abounded, but were effectually countered by an order to be ready to advance for an attack on the Fort de Maulde at twenty-four hours' notice, which was received on November 6th. On the 8th, orders to advance were received, but the Battalion only proceeded again to Quesnoy, a village grossly overcrowded with troops, where it was learnt that the enemy had again started to retire, and where an uncomfortable night was spent preparatory to an early start on the advance the next morning as part of the main body. On this day the Battalion proceeded as far as Peruwelz, passing *en route* through villages whose inhabitants, liberated from the enemy yoke and filled with the joy of their freedom, turned out in their entirety to throw favours of flowers and ribbons, aye, and even the kisses of friendship, to the British troops, who were the visible and immediate cause of the enemy retirement. A tiring day, and a lengthy march, but the distance between villages and the weariness of the way were forgotten at the welcome received from the villagers, and even the most tired braced themselves to march proudly on and show the British soldier at his best before those who had seen none but German soldiers so many weary years. The next morning the Battalion was detailed to form the advance guard and passed in the early morning through the outpost line of the 9th Battalion. The advance continued through Basecles, Quevauchamps and Stambruges, where the canal was crossed, to Neufmaison, the scenes of the previous days being re-enacted with the additional fervour of welcome accorded to the very first British troops to pass through in the wake of the retiring enemy. It was a Sunday and everywhere was heard the joyful (the more so because unaccustomed) sound of Church bells calling the liberated to prayer and praise. No opposition was encountered, and an outpost line was established covering the village of Neufmaison, the enemy being located a mile or two away at Herchies. The next morning, there being no orders for a further advance, the Battalion stood fast on its outpost line, and there was later received about 10.30 a.m. an historic wire from Brigade Headquarters :—" 10th and 12th Battalions B.M. 153 11th inst. Hostilities cease 11.00 to-day aaa Troops will stand fast on the outpost line already established aaa. All military precautions will be observed and there will be no communication with the enemy aaa. Further instructions later aaa. Acknowledge Ends." In the words of the War Diary, " The news was received calmly," a state of feeling for which the total absence of news of the whereabouts of the day's ration was doubtless largely responsible, coupled with the fact that the village had so recently been denuded of eatables by the enemy invader. However, the 10th Battalion band played " God save the King " and other appropriate patriotic airs in the village centre, and the Mayor drank healths in a small supply of cognac with all too few a selection of senior officers. Cavalry passed through the village, riding furiously for Mons, in charge of an officer eager to end the war where he had begun it. Rations eventually turned up about 1 p.m., the rapidity of the advance in the last few days having completely outstripped the ability of supply to cope with the broken down bridges and blown up roads left in his wake by a retreating foe.

CHAPTER VI.

FROM THE ARMISTICE TO THE END.

ON November 13th the Battalion moved back into billets, a great deal more comfortable, at Stambruges, where on the following day was held a Service of Thanksgiving by the Brigade upon the conclusion of an Armistice.

There now began a life of training in the morning, recreation in the afternoon, and educational classes throughout the day. Training consisted mainly of ceremonial, in which most of the Battalion were conspicuously rusty and which was very essential in view of Army Commander's Inspections and the like, and route marches, Football competitions, inter-battalion and inter-company, were organised; a Brigade debating society was started and allowed to die a natural death after one very crowded and well-supported debate on a subject dealing with a comparison between Shakespearean plays and the present-day Revues; entertainments, vocal and instrumental, in the local theatres by the various Battalions were arranged; dances were organised; and even two cinemas were running at one time. On December 20th a move was ordered to Leuze, where the Battalion found itself in quite comfortable billets and remained for the rest of its existence in the Expeditionary Force. Preparations for the celebration of Christmas were put into full swing. After Church Parade, Company dinners followed by concerts were organised and proved a great success. At Leuze a similar programme of training, recreation and education was carried out, the last-named having eventually to cease owing to the inroads made on both teachers and students by the ever-increasing tide of demobilisation. This period was marked by great efforts to deal adequately with the question of the entertainment of the troops. Concert parties on tour visited the town and gave performances, but, while a few possibly equalled, yet none excelled, the very praiseworthy performances of the concert party of the 9th Battalion. Dancing became the vogue and each Company undertook the initiation of those hitherto unversed in its mazes. Boxing was taken up with considerable enthusiasm and the ever-popular football claimed its usual large toll of votaries. Demobilisation set in, and at first in small batches, but afterwards in increasing numbers, the comrades of many a month, aye, and even of many a year, of campaigning, left the Battalion to taste again the sweets of " civvy " life. A large draft of Officers, N.C.O's and men, volunteering for, or compulsorily retainable in, the Army of Occupation, went early in February to the 16th London Regiment, and later in the same month a further large draft joined the 9th Battalion and proceeded with it to join the Army of Occupation at Dürren. Smaller and smaller grew the Battalion, until there were left not enough even to form teams for football and other sports, or to dance. Concert parties and bands were broken up and time hung heavy on the hands of the ultimate cadre, after stores had been collected in a Brigade store, transport had been parked in a Brigade park, and the animals resolved into their various classes and distributed, some for the post-bellum Army, some for England for sale, and some for sale in Belgium.

To face page 249.]

COLONEL W. F. LEESE, V.D.

PART FIVE.

The Depot and
The Reserve Battalion.

CHAPTER I.

THE DEPOT.

ON August 4th, 1914, the strength of the Battalion was roughly 850. During the first days of mobilisation, about 300 recruits presented themselves at Chenies Street for enlistment, of whom 160 were selected and enlisted after an examination by the two regimental medical officers ; thus within a week we were up to establishment, 1012.

On mobilisation the Battalion was billeted at Headquarters, Chenies Street, The Polytechnic, Regent Street, and the Central Y.M.C.A., Tottenham Court Road. It was impossible to provide also for the recruits in such limited quarters, so these were obliged to sleep at their homes and to parade each morning for instruction at the Depot. The training for the recruits was in charge of Captain Wilson and one other officer, two sergeants and one corporal, who were all that could be spared by the C.O. from duty with the Battalion. Fortunately there were several old members of the Battalion among the " recruits," and these supplied much valuable assistance in the preliminary training.

Uniform and equipment had been issued from the Quartermaster's stores within the first forty-eight hours after mobilisation, to fit out those men of the Battalion whose clothing was either unserviceable or short, and very little was left over for the new-comers. Khaki could be served out to a few of them and some others were supplied with rifle-green uniforms, but the majority had to parade in plain clothes.

On August 19th the Battalion left London for Bulls-water Camp, taking with it 60 recruits for whom uniforms had been provided. The training of the remaining 100 men was carried on from Chenies Street.

So events continued until the 3rd September, 1914.

On September 3rd, information was received from the C.O., who was with the Battalion at Bullswater, that 100 men who were either unfit or unwilling to accept the foreign service obligation were returning to Chenies Street. On their arrival a transfer was effected *en bloc* of their uniforms and equipment to the 100 recruits, who were drafted to Bullswater Camp the same evening.

When the Battalion first moved to Bullswater, their strength was about 900. During August, however, the Signalling Section was transferred to the Royal Engineers, a certain number of men received Commissions, and a few on further medical examination were recommended for discharge. Thus the strength of the Battalion at the end of August, 1914, was reduced, approximately, to 800.

Early on the morning of September 4th, 1914, authority was received at Chenies Street to commence raising a 2nd Battalion.

On receipt of this information Captain Wilson communicated immediately with all the evening papers, who gratuitously printed announcements the same afternoon that " the Rangers " were about to raise a 2nd Battalion and would commence recruiting the following morning.

The response was instantaneous ; by 10 a.m. there was a queue outside the Depot of over 200 anxious to enlist, and during that and the subsequent days the queue sometimes numbered as many as three to four hundred. So keen were the men that they would refuse to leave the queue for fear of losing their turn.

The rate of enlistment in those days was regulated by the supply of doctors. Our two regimental medical officers were with the 1st Battalion ; consequently there was no official medical officer available at Chenies Street. This difficulty was overcome by the generous help of local practitioners, who came willingly and without any payment gave as much of their time as they were able to spare. On one occasion no less than twelve were examining recruits simultaneously. In less than a week over a thousand men were medically examined, enlisted and formed into companies. All the men lived at their homes, reporting at Chenies Street daily at 9.0 a.m. Squad drill and Company training took place in the squares and side streets round the Depot, and, in addition to our own Drill Hall, the free use of Central Y.M.C.A. Gymnasium, Tottenham Court Road, and the Gymnasium at Regent Street Polytechnic, was secured for training purposes. Battalion Parades were held in Regent's or Hyde Parks.

This *regime* continued until the 2nd Battalion was moved to quarters in the White City, Shepherd's Bush, in the middle of October.

No uniform, boots or small kit were available until after the 2nd Battalion moved to the White City and even then they were only issued in limited quantities. A monetary allowance was made by the Territorial Force Association for the individual purchase of small kit and necessaries, and later on a further allowance for fair wear and tear of civilian clothing was sanctioned.

The last recruit for the 2nd Battalion was taken on October 23rd, when recruiting was closed down until the raising of the 3rd Battalion in January, 1915.

On January 19th, 1915, instructions were received to commence raising a 3rd Battalion.

Recruiting for the Unit had been closed down for nearly four months.

Only 25 recruits were enlisted during the first week, and about a similar number in the second ; in the third about 40, and so on. The stream of volunteers which had flowed in strongly in the preceding year was now running out. The supply of uniforms had largely increased during the past six months and it was now possible to clothe each man enlisted with a cap, jacket, trousers and puttees.

The new C.O. was appointed in February, 1915. Parades were held in Regent's Park daily, and, if wet, at Y.M.C.A., Polytechnic or Headquarters.

Such was the daily routine until the Battalion left London about the middle of April ; recruiting was still continued, and parties of recruits were sent down clothed and equipped to the Unit two or three times weekly.

It became increasingly necessary as time went on to adopt the traditional methods of encouraging enlistment.

It was of vital importance to secure a band. The 1st Battalion band was now overseas. Accordingly it was decided to form a new brass band, and in response to an appeal to friends of the Regiment the sum of £250 was received with which to purchase the necessary instruments. With this fund a band of 40 instrumentalists was successfully equipped, which throughout 1915 was used chiefly for recruiting purposes. Every day an open air programme was arranged in various parts of London, and sometimes the assistance of well-known singers was secured as an additional attraction. Open air recruiting meetings were also tried from time to time, with varying results. In addition a press campaign was started. Notices of the current doings of the Rangers and also accounts of their history from 1780, in which year the Regiment was raised, appeared in the various daily and weekly newspapers. Recruiting posters were placarded in prominent public positions, and also by kind permission of the proprietors in the large local houses of business.

About mid-summer the most successful scheme of all was inaugurated, viz. : the use of empty offices or shops in various parts of the West End and City as temporary Recruiting Offices.

The Battalion overseas had by now suffered severe casualties and 30 N.C.Os. and Riflemen, all of whom had returned from active service, formed the recruiting staff. Three or four were detailed to each office. So long as a recruiting office was prolific it was kept open, but as soon as it became unproductive it was closed down and a fresh office was opened in some other locality.

On the average about half a dozen of these temporary offices were running at one and the same time.

Through the generosity of the Landlords and Estate Agents we had in all some forty of these offices and shops for different periods, the cost of which to the Rangers and the Government was nil.

Such were some of the efforts made to obtain recruits for the 3rd Battalion from January, 1915, to February, 1916. During this period, 1,982 volunteers enlisted.

On March 2nd, 1916, the " Military Service Act " came into force and voluntary enlistment ceased. From that time onwards recruits were posted to units direct from Great Scotland Yard, Woolwich, the White City, or Stratford.

From March to August, 1916, 1,530 recruits were posted to the Rangers.

On September 1st, 1916, the 3rd Battalion was amalgamated with the Queen Victoria's Rifles under the title of the Reserve Battalion 9th London Regiment.

GENERAL REMARKS, 1914–1917.

The Battalion premises at Chenies Street which were designed and built as peace-time headquarters, were totally deficient in barrack-rooms, washing and sanitary arrangements, and the necessary cooking appliances usually found in Regular Depots. It was thus quite impossible to make arrangements at Headquarters for the accommodation and feeding of troops in any large numbers.

For this reason all recruits whilst in London were sent to their homes nightly.

A Regimental Comforts Fund for the two Battalions Overseas was founded in 1915. This Committee was most successful, and obtained a considerable number of subscriptions, by which it was enabled to send out every week parcels of clothing and comforts to both Battalions.

THE RESERVE BATTALION.

AN IMPRESSION BY ITS C.O.

EARLY in January, 1915, it was decided by the Military Authorities to raise by voluntary enlistment a third Battalion of the " 12th London." The 1st Battalion had been sent to France at the end of December, 1914, and the 2nd Battalion was under training in Sussex.

The preliminary work in the establishment of the new cadre devolved upon Captain K. R. Wilson, Officer Commanding the Rangers Depot at Chenies Street. On his application for assistance, two Officers from the 2nd Battalion—Captain W. H. Wellsman and 2nd Lieut. B. R. D. Bradley—were detached for that purpose.

Colonel W. F. Leese, V.D., who had served in the Old Rangers for thirty years, and had commanded them from 1901 to 1907, was asked by Lord Esher to take the Command of the infant Battalion, and was gazetted on 20th February. Meantime Captain Wilson and his coadjutors had got together a nucleus around which the new body steadily increased in numbers, and by the end of February was nearly 200 strong. As several Battalions were forming their 3rd Lines in the immediate vicinity and had opened recruiting stations close by, the competition for members was decidedly keen, and Tottenham Court Road was the scene daily of persuasive harangues from a number of eager orators. In order to keep up with other units, Colonel Leese arranged with the O.C. 2nd Battalion, Colonel Barham, for the transfer of the remnants of the Regimental Band and the Bandmaster, Mr. F. Benson Ansley, to the 3rd Battalion. The zeal and energy of the latter very soon raised the Band strength to over thirty and brought it to a high state of efficiency. A generous donation from the Mansion House and some private subscriptions enabled the band to purchase new instruments. From the latter end of March, it performed daily in the neighbourhood and was the means of inducing many recruits to join. The daily musters for training in Regent's Park grew stronger and stronger day by day, and by the middle of April the new unit numbered about 400. One of the most fortunate things that happened to it was the discovery that Sergeant-Major McCarthy, K.R.R., who had served in the old Rangers for some fifteen years, was to be found at the Rifle Depot, Winchester, and by the courtesy of the O.C. at Winchester he was transferred to the 3/12th. As Sergeant-Major McCarthy had been assisting in the training of a new service Battalion for eighteen months, he was thoroughly up to date, and, soaked as he was in both Rifle and Ranger traditions, his influence on the young Rangers was invaluable. In fact, to his zeal, tact and sympathy, was largely due the excellent spirit which reigned from first to last in the Battalion.

Meantime the time and energies of the Commanding Officer were largely occupied in the selection of Officers from the numerous applicants for Commissions. Amongst the first recommended to Territorial Force Association for promotion was Mr. G. G. B. Brotchie from the Inns of Court O.T.C. This gentleman on being gazetted was appointed acting Adjutant and in due course was confirmed in the appointment. All who served with him will agree that no better selection could have been made.

As it became evident that the embryonic stage of the new unit must soon come to an end, the selection of a thoroughly competent Quartermaster had to be decided on, and fortunately for the Battalion the choice of the C.O. fell upon Mr. Charles Harvey, who had served with credit and distinction for over twenty years in the R.G.A. and, after experience as

Quartermaster-Sergeant and acting Quartermaster in various parts of the world, had retired to civilian life shortly before the war. From first to last Mr. Harvey was an unqualified success. His knowledge of every detail never failed, and his efficiency may be gauged by the fact that after service in four different localities—Tadworth, Richmond, Sheen and Fovant—during eighteen months the total deficiencies chargeable to the unit on its amalgamation with the 9th and 11th London were under £20. The staff being now organised, preparations began for the first "move." A second Company was formed early in April and Captain Douglass Mathews was transferred from the 2nd Battalion to take command. By the end of April the unit numbered approximately 400, including 14 Officers, and had sent its first draft of 100 men with 4 Officers to the 2nd Battalion at Crowborough. Early in May, it marched by road to the new Camp at Tadworth, adjoining Epsom Downs, having been inspected a few days previously at the Horse Guards by General Sir R. Pole-Carew, K.C.B., and complimented on its physique and steadiness on parade.

The organisation of a new unit on virgin ground, where no camp had hitherto stood, was no light task and gave full play to the loyalty and adaptability of all concerned. The difficulties were, however, tackled with the traditional "Ranger Spirit," and speedily surmounted. Friendly rivalry with neighbours going through the same trials kept every one up to the mark, and the youngsters began to soak in camp lore like so many sponges. In a short time the camp was a home, and weekly and bi-weekly drafts from Headquarters soon brought the numbers to nearly 600. True, training was a conundrum which probably only Britishers could have solved. The arms of the Battalion consisted of about 100 "D.P." rifles—many without bayonets. Equipment was largely imaginary, and just as the organisation for 600 men was complete the powers discovered that there weren't tents enough to go round, and ordered a reduction of the personnel in camp to 300 men and 11 officers. The remainder were to be sent back to London !

The request of the C.O. to be allowed to buy tents—in good preservation, which were being offered cheaply by London dealers—was turned down, and things looked pretty gloomy until the energy and determination of Major-General Sir Francis Lloyd, who came down specially to see how things were, got the matter straightened out. After some weeks of unsettlement, tents came back from somewhere and training proceeded, but as all musketry practice beyond 100 yards had to be gone through at Purfleet much time was lost.

Another complication came in the shape of invalids from the 1st Battalion which had been badly cut up in France. The Military Authorities seemed unable to make up their minds as to how these men were to be treated. The idea apparently was that automatically they became, on return to England, members of the 3rd Battalion, to which they were sent on discharge from Hospital ; but as the fact of their existence was frequently not notified to the O.C. 3rd or the O.C. Depot there were continuous unexpected driblets of these poor fellows crawling into Camp after reporting casually at Chenies Street.

After eleven weeks at Tadworth the 3rd Rangers began to consider themselves almost old residents and had settled down to serious and regular training. Then, as usual, came a bomb in the shape of an order to move at short notice to another new camp on the borders of Richmond Park. All the pet embellishments and conveniences hewed out of the unfriendly chalk at grievous labour, had to be handed over to unsympathetic and bargain-hunting successors who got, for practically nothing, what had cost the

R 2

Rangers nearly £100—from Regimental and private funds. Small blame to the successors! It was the fortune of war. However, on 2nd August the Battalion moved off with its tail up and started its second camp in a "pretty green field" on the borders of Roehampton on the Kingston Road. Beyond having to start everything afresh, and the polite attentions of General Monck, who conscientiously kept the Battalion up to the mark, the next three months were uneventful. The Rangers were in aristocratic company, their camp fellows being the 3rd Queen Victoria and 3rd Civil Service Rifles. The Battalion increased to nearly nine hundred strong, notwithstanding a succession of drafts to the front. One of the best of the Rangers' friends rejoined it there, Rev. R. S. de Courcy Laffan, M.A., Rector of St. Stephens, Walbrook, E.C., who for several years had been Chaplain to the old Rangers and had expressed his wish to resume his relations with his comrades of other days. Pressure of duties prevented his going to Tadworth, but from the opening of the Richmond Camp he served as Honorary Chaplain, not only giving his whole time without pay to the work, but supplying at his own expense Church tent and furniture. His influence both amongst Officers and men was more than beneficial, and accounted largely for the high moral tone both of the "Lines" and the Officers' Mess. Apart from the regular Battalion training staff and the raw material, there was a regular stream of "Returned Expeditionary" Officers and men. At one time the latter numbered nearly 200, suffering from trench feet, rheumatism, wounds and nervous general breakdown. Amongst the Officers temporarily attached—either then or later, were Major Tucker, Captains Worthington, Tattersall, Wyatt, Jones and Edgell, and Lieutenants Stein, Hunter, Wakefield, Perkins, Stuckey, Moss-Vernon and Wheeler-Holohan.

As time went on and the summer waned, the disadvantages of the camp in the " pretty green field " began to manifest themselves. The men's Lines were fairly high but the Canteen, Mess and Church tents, stores and kitchen, were on a level with the Beverley Brook, which overflowed from the Autumn rains and turned the lower portion of the camp into a swamp. Every hollow filled with water, and the floor of the Mess tent was practically afloat. Depressed Officers sat in the damp with paraffin stoves between their knees, and consoled themselves with the thought that things were much worse in France. The Authorities for once were slow to move, and it was not until about November 17th that the units of the Camp were ordered into billets at Sheen. It was time. On the last night a storm of wind with a deluge of rain levelled, amongst other things the Mess tent, Church tent and Y.M.C.A., and the Battalion took its departure, leaving very much of a wreck behind it, with a decidedly low-spirited Camp Guard to " hand over " whenever the weather might moderate and allow things to dry.

Billets were a new experience, and, for a change, a decidedly pleasant one. The Battalion, over eight hundred strong, was distributed amongst some three hundred houses, whose inhabitants at first by no means welcomed this irruption into their privacy. Still, before long, they became reconciled. The " Boys " were so good, and gave so little trouble, that in a short time they became welcome guests, and many were the testimonials and notes of regret received by the C.O. when the time came to part. The Officers were billeted together in a large empty house, " Hindley," in which they had the privilege of using the billiard room, and were extremely comfortable. Amongst the many benefactors to the Regiment whilst at Sheen, none showed themselves quite so devoted as Mrs. Belville.

This good lady, with her husband and her daughter, opened a free canteen in the pavilion on Sheen Common, and daily, in all weathers, served coffee and cakes to the men after breakfast, about 10.30 a.m. The Rangers were not ungrateful, and on their departure, subscribed for a bronze statuette of a Ranger, with the following Inscription on the base :—

" Presented to Mrs. Belville by the Officers, N.C.Os. and men of the 3rd (Reserve) Battalion, 12th London Regiment (The Rangers) in gratitude for her great kindness to them during their stay at East Sheen— November, 1915–January, 1916."

The figure, with the pedestal, is about 14 inches high and will be, no doubt, a valued souvenir of her patriotic services.

Another act of recognition on the part of the Battalion was a leaded glass panel with inscription (designed by Captain Wheeler-Holohan), placed in the porch of Christ Church (East Sheen), a church which was placed at the disposal of the 9th and 12th Battalions every Sunday morning during their stay. A similar panel—to match—was given by the 9th (" Queen Victoria's ").

On the whole, the training at Sheen was probably as valuable as any that the Battalion received ; billets were a good test of discipline ; bombing, trench work and miniature range firing (in and out of doors) were carried on, and long range practice was done by a succession of detachments at Purfleet.

At the turn of the year there were rumours of another change, and a few days later (middle of January) the Battalion was ordered to proceed to Fovant, Salisbury, to form a portion of the 1st London (Territorial) Infantry Division. The descriptions brought back by the Adjutant and Quartermaster, who went down to explore, were not such as to inspire joy at the change. Comfort (comparative) appeared to depend on which camp was

allotted to the Unit—and it got the worst. The
hutments had just been vacated by two Brigades of
Northern Field Artillery. The Parade ground had
beer. used for months for the picketing of several
hundreds of horses and mules. It was approximately 12 to 15 inches deep in fœtid mud, semi-
liquid, and water-logged. The men's quarters were
dirty and much damaged by wanton ragging on the
part of the late occupants. On the other hand the
Officers' quarters were comfortable and in good order.

It took quite a month to clean up, and it was
nearly three months before the parade ground
could be used for infantry purposes. Of course the
training suffered, and moreover the supply of high-
class volunteer recruits was giving out. The
" Derby " scheme was being tried with varying
success and brought in a heterogeneous crowd—
College Professors and dustmen side by side, boys
nominally 18 and men of 40, stalwart porters and
weedy tailors fresh from fifteen years cross-legged
on the bench. Homogeneous training was impossible.
The plethoric and anæmic, the athlete and the weed,
could not stand the same push—but eleven
weeks was the time prescribed for turning the
raw material—good, bad and indifferent—into a
soldier. Drive from Headquarters—spurred by the
necessity which knows no law—reacted on Army,
Divisional and Brigade Commanders. Everybody
was harried—Inspecting Officials, Military and
Medical, came in procession through the camps,
trying to achieve what appeared to be the impossible. Yet wonders were performed. Officers
and men worked hard, and the new stuff was as
eager to do its duty as the old had been. There
was no grousing and (in the Rangers) practically no
" crime." Absentees were very few and disorder
unknown. One of the remarkable phenomena was
the profusion of musical and theatrical talent in the
Battalion, and many of the weekly concerts could

hardly have been excelled in a high-class London Hall. But the system was approaching its end. The distinction between " Regular " and " Territorial " was fading away. Conscription, stark and undisguised, was coming into its own. The Territorial's privilege of serving abroad only in his own unit, was standing in the way of symmetrical reinforcements. Side by side might be two Reserve Battalions—the one harassed to supply drafts to its depleted first line—as happened in the Rangers' case—the other—whose 1st Battalion had suffered little—full of trained men not needed at the front— who refused—as was their right—to be drafted to other units. The high hand had to be applied, and the destruction of the Battalion *esprit de corps* was decided on. The amalgamation of several reserve units into one seemed the easiest way of accomplishing this. The O.C. 3rd Rangers was retired at the end of June, 1916, under the age clause. The Officer commanding 3/9th was transferred to other duties and in eight weeks (during which the Command was held by Lieut.-Colonel Challen (wounded from 1st Battalion)), the 3rd Rangers had ceased to exist and a new unit composed of the 9th, 11th and 12th Battalions took over all three. The old Second in Command, Major Douglass Mathews, applied for and obtained Staff work—which he worthily and efficiently performed until May, 1919. Captain Brotchie (the Adjutant) transferred to the Mechanical Transport. The Quartermaster, after declining the Quartermastership of the combined unit, was appointed to the Royal Air Force, in which he holds the rank of Major. The Chaplain had been appointed to the head of St. George's House, Aldershot, on full pay—a worthy acknowledgment of his devoted services. The Sergeant-Major resumed his pension.

Of the 76 Officers who served for longer or shorter periods with the Battalion, twelve were

killed in action and more than half the remainder
wounded or otherwise disabled, permanently or
temporarily, by the casualties of War. Of the men,
only the Regimental Records will, one day, reveal
the names of the fallen and the survivors.

Of many episodes—pathetic and otherwise— no
record has been kept, but any description of the
doings of the 3rd Battalion would be incomplete
without the mention of at least two names. In
February, 1915, three Officers of the 1st Battalion
were killed in action—Major Hoare, Captain L. F.
Studd and Lieut. C. E. Beausire. The Polytechnic
Institute had been—and is—an invaluable supporter
of the Rangers, and Captain Studd was the only son
of the gentleman whose name has been so prominent
in its Foundation and Management. Within a very
few days of his death, his father called at Headquarters and in an interview with the C.O. said " My
boy has gone, and I have no other. Will you allow
this boy—my nephew—to take his place ? " Needless
to say that offer was accepted with gratitude and
the nephew, Lieut. R. E. K. Bradshaw, was gazetted
on the 21st March. In due course he was transferred
to the 1st Battalion in France—where he also met
his death later—in action on 1st July, 1916.

The other name is that of Miss Alice Laking.
This generous and devoted lady, a prominent artiste
and well-known singer, allied herself to the Rangers
from the beginning of the war and, throughout its
continuance, was unsparing in her efforts for recruiting and for the entertainment of the men in
training. She sang in public—even in the street—to
attract recruits and organised a succession of the
highest class professional Concert parties both at
Tadworth and Richmond. The departure of the
Battalion for Salisbury necessarily severed the
personal connection between her and the unit,
but for long after that date her efforts continued
in aid of prisoners and for the supply of " comforts "
for the men in the fighting line.

NOTE.—*The Editors accept no responsibility for the accuracy of this Honours List, which they have obtained from the responsible authorities. The Editors understand that it has been compiled from Official sources, but that, owing to the manner in which Honours Lists were issued in the " London Gazette " during the War, absolute accuracy cannot be guaranteed.*

HONOURS AND AWARDS.

Companion of the Order of St. Michael and St. George.
Lieut.-Col. A. D. BAYLIFFE, T.D. (L.G., 23.6.15).
Lieut.-Col. (Hon. Col.) A. S. BARHAM (L.G., 1.1.18).

Distinguished Service Order.
Captain CLIVE HARDY (L.G., 19.11.17).
2nd Lieut. E. S. KNIGHT (L.G., 4.2.18).
Major (T./Lieut.-Col.) S. CHART (L.G., 26.7.18).

Officer of the Military Division of the Most Excellent Order of the British Empire. .
Captain (A./Major) G. W. MONIER WILLIAMS (L.G., 3.6.19).
Lieut. J. M. TROUTBECK (L.G., 3.6.19).

Military Cross.
Captain W. K. VENNING (D.C.L.I. Adjutant). (L.G., 23.6.15).
5472 C.S.M. (A./R.S.M.) P. KEARNEY (Rifle Brigade P.S.), (L.G., 27.7.16).
Captain (T./Major) G. W. MONIER WILLIAMS (L.G., 1.1.17).
Captain (T./Major) W. G. WORTHINGTON (L.G., 1.1.17).
Lieut. (T./Major) J. K. DUNLOP (Attached M.G. Corps), (L.G., 1.1.17).
2nd Lieut. (T./Lieut.) D. HIGGINS (L.G., 1.1.17).
Qmr. and Hon. Lieut. W. T. LINDOP (L.G., 4.6.17).
2nd Lieut. (A./Captain) S. F. FOOKS (L.G., 4.6.17).
2nd Lieut. (A./Captain) W. M. BARRETT (L.G. 18.6.17).
2nd Lieut. F. O. BARON (S. Lancs. Attached), (L.G., 18.6.17).
2nd Lieut. J. J. I. CUNNINGHAM (L.G., 18.6.17).
T./Captain J. D. HART, M.B. (R.A.M.C. Attached), (L.G., 18.7.17).
2nd Lieut. S. G. BEER (L.G., 18.7.17).
2nd Lieut. H. C. A. GALBRAITH (L.G., 26.9.17).
2nd Lieut. E. C. V. FOUCAR (L.G., 26.9.17).

Lieut. (A./Captain) G. B. Best (L.G., 19.11.17).
Captain H. W. Wightwick (L.G., 25.4.18).
T./Lieut. L. B. Burtt (L.G., 3.6.18).
Lieut. A. O. Colvin (L.G., 3.6.18).
Lieut. (A./Captain) D. C. B. Copeland (L.G., 3.6.18).
Rev. (T./Chaplain 4th Class) K. J. F. Bickersteth (L.G., 1.1.18).
Lieut. (A./Captain) G. C. W. Harker (D.R.O. 2287, 18.1.18).
Lieut. (A./Captain) K. G. Anderson (L.G., 22.6.18).
Captain F. P. G. Telfer (Attached Tank Corps), (L.G., 26.7.18).
Rev. W. H. Carew, B.A. (Army Chaplains Dept. Attached), (L.G., 16.9.19).
Lieut. (A./Captain) L. K. Spencer (L.G., 16.9.19).
2nd Lieut. L. Duckett (L.G., 7.11.18).
Captain (A./Major) H. Infeld (Emp. " Q " Spec. Coy., R.E.) (L.G., 1.1.19).
2nd Lieut. R. V. Moore (Attached 2/15th Lond. Regt.) (L.G., 1.2.19).
2nd Lieut. A. W. Sanger (Attached 2/5th Lond. Regt.) (L.G., 8.3.19).
Captain S. R. Moss Vernon (A.O. 3/1, 5.5.19).
Lieut. W. G. Parker (A.O. 3/1, 5.5.19).

Awarded a Bar to Military Cross.

2nd Lieut. S. G. Beer (L.G., 4.2.18).

Distinguished Conduct Medal.

2855 Rfm. D. P. B. Hegarty (L.G., 22.9.16).
4014 Rfm. A. Perkins (L.G., 22.9.16).
473214 Rfm. J. Hudson (L.G., 28.3.18).
474088 L./Cpl. J. O'Hara (L.G., 28.3.18).
470722 Sgt. A. G. Meacham (L. G., 26.6.18), (Attached T.M.B.)
470892 Sgt. (A./C.S.M.) U. J. Lee (L.G. 21.10.18).
470041 C.S.M. H. Brandon (L.G., 16.1.19).

Military Medal.

1416 Cpl. C. S. Strickland (L.G., 1.9.16).
2574 L./C. A. J. P. Savill (L.G., 1.9.16).
4011 Rfm. F. Bartleman (L.G., 1.9.16).
3200 C.S.M. H. A. Graham (L.G., 27.10.16).
1523 C.S.M. W. J. Hornal (L.G., 27.10.16).
2516 Sgt. H. A. W. Backhoff (L.G., 27.10.16).
3157 Sgt. A. J. N. Sievwright (L.G., 27.10.16).
1575 Sgt. N. Marriot (L.G., 27.10.16).
1325 L./Sgt. A. M. Copping (L.G., 27.10.16).

2786 Cpl. W. BLABER (L.G., 27.10.16).
1413 Cpl. C. E. GIBBLING. (L.G. 27.10.16).
1774 Rfm. C. GREGORY (L.G., 27.10.16).
2232 Rfm. W. J. McLAREN (L.G., 27.10.16).
1624 Rfm. H. G. SALISBURY (L.G., 27.10.16).
1551 Rfm. W. E. TAUNT (L.G., 27.10.16).
7615 Rfm. W. E. MILLS (L.G., 6.1.17).
2186 Sgt. J. G. WATSON (L.G., 12.3.17).
471215 Rfm. J. NORRIS (L.G., 26.5.17).
470369 Sgt. A. R. NEIL (L.G., 18.6.17).
470722 Cpl. (A./Sgt.) A. G. MEACHAM (L.G., 18.7.17).
472863 Rfm. G. SWAINSTON (L.G., 18.7.17).
472284 Sgt. H. G. HARRIS (L.G., 28.9.17).
470662 C.Q.M.S. T. H. PALMER (L.G., 28.9.17).
2420 Sgt. H. E. BENNETT (L.G., 28.7.17).
2260 Rfm. J. E. LACEY (L.G., 28.7.17).
473941 Rfm. S. E. POCOCK (L.G., 18.10.17), (Attached M.G.C.).
471108 Sgt. H. C. J. HAWKINS (L.G., 2.11.17).
473669 Rfm. W. PHILP (L.G., 2.11.17).
472646 Rfm. J. W. G. PINNER (L.G., 2.11.17).
470831 Sgt. E. J. DUNSTONE (L.G., 19.11.17).
472276 Cpl. C. M. ELLISON (L.G., 19.11.17).
470736 Cpl. (A./Sgt.) E. B. C. KERRY (L.G., 19.11.17).
471035 Sgt. C. L. OWEN (L.G., 19.11.17).
472142 Rfm. E. POWELL (L.G., 19.11.17).
470856 L./Cpl. G. J. REELAND (L.G., 19.11.17).
470943 Cpl. W. G. SUTTON (L.G., 19.11.17).
471826 Cpl. (A./Sgt.) C. E. WINTERFLOOD (L.G., 19.11.17).
471112 Rfm. W. J. ADAMS (L.G., 12.12.17).
470966 L./Cpl. F. W. ALDRIDGE (L.G., 12.12.17).
471069 Rfm. W. G. BAKER (L.G., 12.12.17).
472037 Rfm. S. COLLYER (L.G., 12.12.17).
470901 Cpl. H. C. CORLEY (L.G., 12.12.17).
472987 Rfm. H. A. CORNELIUS (L.G., 12.12.17).
471827 Rfm. C. T. CRUMP (L.G., 12.12.17).
472329 Rfm. W. A. DYKES (L.G., 12.12.17).
470685 L./Sgt. W. J. HARPER (L.G., 12.12.17).
472331 Rfm. A. L. HILL (L.G., 12.12.17), (Attached T.M.B.).
474415 Rfm. H. H. JONES (L.G., 12.12.17).
471036 Sgt. J. H. LAND (L.G., 12.12.17).
472130 Rfm. R. H. LANSBURY (L.G., 12.12.17).
471840 Rfm. J. LINKINS (L.G., 12.12.17).
470449 Rfm. G. J. MARSHALL (L.G., 12.12.17).
472041 Rfm. A. MURPHY (L.G., 12.12.17).
472826 Rfm. A. F. PARRISH (L.G., 12.12.17).
470051 Rfm. C. H. J. PIPE (L.G., 12.12.17).
472353 Rfm. R. RADLEY (L.G., 12.12.17).

471825 L./Cpl. N. T. Ratcliffe (L.G., 12.12.17).
470673 Rfm. C. W. Reynolds (L.G., 12.12.17).
470173 C.Q.M.S. A. N. Spargo (L.G., 12.12.17).
470332 Rfm. A. E. Walker (L.G. 12.12.17).
471270 Rfm. A. J. Wingrove (L.G., 12.12.17).
471164 L./Cpl. T. E. Wood (L.G., 12.12.17).
393615 Rfm. E. G. Newman (L.G., 12.12.17).
474405 Rfm. L. Barrett (L.G., 14.1.18).
474382 Rfm. P. Carpenter (L.G., 4.2.18).
470458 L./Cpl. R. H. Shipley (L.G., 23.2.18).
A./202188 Rfm. R. Nesbit (L.G., 23.2.18), (K.R.R.C. Attached).
473250 L./Sgt. (Sgt.) H. Avern (L.G., 13.3.18).
470410 Sgt. H. H. Clarke (L.G., 13.3.18).
470801 L./Cpl. F. F. Smith (L.G., 13.3.18).
473108 Rfm. H. Ward (L.G., 13.3.18).
470428 Rfm. W. H. Wiltshire (L.G., 13.3.18).
A./203410 Rfm. T. H. Brett (L.G., 13.3.18), (K.R.R.C. Attached).
473756 Rfm. W. G. Flawn (L.G., 13.3.18).
472081 Sgt. A. V. Coombs (L.G., 29.8.18).
474411 Rfm. A. Hiles (L.G., 29.8.18).
472163 Cpl. A. G. Ives (L.G., 29.8.18).
470778 Sgt. H. J. Moore (L.G., 29.8.18).
470395 Rfm. C. Turner (L.G., 29.8.18).
472098 Sgt. A. E. Bulling (L.G., 24.1.19).
472120 Sgt. P. A. Fickling (L.G., 24.1.19).
470095 Sgt. V. W. France (L.G., 24.1.19).
473307 Sgt. J. Garrard (L.G., 24.1.19).
470848 Sgt. R. J. Mason (L.G., 24.1.19).
472154 Sgt. W. Radley (L.G., 24.1.19).
470231 Sgt. W. J. Tombleson (L.G., 24.1.19).
471684 Rfm. H. W. Bull (L.G., 24.1.19).
471823 Rfm. G. A. Tietjen (L.G., 24.1.19).
472112 Rfm. G. T. Stephens (L.G., 11.2.19).
470619 Rfm. P. N. Tremain (L.G., 11.2.19).
471809 Rfm. A. R. Thirkell (L.G., 11.2.19).
471469 Rfm. (A./L./Cpl.) A. B. Flight (L.G., 13.3.19).
71103 Rfm. W. Lyons (L.G., 13.3.19).
474306 Rfm. H. P. Quirk (L.G., 13.3.19).
474681 Rfm. J. R. Fletcher (L.G., 29.3.19).
474596 Rfm. J. Wild (L.G., 29.3.19).
470762 Rfm. (A./L./Cpl.) P. Sankerwitch (L.G., 14.5.19).

Meritorious Service Medal.

471276 Cpl. W. Brown (L.G., 4.6.17).
470041 C.S.M. H. Brandon (L.G., 17.6.18).

470011 C.Q.M.S. G. DODDS (L.G., 17.6.18).
470848 Sgt. R. J. MASON (L.G., 17.6.18).
472567 T./R.S.M. W. CHATFIELD (L.G., 29.8.18).
473680 Sgt. E. J. BOND (L.G., 18.1.19).
470321 Cpl. (L./Sgt.) G. R. GREEN (L.G., 18.1.19).
470285 Rfm. (A./Sgt.) S. W. YOUNG (L.G., 19.1.19).
470001 R.Q.M.S. C. CORY (L.G., 3.6.19).
470941 Sgt. F. W. KENDAL (L.G., 3.6.19).
470791 Sgt. C. R. PARSONS (L.G., 3.6.19).
471132 Cpl. R. C. HYLAND (L.G., 3.6.19).
473505 Rfm. (A./C.Q.M.S.) W. DULLAGE (L.G., 3.6.19).

Mentioned in Despatches.

Lieut.-Col. A. D. BAYLIFFE, T.D. (L.G., 22.6.15).
Captain W. K. VENNING (D.C.L.I. Adjutant), (L.G. 22.6.15).
Lieut. (T./Captain) J. K. DUNLOP (L.G., 1.1.16).
2nd Lieut. J. M. TROUTBECK (L.G., 1.1.16).
Lieut.-Col. A. D. BAYLIFFE, C.M.G., T.D. (L.G., 4.1.17).
Captain (T./Major) L. F. JONES (L.G., 4.1.17).
Lieut. (T./Captain) S. W. GREEN (L.G., 4.1.17).
2nd Lieut. (T./Lieut.) D. C. B. COPELAND (L.G., 4.1.17).
2nd Lieut. (T./Lieut.) L. H. K. NEIL (L.G., 4.1.17).
2914 Sgt. P. C. WORTHINGTON (L.G., 4.1.17).
Captain (T./Major) J. K. DUNLOP, M.C. (L.G., 25.5.17).
2nd Lieut. A. O. COLVIN (L.G., 25.5.17).
Lieut.-Col. (Hon. Col.) A. S. BARHAM (L.G., 24.12.17).
Captain (A./Major) L. C. BENNS (L.G., 24.12.17).
Captain V. L. BURNSIDE (L.G., 24.12.17).
Major S. CHART (L.G., 24.12.17).
2nd Lieut. K. H. S. CLARK (L.G., 24.12.17).
2nd Lieut. A. O. COLVIN (L.G., 24.12.17).
Captain C. HARDY, D.S.O. (L.G., 24.12.17).
Lieut. A. F. SARGEAUNT (L.G., 24.12.17).
Captain F. WALLER (L.G., 24.12.17).
2nd Lieut. D. M. C. WOODRUFFE PEACOCK (L.G., 24.12.17).
470321 L./Sgt. G. R. GREEN (L.G., 24.12.17).
470139 Cpl. S. H. SHERIFF (L.G., 24.12.17).
470278 Sgt. L. W. STOTT (L.G., 24.12.17).
470746 Rfm. (A./Cpl.) A. J. TASKER (L.G., 24.12.17).
· Lieut. (A./Captain) K. G. ANDERSON (L.G., 25.5.18).
Major (A./Lieut.-Col.) S. CHART (L.G., 25.5.18).
Lieut. (A./Captain) N. P. DE SAULLES (L.G., 25.5.18).
2nd Lieut. E. S. KNIGHT, D.S.O. (L.G., 25.5.18).
Lieut. (A./Captain) R. B. LOVELESS (L.G., 25.5.18).
470026 R.Q.M.S. E. BATTEN (L.G., 25.5.18).
470445 C.S.M. G. B. LEMAN (L.G., 25.5.18).
470285 Rfm. (A./Sgt.) S. W. YOUNG (L.G., 25.5.18).

Captain S. A. S. MALKIN (R.A.M.C. Attached), (L.G., 25.5.18).
Major (T./Lieut.-Col.) S. CHART (L.G., 13.12.18), (Attached 18th Entrenching Bn.).
Captain (A./Major) G. W. MONIER WILLIAMS, M.C. (Attached R.E.), (L.G., 30.12.18).
Captain S. A. S. MALKIN (R.A.M.C. Attached), (L.G., 30.12.18).
Lieut C. ROCHFORD (L.G., 30.12.18).
472382 Sgt. F. CHARLTON (L.G., 30.12.18).
470780 C.S.M. E. CLAYFIELD (L.G., 30.12.18).
Captain (A./Major) C. HARDY, D.S.O. (Attached 25th Bn. Liverpool Regt.), (L.G., 10.7.19).
Captain (A./Major) G. W. MONIER WILLIAMS, M.C. (L.G., 10.7.19).
Captain H. W. WIGHTWICK, M.C. (L.G., 10.7.19).

ALLIED DECORATIONS.

Croix de Guerre (French).
Lieut. E. R. CRASSWELLER (L.G., 7.1.19).

Croix de Guerre (Belgian).
471912 L./Cpl. E. BLABY (L.G., 12.7.18.)
471834 Sgt. H. J. HADDOCK (L.G., 12.7.18).
470139 Cpl. S. H. SHERIFF (L.G., 12.7.18).
Captain (A./Major) A. F. SARGEAUNT (L.G., 4.9.19).

The Italian Military Order of Savoy (Cavalier).
Lieut.-Col. A. D. BAYLIFFE, C.M.G., T.D. (L.G., 26.5.17).

The Serbian Order of the White Eagle (With Swords).
Captain J. EDGELL (L.G., 9.3.17).

The Russian Order of St. George, 4th Class.
1624 Rfm. H. G. SALISBURY, (L.G., 25.8.15).

The Russian Cross of St. George, 4th Class.
2855 Rfm. D. P. B. HEGARTY (L.G., 15.2.17).

The Russian Order of St. Anne, 4th Class (Inscribed " For Valour in War ").
Lieut. J. K. DUNLOP (L.G., 25.8.15).